"This preeminent guide on teaching for justice in the elementary classroom is a rare and invaluable gift to those of us working—too often in isolation—to invite young children to struggle mightily alongside us for a better world. Speaking as scholars, educators, mothers, and human beings, the authors offer the support and inspiration we need to skillfully practice anti-oppression in our classrooms and to prepare children to carry that practice into their lives outside of school."

—**Carla Shalaby,** author of *Troublemakers: Lessons in Freedom from Young Children at School*

"No one should step into a classroom without first reading *Social Studies for a Better World*. The book sings with possibility about creating classrooms of justice and kindness. It is utopian in the absolute best sense of the term. So many teaching books are dry as dust, and pedagogically unhelpful. But Noreen Naseem Rodríguez and Katy Swalwell, former classroom teachers, know what they are talking about. Inviting, warm, and deeply humane, *Social Studies for a Better World* is the book that all teachers need in these hard times."

—**Bill Bigelow,** Curriculum Editor, Rethinking Schools

"Brilliantly conceptualized, *Social Studies for a Better World* offers essential insights for understanding the ability of social studies to help students decipher the past and make sense of the present. Equally important, it provides an easy to follow blueprint for classroom implementation. This is essential reading for anyone who believes in the power of social studies to transform society."

—**Hasan Kwame Jeffries,** host of the podcast "Teaching Hard History," and Associate Professor of History, The Ohio State University

"With the increased scrutiny on educators who aim to teach from an anti-oppressive stance, precise tools and strategies for liberatory education are needed now more than ever. Enter *Social Studies for a Better World*. By critiquing social studies as it is while sharing a vision for what it could be, Rodríguez and Swalwell provide elementary educators with creative solutions for transforming the discipline. This book is a must-have resource for current and aspiring teachers."

—**Bree Picower,** author of *Reading, Writing and Racism: Disrupting Whiteness in Teacher Education and the Classroom*

# SOCIAL STUDIES
## for a BETTER WORLD

### An Anti-Oppressive Approach
### for Elementary Educators

## Norton Series on Equity and Social Justice in Education

Cheryl E. Matias and Paul C. Gorski, series editors

Norton's Equity and Social Justice in Education series is a publishing home for books that apply critical and transformative equity and social justice theories to the work of on-the-ground educators. Books in the series describe meaningful solutions to the racism, white supremacy, economic injustice, sexism, hetero-sexism, transphobia, ableism, neoliberalism, and other oppressive conditions that pervade schools and school districts.

*Learning and Teaching While White*
Jenna Chandler-Ward and Elizabeth Denevi

*Ableism in Education*
Gillian Parekh

*Public School Equity*
Manya C. Whitaker

*Social Studies for a Better World*
Noreen Naseem Rodríguez and Katy Swalwell

*Equity-Centered Trauma-Informed Education*
Alex Shevrin Venet

Norton Books in Education

# SOCIAL STUDIES
## for a BETTER WORLD

An Anti-Oppressive Approach
for Elementary Educators

Noreen Naseem Rodríguez
Katy Swalwell

**W. W. NORTON & COMPANY**
*Independent Publishers Since 1923*

Copyright © 2022 by Noreen Naseem Rodríguez and Katy Swalwell

All rights reserved
Printed in the United States of America
First Edition

For information about permission to reproduce selections from this book, write to
Permissions, W. W. Norton & Company, Inc., 500 Fifth Avenue, New York, NY 10110

For information about special discounts for bulk purchases, please contact
W. W. Norton Special Sales at specialsales@wwnorton.com or 800-233-4830

Manufacturing by Lake Book Manufacturing, Inc.
Production manager: Katelyn MacKenzie

Library of Congress Cataloging-in-Publication Data

Names: Rodríguez, Noreen Naseem, author. | Swalwell, Katy M., author.
Title: Social studies for a better world : an anti-oppressive approach for elementary educators
/ Noreen Naseem Rodríguez and Katy Swalwell.
Description: First edition. | New York, N.Y. : W. W. Norton & Company, 2022. |
Series: Equity and social justice in education series | Includes bibliographical references.
Identifiers: LCCN 2021009006 | ISBN 9781324016779 (paperback) |
ISBN 9781324016786 (epub)
Subjects: LCSH: Social sciences—Study and teaching (Elementary) |
Social sciences—Curricula. | Marginality, Social. | Oppression (Psychology)
Classification: LCC LB1584 .R64 2022 | DDC 372.89—dc23
LC record available at https://lccn.loc.gov/2021009006

W. W. Norton & Company, Inc., 500 Fifth Avenue, New York, N.Y. 10110
www.wwnorton.com

W. W. Norton & Company Ltd., 15 Carlisle Street, London W1D 3BS

2  3  4  5  6  7  8  9  0

Dedicated to Lucia, Sofia, Thea, and Beau

*Remember that consciousness is power. Consciousness is education and knowledge. Consciousness is becoming aware. It is the perfect vehicle for students. Consciousness-raising is pertinent for power, and be sure that power will not be abusively used, but used for building trust and goodwill domestically and internationally. Tomorrow's world is yours to build.*

—YURI KOCHIYAMA

# Contents

## Part I
### Why Social Studies Can Change the World    I

## Part II
### Common Pitfalls and Creative Solutions    45

# • Acknowledgments •

Each night at dinner, Katy's family joins hands and says, "Thank you to all the people, plants, and animals who made this food possible. Let's do right by them and do good things with this energy." In that spirit, we offer deep gratitude for who and what has made it possible for us to bring this book into being. This includes our positions as academics and teacher educators expected to serve the common good, our partners' unconditional support and sharing of household duties, our graduate mentors and teachers at every stage who nurtured our confidence in our abilities as thinkers and writers, our past and present colleagues and students who inspire us every day, and scholars and educators we have never met but whose words have forever changed us. We cite many of them in this book, and intentionally draw from work that not only represents exceptional scholarship and practice but lifts up the voices of people who we admire and respect—especially Indigenous women, Black women, and women of color who academic gatekeepers have ignored, exploited, or appropriated for far too long.

There are many people who have supported us along our journey to create this book. Thanks to the staff and editors at W. W. Norton, Carol Collins, Marne Evans, Paul Gorski, and Jamie Vincent, and our tirelessly supportive colleagues at Iowa State University, especially our SCS co-conspirators Gabriel Rodriguez and Nicolas Tanchuk. Many of the ideas fleshed out in this book emerged from conversations and work done in collaboration with the Glorious Ladies of Social Studies (GLOSS)—Erin Sears, Jenny Sinclair, and Stefanie Wager—and our badass crew of social studies mentors and friends: Erin Adams, Sohyun An, Michael Apple, Janel Anderson, Bill Bigelow, Chris Busey, Diana Figueredo, Delandrea Hall, Diana Hess, Anne-Lise Halvorsen, Jenni Gallagher, Esther Kim, LaGarrett King, Deborah Menkart, Sarah Pamperin, Katie Payne, Lakota Pochedley, Leilani Sabzalian, Cinthia Salinas, Simone Schweber, Sarah Shear, and Amanda Vickery.

We also draw mightily from the scholarship, advocacy, and passion of Cati de los Ríos, Paul Gorski, Ki Gross, Rita Kohli, Stephanie Jones, Bettina Love, Bree Picower, Carla Shalaby, Daniel Spikes, Tran Templeton, Jenice View, Christina "V" Villarreal, Quentin Wheeler-Bell, Maisha Winn, and Connie Wu. As we finalized our text, we entrusted it with future, current, and former educators who we knew would be critical friends and would push us to do better: Lisa Brown Buchanan, Maddi Considine, Anna Falkner, Mohit Mehta, Tiffany Mitchell Patterson, Corey Sell, Nina Sethi, Jesica Sidler, Leah Slick-Driscoll, Zipporah Smith, and Delana Vogel. Our book is infinitely better thanks to your time, care, and critiques. A final thanks to Tahira Ali for helping with revisions and references.

# • Prologue •

Where and when we wrote this book is important. We wrote this book on the ancestral lands of the Báxoǰe, Očhéthi Šakówiŋ, Sauk, and Meskwaki. Through forced removal, land cessions, and land sales with Native Nations in the 19th century, settlers cut, drained, and cleared most of the tallgrass prairie, wetlands, and forest to build what we now call Ames and Des Moines, Iowa. We worked at a land-grant institution that exists only because of the U.S. federal government's policies displacing Native Nations. Our presence here is the result of settler colonialism, which includes ongoing exclusions and attempted erasures of Native Peoples who have been and continue to be stewards of the land, air, water, and all who inhabit them. We commit to joining in that stewardship while honoring Native sovereignty, and educating young children in our care to do the same.

We finished this manuscript at the end of 2020, a year filled with incredible chaos and trauma, including a life-threatening global pandemic that exacerbated existing racial and class and gender inequities, devastating natural disasters like wildfires and hurricanes amplified by climate change, increasingly polarized elections coupled with disturbing efforts to disenfranchise voters, seemingly nonstop political scandals, a massive financial crisis, horrifying family separations of asylum seekers at the hands of the federal government, and ongoing anti-Black police brutality leading to an international uprising for racial justice. It was an exhausting, often terrifying year that only intensified our commitment to anti-oppressive social studies for young learners.

Young people in a diverse democracy with a slew of injustices and complex social problems *must* be given opportunities to grapple with all of these issues, to nurture meaningful relationships of mutual obligation, and to develop a skill set that enables and inspires them to build a better world. We believe the education of young people is an important long-term strategy to tackle challenges in health care, our environment, financial systems, politics, immigration, human rights, civil rights, and criminal justice. Not to put all of that burden on their shoulders—there is *so much* we need to be doing as adults in the here and now to address these problems—but engaging with youth around these issues (to both inspire them and be inspired by them) is certainly an important part of that work. This book lays out our vision for an elementary education that helps young people find value in learning about the world through the social studies disciplines and to help make their communities more just, equitable, and healthy.

While we share a clear passion for anti-oppressive social studies, we came to it along very different paths. Katy was an unabashed social studies nerd from the jump, soaking up anything related to history and politics and poring over a dog-eared atlas during cross-country family road trips. More often than not, she saw herself reflected in the curriculum as a white, Catholic, cisgender, straight, English-speaking descendent of Midwestern settlers—though, she remembers the righteous fury she and two friends felt standing up to a teacher who suggested women's contributions were a footnote to history. As an undergrad, Katy tacked on a teaching major to history and Spanish degrees as an employment safety net only to fall in love with the profession. A methods instructor blew her mind when he assigned Howard Zinn's (1980/2013) *A People's History of the United States* and other texts that centered counter histories. After several years teaching middle and high school history and economics, she started working in elementary social studies as a graduate student at the University of Wisconsin–Madison and hasn't looked back.

Unlike Katy, Noreen was mostly apathetic about social studies until her 10th-grade U.S. history class, when her teacher randomly asked her, "Where are your people from?" As a Pakistani/Filipina American, the isolated nature of the question (no one else was asked) and the emphasis on her ethnoracial ambiguity made clear to her that she was viewed as an outsider. For the remainder of the school year, Noreen fully disengaged from the class and opted to not take any other history classes unless they were required. She experienced what many Black, Indigenous, and People of Color (BIPOC) felt, and continue to feel, in school: a distinct disconnect from what is presented as U.S. history, because it focuses largely on landed white men and rarely attends to BIPOC in ways that recognize them on their own terms and in their own voices. While Noreen was always fascinated by the histories of her Asian ancestors, they were never acknowledged in school. She took a couple of classes about South Asian history in college, but was focused on bilingual elementary education, Spanish, and linguistics. Late in her teaching career, she participated in the Tejano History Curriculum Project, which sought to infuse fourth grade Texas history with Tejano narratives. That collaboration with professors at the University of Texas at Austin led her to pursue a doctorate focused on social studies education. Not until her first year in that program did Noreen learn about Asian *American* history. It was life changing and life giving for her, and she's been compelled to learn more about BIPOC histories and anti-oppressive approaches to social studies ever since.

As scholars, we have produced research on diverse children's literature, the inclusion of Mexican and Asian Americans in the curriculum, disrupting Islamophobia in elementary schools, the experiences of teachers of color, the power of anti-racist local history, current and controversial events, economic and racial injustice, and anti-oppressive education in "elite" schools. As teacher educators, we have over two decades of combined experience crafting professional development for in-service teachers and methods courses for preservice teachers. As colleagues in the Iowa State University School of Education, we became fast friends who dreamed of laying out our vision for what elementary social studies can and should be. We are humbled and thrilled to share that in this book.

To be clear, we are *still* growing and learning as social studies educators and know this book has limitations. For example, we admittedly are more familiar with teaching about race, ethnicity, religion, language, and class than other aspects of identity, and need to keep learning more about other dimensions of the human experience. In fact, we are striving to be less anthropocentric (human-centered) as our sense of community and obligation goes beyond human life. And, given that our educational experiences have been in the United States, we don't want to presume that what we explain here would make sense in other cultural and national contexts.

We also note that our love of social studies is not purely academic or professional—it is *deeply* personal. Since we were young, we have been concerned with and curious about the ways in which we and our loved ones have struggled with systemic oppression like sexism, ableism, racism, economic disparity, xenophobia, homophobia, and Islamophobia. As we've learned and lived more, we've engaged in deep, sometimes painful, critical reflection about how we have internalized and even reproduced that oppression ourselves. As members of families with deep ideological divides, we increasingly believe in the importance of open dialogues across difference and the complexity of balancing that with clear stands against bigotry and ignorance. As mothers of young children, our responsibility to past and future generations feels even more profound, and our commitment to building a better world is fueled in large part by our love and hopes and dreams for them. We want to model for our children how to recognize the humanity of others and for them to feel their obligations and connections to the world in their bones.

This book represents our best attempt to do right by all those who have invested in us, and to help launch the next generation of innovative, imaginative, anti-oppressive social studies. Part 1 lays the foundation for our vision by providing an overview of the social studies disciplines (Chapter 1) and articulating the philosophy that drives our approach (Chapter 2). Part 2 identifies four common problems we've noticed in elementary social studies and applies our framework to transforming them: *normalization* (Chapter 3), *idealization* (Chapter 4), *heroification* (Chapter 5), and *dramatization and gamification* (Chapter 6). Part 3 examines how to build and sustain anti-oppressive social studies in classrooms in terms of planning curriculum (Chapter 7) and responding to resistance (Chapter 8). Appendix A offers an organized list of the resources we recommend in each chapter. For additional suggestions and supplements for each chapter, check out www.ssfabw.com. Appendix B includes reproducible worksheets for educators to apply the ideas from this book. Throughout, we pose questions about what you would do in the face of likely dilemmas and, at the end of each chapter, we offer ideas to apply what you're learning. Read it front to back, dive into something that intrigues you in the middle—whatever works for you to help you critically reflect on your own practice and act.

A few notes about the choices we made in this book. First, we were careful with our words. For example, we capitalize Black and Brown, but not white. "White" represents racial domination and, as such, ought not to be capitalized, while Black and Brown represent deep political and social movements for liberation so capitalizing them honors that (Gotanda, 1991). In some cases, we use the term *BIPOC* (Black, Indigenous, People of Color), which reflects the diversity within groups of color and respects the distinct but interrelated forces of anti-Blackness, settler colonialism, and racism and xenophobia. We also use the terms *Indigenous*, *Native*, and *Native American* interchangeably; like the other group terms mentioned, however, these fail to adequately acknowledge rich intergroup diversity within and among sovereign Peoples and Nations. None of these group identifiers are biological categories; rather, they are social constructions with shifting criteria for belonging. That said, the "box" one checks or is put into has enormous and very real consequences on our lives.

Similarly, our anti-oppressive approach drives us to disrupt linguistic hierarchies that view languages other than English as "not normal" or "foreign." Throughout this book, we opt not to put words in languages other than English in italics (unless they are cited in this format) and offer definitions as needed for clarity. In addition, we've done our best to avoid ableist language. In Chapter 7, we use the term "blind spot" in direct citation from Gultekin and May (2020) while encouraging educators to consider alternatives like "deliberately ignore" that use blindness as a metaphor. For more information about ableism in language, check out Lydia X. Z. Brown's blog (www.autistichoya.com).

Lastly, as lovers of children literature, we wrestled with which texts to include by title in this book. The books that are listed here are from independent publishers and while they may or may not be widely known among educators, they offer vital counter narratives that support anti-oppressive social studies. We encourage you to check out our website (www.ssfabw.com) for *many* more titles and a slew of recommended resources for all the topics (and more!) included in this book.

Whether you're an in-service teacher engaged in professional development, an instructional support specialist or administrator interested in trying something new, or a methods student learning how to teach, we hope you will find ideas in these pages to push and support your practice. You may not love history or language or any of the social studies like we do—at least not yet. That's okay. Maybe your teachers made social studies dull or dry or shallow. Maybe they actively denigrated you through what they included or left out. Maybe they taught in a way that made you feel stupid or ignorant or invisible or inferior. That's on *them*, not the disciplines. We can and must do better.

We wish you happy reading and the best of luck as you work with students to build a better world.

# SOCIAL STUDIES
## for a BETTER WORLD

# Part I

# Why Social Studies Can Change the World

These first two chapters introduce you to the foundation of our vision for elementary social studies—both how we define what the "social studies" are *and* the belief systems that we bring to our work toward building a better world. While explicit time for social studies is increasingly less common in elementary school daily schedules, these disciplines are nonetheless the heartbeat of every classroom. From explicit content and instructional time to the ways an educator establishes a classroom community, engages with families, and empowers students to be themselves and stand up for themselves and others inside and beyond school walls, social studies can be found across the content areas and throughout the school day.

In Chapter 1, we outline the five major disciplines of social studies: history, economics, behavioral sciences, civics, and geography. As we summarize each of the five disciplines, we explore the empirical and normative questions that guide them. Empirical questions can be answered with evidence, but our answers may vary based on our perspective and experience. Normative questions, ideally rooted in evidence, are about what matters to us and are based on our priorities, values, and ethics—we may never agree, but we seek to understand each other's positions. We also consider the types of narratives that are taught and learned in each discipline. Dominant narratives are those stories we understand as "common sense," told by those in power to maintain the status quo and bolstered by messaging commonly found within institutions like the media and school. In contrast, counter narratives are stories with deeper complexity and accuracy that reveal inequities and injustices by offering a broader range of perspectives. Both types of narratives are found in every discipline, and it is important for educators to recognize who and what is left out of the dominant narrative as well as to know where to find the counter narratives that are often missing from the elementary curriculum.

Chapter 2 explains our philosophy behind anti-oppressive elementary social studies and outlines the better world we are imagining and how we hope to build it. We stress that there is no "neutral" approach to teaching social studies—every resource out there is rooted in *some* understanding of what the education of young children ought to be about, whether it is clearly stated or not. We clarify why we find concepts like anti-racism, social justice, diversity, inclusion, and tolerance to be important yet incomplete, and detail our guiding philosophy of mutual concern from across time and around the world that emphasizes our connections and obligations to all beings. We draw from educational scholarship about intersectionality, funds of knowledge, and transformative justice to explain the kinds of relationships we hope to build with students and their families and offer advice for addressing two major fears that the preservice teachers we work with often express: teaching controversial issues and being accused of indoctrination.

In Part I, we want to make clear what the social studies are and why they can change the world. The remainder of the book explores *how* to make it happen. In the words of abolitionist Mariame Kaba (2021), "Changing everything may sound daunting, but it means there are many places to start" (p. 5) Indeed, there is a great deal of work to do. But together we believe it is possible and elementary schools are the perfect place to start.

# The Social Studies

efore we get into the specifics of how anti-oppressive social studies education can help youth build a better world, we want to make sure readers have a solid understanding of what the social studies actually are. Think of each discipline as a set of questions—almost like a pair of goggles that allow us to process different information. Just like sonar uses sound or infrared senses heat to create a fuller picture of our physical world, the disciplines offer distinct but complementary ways of understanding our social world. It is important to remember that *none of these disciplines are acultural or fixed*. Instead, each helps us engage in a dynamic conversation about our world—how it is *and* how it should be.

## Types of Questions

There are two types of disciplinary questions: *empirical* and *normative*. Empirical questions can be answered with evidence. When did something happen? Where did something happen? Sounds simple, right? Sometimes it is. But—maybe we don't have enough evidence *yet* to definitively answer a question. Or maybe there is enough evidence, but people question the credibility of the data. Or maybe there are disagreements about how to describe or define something. Just because it is "empirical," doesn't mean that it is resolved. Ultimately, empirical questions are important guides for social scientists as they provide the foundation for all of us to be informed as we grapple with which social problems to solve and how to solve them. In other words, facts matter. And, ideally, we're all wrestling with the same facts—*real* facts, not "alternative" facts or misinformation propping up conspiracy theories. Even when we rely on solid, good information, we will not always agree, of course—in fact, we need a range of different perspectives and ideas to help us solve the real problems we have in our world.

Normative questions, on the other hand, are questions about what matters to people or what *should* happen rather than what *does*. These are questions about priorities, values, and ethics. Ideally, we use high-quality evidence to justify our positions and are willing to change our minds if new data emerges. But we know that is not always the case. Ultimately, normative questions are "forever struggles"—while they may be answered in the sense that enough people agree to make an issue appear "closed," there is no way to permanently shut the door on them. Both empirical and normative questions are at the heart of the social studies disciplines, and should be the heart of our curriculum with elementary students.

## Dominant and Counter Narratives

For each discipline, we reference *dominant* and *counter* narratives, two types of stories about how the world works (Takaki, 2012). These might be literal stories we tell youth, but these can also be our worldviews about what seems natural or logical. In the United States, this means centering heterosexuality, cisgender identities, maleness, Christianity, whiteness, able-bodiedness, middle- and upper-class positions, documented status, the English language, the Global North, settlement, and colonialism, for example, as the norms or most important perspectives. We will talk about these more throughout this book—for now, it is enough to understand that dominant narratives are those stories (or worldviews or logics) that make the "common sense" of the people and systems enacting oppression seem natural or legitimate. By oppression, we mean exploitation, marginalization, powerlessness, cultural domination, and violence (Young, 1990). Dominant narratives are reinforced by all sorts of messages in schools, popular media, and other institutions. Those who are deeply invested in maintaining that power want to ensure no one questions it. Sometimes, dominant narratives are just straight up inaccurate—but the story they tell helps keep oppression humming along. Sometimes, they are only *partially* true, leaving out important information or perspectives that would cast suspicion on their integrity.

Counter narratives, on the other hand, are stories that question and complicate the status quo. The information and perspectives that counter narratives provide let us better understand how things actually are, wonder why things are that way, and imagine how things could be better by centering the lives of those who are experiencing oppression. Counter narratives offer more accuracy and complexity than do dominant narratives in understanding how the world works and they help us situate dominant narratives as constructions that perpetuate inequities and injustices. As you will read, *every* discipline has the potential to reinforce dominant narratives. Every discipline also has the ability to complicate or challenge them through counter narratives. It may seem abstract now, but we will give specific examples as we move through the chapter.

With that, let's jump into the disciplines: *history, economics, behavioral sciences, civics,* and *geography.* You may be cringing as you read that list—maybe the memory of an econ class makes you shudder or you start sweating as you think about identifying places on a map without an app. Give us a chance! We promise that these are all incredibly interesting and appropriate disciplines for young children. See Table B.1 *Empirical and Normative Questions in the Disciplines* and Table B.2 *Disciplinary Concepts and Tools* in Appendix B to help keep everything straight as you read.

## The Disciplines

### History

Let's start with history—the discipline most people associate with social studies. Many of us learned history as a chronological march through time, memorizing dates and famous people deemed important by our textbooks or teachers. While some may enjoy history-as-trivia, the discipline is way more contentious and fascinating. Remember our question goggles? For history, some of the most fundamental questions are *What happened in the past? Why? What stories do people tell about the past? Why?* These are empirical questions—but even though they can be answered with evidence, there is not always agreement among experts. Or, sometimes there *is* agreement among experts but myths persist among the general public—which is prime territory for a teacher, who has the responsibility to clear up any misconceptions. Take the classic case of the U.S. Civil War. Historians are clear: The breadth and depth of evidence showing that the South seceded in order to preserve the institution of slavery is overwhelming. Nevertheless, some Americans wrongly insist that it was about states' rights (Loewen, 2008). Our job as social studies teachers is to help clear away the cobwebs of confusion when there *is* clarity to be had, and to help students see the complexity and nuance when there is not.

Historians' most important normative questions are *Whose history matters?* and *What stories should get told?* Let's be very clear: This is contentious. Our stance is that we ought to center counter narratives—stories that matter to and include the diverse experiences and perspectives of marginalized communities (the poor, women and gender nonconforming people, Black and Brown people, Indigenous Peoples and Nations, LGBTQIA+ [lesbian, gay, bisexual, transgender, queer, intersex, and asexual] people, differently abled people, non-Christians, residents of the Global South, etc.). This is in contrast with continuing to *only* tell the stories that have mattered to or privilege the experiences of dominant groups (the wealthy, men, white people, settlers, straight people, able-bodied people, Christians, residents of the Global North, etc.). This means attending to the often overlooked contributions and joys of these communities as well as to their struggles navigating systems designed to exclude or exploit them. It also involves looking at the actions people in dominant groups have taken to maintain those systems of exclusion and exploitation (Leonardo, 2004). That said, we fully recognize that the question of whose history matters is normative, which means that there will be people who disagree with us about whose perspectives to include, whose stories to center, and who should decide any of this (Evans, 2004).

For example, *The New York Times* launched *The 1619 Project*, an educational resource designed to center the consequences of Africans' enslavement in North America beginning in 1619, as well as the contributions and experiences of Black Americans in order to better understand U.S. history. This was in response to decades of research documenting the inaccuracy and absence of Black history in K–12 schools (Banks, 1971; L. J. King, 2017) coupled with ongoing ignorance about anti-Blackness (Dumas, 2016). Another group of historians, however, claimed this approach encourages a victim mentality among Black people. They launched *1776 Unites* to celebrate the opportunities created for Black Americans through capitalism, starting this history with the American Revolution in 1776. We reject that responsible teaching about the consequences of enslavement encourages a victim mentality and have questions about capitalism's track record of doing right by Black communities (Marable, 2015). We greatly appreciate *The 1619 Project*'s resources and align with education scholars LaGarrett King and Crystal Simmons's (2018) premise that a better world will be built when teachers resist singular narratives to explore peoples' full humanity in history. Revealing a broader scope to students "requires an exploration into the complexities of being human . . . that do not always align with the celebratory prisms most histories present" (p. 110).

Regardless of their positions on these normative questions, historians' primary concepts within the discipline of history include *chronology, cause and effect, change and continuity*, and *turning points*. The most common tools include *primary sources* (letters, diaries, photographs, etc.) and *artifacts* that preserve information from the past. None of these tools are neutral—what sources exist depends on who has controlled their preservation and curation (museums, archives, etc.). These collections always reveal a particular politics that often uphold what those in power deem to be most important and valuable. In other words, not everything that has mattered has been documented or preserved. This doesn't mean that what does exist is inherently oppressive garbage—just that we must always be mindful of which sources we use and how we contextualize them for students.

In addition, we want to point out that *all* children can and should engage with primary sources, including the very young (Savage &

Wesson, 2016), students who are differently abled (De La Paz et al, 2007), and emergent bilingual students (Salinas, Fránquiz, & Guberman, 2006). You will be astonished by students' insights as you ask them to engage in close observation ("What do you notice?"), make inferences ("What's going on here, and what makes you say that?"), and find connections ("How does that relate to what we're learning about?"). Ultimately, it's our job as thoughtful social studies educators to help *all* students think more critically about the consequences of remembering—or forgetting—certain stories and telling them in certain ways.

All of this is intended to cultivate students' historical-thinking skills. As social studies education professors Peter Seixas and Carla Peck (2004) outline, historical thinking is the construction of narratives that help us make sense of how our world came to be. It includes *determining significance* by identifying which events and people we deem worthy of our attention; *establishing credibility* through the critical analysis of historical accounts to determine whose word we should take and why; *orienting ourselves as historical subjects* by understanding how our notions of "progress," "decline," "continuity," and "change" are relative to our own identities and experiences; *applying empathy and moral judgment* by grounding evaluations of people's actions in light of what shaped and constrained them (societal pressures, cultural values, etc.) while upholding a belief in a "historically transcendent" (Seixas & Peck, 2004, p. 113) recognition of everyone's humanity; and *acknowledging the range of human agency* by noting the power dynamics within a historical moment while not discounting how even the most oppressed of people have found ways to act, resist, and create. Whew!

As an example, let's consider how we might teach about when Christopher Columbus and the men who accompanied him landed in the Caribbean. As we (de)construct a historical narrative around this event with our students, we inevitably determine who and what is significant. The dominant narrative celebrates the colonization of the "New World" by focusing on the bravery and scientific knowledge of Columbus and his men in securing the "West Indies" for Spain. While recognizing this event as a huge turning point because of the settlement that occurred after 1492, a more nuanced and accurate counter narrative would not start the story with Columbus, but rather with the long histories and diversity of Indigenous Peoples who lived on Turtle Island or Abya Yala. It would acknowledge that Columbus was not the first "explorer" by including others from Asia, Africa, and Europe who came *before* 1492 and highlighting the different relationships they built with Indigenous Peoples. It would also consider a range of primary sources documenting what happened (the diaries of Columbus justifying abuse, letters to Spain from Bartolomé de las Casas who was horrified by the expedition's violence, oral traditions of the Taíno, etc.), and questioning how best to remember Columbus through observances of holidays, names of places, or memorial statues. Notice how we never recommended making crafts of the Niña, Pinta, or Santa Maria? Let's nip that in the bud right now.

## Economics

Ah, economics. Notoriously the most loathed and anxiety-producing of the social studies disciplines. Fear not! This is actually the discipline *most* well-suited to the education of young children. Seriously. If you think about it as the gross domestic product or the stock market, then it doesn't make much sense to teach at the elementary level. When we put on our economics goggles, however, we suddenly recognize how even the youngest of children "think like economists" all day, every day. The most important questions economists ask are *What is scarce, and why?* and *How do people allocate scarce resources?* or, translated for kid-speak: *What do we want and need? Is there enough of what we want and need? What do we do when there isn't enough? What are the consequences of our decisions?* The normative side to these questions involve the classic normative word "should": *What should people want and need? What should we do when there isn't enough? What consequences are fair and just?*

As parents of young children in addition to being teachers, we can tell you that kids apply economic thinking *very* early: "That's not fair! Why does Sofia get to stay up late, but I have to go to bed?" or "It's my turn on the swings!" These examples highlight the fundamental conceptual tools for economists: *scarcity* (not enough of something) and *needs and wants*, which includes understanding *goods and services* (what we need or want); *production, distribution, and consumption* (how we get what we need and want in consideration of what is fair and just); *opportunity costs* (what we give up or forego to get what we need or want); *incentives* (what motivates someone for a particular need or want); and *independence and interdependence* (how we work alone and together to fairly meet people's wants and needs). Economic tools include a variety of ways to make *decisions* and consider or document their *consequences* (decision trees, cost-benefit and impact analyses).

Despite their readiness, elementary students rarely learn explicitly about economic thinking. That doesn't mean they aren't constantly learning implicit economic lessons, of course. For instance, the ubiquitous classroom management strategy of offering prizes or shopping in a class store can negatively impact students in poverty and reinforce capitalist consumption (Lagerwerff, 2016). Picture books tend to feature upward mobility in characters' celebratory story arcs (Forest, 2014). And let us get on a soapbox for a moment to share how frustrated we are with how "needs and wants" so often gets taught at the elementary level. It is not, we repeat NOT, a preset list where humans' needs are air, food, water, and shelter, and wants are things like a computer or a boat. *Needs and wants can only ever be understood in the context of specific situations* (S. Gallagher & Hodges, 2010). If I'm drowning, water is not a need, right? Maybe that boat would be what I *need* to save my life—it isn't a *want*. The fundamental reason we teach students how to identify wants and needs in context is so that they can prioritize to make sound decisions. For the record, this prioritization is not just situational like in our drowning example—it's also cultural. In some communities, the needs of future generations or the community trump any one person's immediate, individual concerns. Point being, there is rarely a "right" decision—but often only decisions that are better or worse, given all of these factors. It's our job to teach youth how to juggle them in a considerate way.

Every discipline should help students step back from what may be "normal" to them in order to imagine a different and better world—in other words, we need to consider what the dominant narratives are relative to these disciplinary questions and make sure we're attending to the counter narratives. With regard to economics, this means considering how we use and distribute resources, who gets to decide the consequences of those choices on the world around us, and how we may want to do things differently. It means noticing and questioning the dominant narratives of capitalist logics about individual ownership, consumption, and individualism through maxims like "bigger is better," "pull yourself up by your bootstraps," or "if you work hard you will get ahead" (Swalwell, 2021). Early childhood educators Ann Pelo and Kendra Pelojoaquin (2006) detail how some of their preschool students were frustrated with the power dynamics of the rules their classmates had created for Lego play (who could have which pieces, what they could be used for). Pelo and Pelojoaquin harnessed this teachable moment to talk about power and ways that different groups in their community created rules about ownership and shared use of resources. Professor Erin Adams's blog (erinonecon.net) is filled with additional ideas for how to apply these concepts in elementary classrooms.

To build a better world, we have to teach students to evaluate the status quo and dream up alternatives. Thinking like economists is *essential* to this project, especially when it comes to considering how we are all connected, and how we might better take care of each other and the planet. Students can easily apply economic thinking as they study issues like labor rights, animal rights, health care, gentrification, sanitation, pollution, housing, and mutual aid efforts at the local, national, and global levels in the past and present—and consider what better solutions might be for the future. Support for teachers to do this exists, especially around issues related to sustainability and collective organizing with rich opportunities for integration with math and science. Take the teacher's guide for the United Nations' Sustainability Goals or *A People's Curriculum for the Earth* (Bigelow & Swinehart, 2014). Picture books are also great resources, whether you teach an old standard through the lens of economic justice (J. L Gallagher & Kelly, 2019) or you include books that are dedicated to examples of collective organizing. Check out our website www.ssfabw.com for specific recommendations.

**FINANCIAL LITERACY**

Many states now have financial literacy standards that tend to present financial behavior as objectively "good" or "bad," take for granted the accumulation of wealth as the primary goal, ignore the vastly different financial contexts and consequences facing different communities, and omit the ways financial institutions exacerbate inequalities and prey on people in poverty (Adams, 2020b; Sonu & Marri, 2018; Whitlock, 2019). Unsurprisingly, for-profit financial institutions' lobbying is often why such standards exist. Financial literacy is important, but it is *not* the solution to poverty as many standards imply; most people aren't in poverty because of "bad" financial decisions but rather because of long-standing structural inequalities and exploitation. A "critically compassionate" financial literacy education, on the other hand, *does* take these injustices into account (See Blue, O'Brien, & Makar, 2018; Lucey, 2018).

Notice we have not used the word *money*. Sure, money is one resource that can be scarce, but economics is so much more than that. Financial literacy standards focused on money management are not meant to replace "economics" as the science of decision-making and deliberating about fairness and justice. And what young person doesn't want to make decisions or deliberate about fairness and justice? Furthermore, what diverse democracy with vast inequalities doesn't need people who can do that well?

## Behavioral Sciences

Closely related to economics are the behavioral sciences, which include *psychology*, *anthropology*, and *sociology*. Broadly speaking, psychologists study the human mind and behavior (emotions, mental health), anthropologists study the practices of cultural groups (rites of passage for the Amish, biker-gang slang, etc.), and sociologists study social groups and inequality (the experiences of wealthy Black women, transphobia). These subdisciplines influence each other quite a bit and it can be fuzzy where one stops and another begins. Their empirical questions include, but are not limited to, *What identities exist, and what diversity exists within those identities? How do people interact within and across groups, and why? Who has power and who doesn't, and why? What disparities exist and why?* and *How do advantages and disadvantages compound for people with intersecting dominant and marginalized identities?* The normative questions are, *What identities should be recognized? How should people interact? Who should have power?* and *What should we do about inequities, especially those that exist across various intersections of identities?*

The most important concepts of these disciplines include: *social identities* (race, class, gender, sexual identity, ability, nationality, etc.), *power* and *oppression* and *patterns of disparity* (racism, classism, sexism, homo- and transphobia, ableism, xenophobia), *culture* and *cultural universals* (rites of passage, traditions, family structures. etc.), and *intersectionality*, *stereotypes*, and *perspective-taking*. The tools behavioral scientists use include *ethnography* (qualitative analysis of a group or place over a long period of time), *content analysis* (examining a text for what it leaves out and how it presents what it includes), *interviews*, various strategies for *identifying and interrupting bias* (implicit bias tests, critical self-reflection activities), and *statistics* to track trends and patterns (data charts). Ultimately, the behavioral sciences help teach *open-mindedness*: making cross-cultural interactions ordinary for students, challenging stereotypes and overgeneralizations of people in situations different from our own, valuing the knowledge of "ordinary" people, and teaching the habit of seeking out multiple perspectives (Merryfield, 2012).

Young people are ready to engage in behavioral science questions, both to learn about themselves and others. Even very young children are well aware of their various identities, can detail their family structure, and participate in (or even create) cultural traditions. They also have understandings of social hierarchies, their place in them, and the impact of current events on them—especially if they are in positions that make them vulnerable to violence or harm. Consider the child living in fear that his parents will be deported (Flannery, 2017), the preschooler worrying about their parent who was deployed overseas (Paris, DeVoe, Ross, & Acker, 2010), the transgender student fighting for access to the girls' restroom (Martino & Cumming-Potvin, 2016), the Black boy learning survival strategies from his parents (Sanders & Young, 2020), the child taking responsibility for their family's food insecurity (Fram et al., 2011), or the girl trying to avoid bullying related to her autism (Malecki, Demaray, Smith, & Emmons, 2020). It's really just children with dominant identities who we "protect" from the oppression that marginalized children live every day. We aren't bursting the bubble of childhood when we validate marginalized students' experiences through the explicit curriculum, nor are we doing any favors for kids who are unaware when we try to shelter them.

To be clear, attending to oppression in elementary social studies doesn't mean that we exclusively focus on trauma—that would be unethical and utterly exhausting. We want to complement counter narratives' frank look at forces of oppression with "looking for the helpers," as Mr. Rogers's mother famously advised, and learning about the incredible resistance and survivance of communities across time (for example, Sabzalian, 2019; Vizenor, 1999). We also want to make space for students to enjoy and explore what professor Özlem Sensoy and writer Robin DiAngelo (2017) call *personal identities* (hobbies, interests, etc.) as well as *structural identities* (race, gender)—and examine how both are intertwined (Wheeler-Bell, 2021). Sara Ahmed's (2019) book *Being the Change: Lessons and Strategies to Teach Social Comprehension* has suggestions for exploring identities with youth in multiple ways. To be clear: there is no room in our classrooms for dominant narratives that position some identities or communities as "normal" or "better" than others—even those seemingly benevolent dominant narratives that preach "acceptance" or "tolerance." Inherent in that approach is still the damaging idea that what is being accepted or tolerated is strange, atypical, or exotic.

Another helpful resource for elementary students to articulate their lived knowledge in ways that both celebrate their identities and unpack related forms of oppression (Ching, 2005) is through a chart Katy created while partnering with third-grade teacher Zipporah Smith (see figure). In this chart they defined different categories related to identity that serve as mechanisms for distributing resources and power in various contexts (namely, age, social class, gender, race, ethnicity, language, sexuality, ability, and religion). They stressed that none of these categories are natural or fixed, but each one may hold powerful meaning in particular moments and places. The third graders provided examples of each category, then articulated the difference between groups that tend to experience advantage with institutional power and those who tend to experience disadvantage or oppression. Students had *many* ideas about what should go in each box based on their own lived experiences. The class illustrator even creatively drew pictures to represent the discussion, including a person wearing roller skates with rocket boosters to represent "advantage." Third-grade genius! Lastly, Katy identified herself in each category to model how to reflect on one's socially constructed identities in relation to institutional power, and what that means for our responsibilities to care for each other (Table B.3 *Identity and Power Chart* in Appendix B).

Not only does a chart like this provide an opportunity for community building and self-awareness, but it lays the foundation for the academic vocabulary to apply across the school day. It may seem nerve-wracking to attend to questions of power and oppression with young children in this way, but the research is abundantly clear that the best

| "IDENTITY" Who you are... | definition / picture | POWER / ADVANTAGE | OPPRESSED / DISADVANTAGE | MS. SWALWELL |
|---|---|---|---|---|
| AGE | Babies, Toddlers, Youth, Teens, Adults, Elderly | Adults, Teens | Elderly, youth, Babies | Adult |
| SOCIAL CLASS | Poor, Middle Class, Rich | Rich, middle class | Poor | Middle Class |
| GENDER | Boys, Girls, Transgender | Boys | Girls | Girl |
| RACE | White, Black, Brown, Biracial, Multiracial | White | People of Color "racist" | White |
| ETHNICITY | Nation/Culture, Laotian, Nepali, Mexican, Italian, American, African American | European Americans | xenophobia, everyone else | European American |
| LANGUAGE | English, Lao, Nepali, Spanish, Swahili, Urdu, French, Korean | English | all other languages | English, Spanish "bilingual" |
| ABILITY | Blind, Deaf, Paraplegic, brain injury, Learning disability, Disease, Down syndrome | Able-bodied | People who are differently abled, Glasses | Celiac disease |
| SEXUAL ORIENTATION | "Straight", Gay, Lesbian, Bisexual, LGBTQ | Straight | LGBTQ "homophobic transphobic" | Straight |
| RELIGION | Christian, Jewish, Agnostic, Muslim, Atheist, Buddhist, Hindu | Christian | overweight | Agnostic (Christian) |

Identity Chart Created With Third Graders (PHOTO BY KATY SWALWELL)

way to help disrupt injustice is to frankly confront it in ways that take students' questions and experiences seriously (Winkler, 2009).

Many resources explore what this could look like when teaching elementary students about power and oppression including (but not limited to!) white supremacy, anti-Blackness, racism, ethnocentrism, and xenophobia (An, 2017; Brown & Brown, 2011; Pearcy, 2020; Randolph & DeMulder, 2008; Rodríguez, 2018a); anti-Semitism and Islamophobia (Bajaj, Ghaffar-Kucher, & Desai, 2016; Rodríguez, 2018b); heteronormativity, homophobia, transphobia, sexism, and gender variance (Butler-Wall, et al., 2016; Falkner & Clark, 2018; Tschida & Buchanan, 2017); settler colonialism (Finchum, 2006; Kaomea, 2005); consent (Kleinrock, 2018); and war (Connor, 2003).

In addition to scholarship, our students and the local communities in which we teach are also fantastic resources for teaching kids to think like behavioral scientists (Au, 2009). There are an infinite number of teachable moments and connections to make with students' families, communities, interests, and concerns. For example, second-grade teacher Rachel Hanes created a climate justice unit inspired by a student's family sharing their Nez Perce and Lakota cultural practices, which included protests against the Dakota Access Pipeline at Standing Rock (Hanes, 2020). And third-grade teacher Chelsea Vaught (2017), recognizing that "students' lives and the policies surrounding their identities are always present" (p. 24), found ways to support her Somali American Muslim student who was understandably worried about Islamophobic and xenophobic responses if he included stylized Arabic script in a printmaking project highlighting his cultural identities.

We must constantly be on the lookout for those *problematic* teachable moments when the curriculum includes a dominant narrative, even in implicit or unintended ways that can tokenize a student or put them in a tough spot—the morning meeting question we ask ("Where did everyone go for spring break?"), the way we address our class ("Okay, boys and girls!"), how we frame the experiences we offer ("Let's try this weird new food!"), to name a few. Knowing ourselves well enough to check our own biases and "commonsense" assumptions as well as learning about the demographics and histories of where we teach, collaborating with local organizations, and building relation-ships with families are essential to strengthening our understanding of counter narratives and helping children learn the value of thinking like behavioral scientists. This demands balancing attention to local communities with connections to people and places across the globe—keeping in mind that many children already have rich transnational and transcultural experiences that get ignored when teachers center native-born, U.S.-centric perspectives. Remember, a curriculum that emphasizes dominant narratives framing cross-cultural interactions as scary or strange and reinforces stereotypes that essentialize or rank communities does nothing but reinforce inequity.

## Civics

When we introduce civics as a social studies discipline, we often hear teacher candidates say, "Oh, I don't like politics!" There's a lot to unpack there. First and foremost: If you are a teacher, then you are engaged in a super-political profession. Whether conscious of it or not, "teachers per-petuate values, beliefs, myths, and meanings about the world" (Darder, 2017, p. 55) and socialize students accordingly. Decisions about what to teach are inherently political because we have to make decisions about what to include and exclude. Schools themselves are political sites, and often function to condition students to dominant norms and the polit-ical climate of the day (Darder, 2017).

Remember—being *political* is different than being *partisan*. The former refers to any decision about how to live together while the lat-ter refers to the work of political parties. Teachers, especially in public schools, should not use their position to promote a partisan agenda—though learning *about* political parties is useful, of course, and teachers should promote civic skills and virtues like critical thinking, the build-ing of community, and the development of opinions rooted in high quality evidence. Are those increasingly partisan values? Sadly, yes. But that doesn't mean we abandon them.

Fundamental empirical questions related to civics include *Who is in our community? How do people govern themselves? What are a commu-nity's rules and consequences for breaking them? How does social change* *occur?* and *What tools do people have to identify and solve a problem?* Fundamental normative questions include *Who should be in our circle of care and concern?* and *What does that mean for our obligations for how to treat others, and expectations of how others will treat us?* How should people govern and organize themselves? What are fair and just rules and consequences? What social change should occur?* and *What is a problem in our community, and how should we solve it?*

Tools for thinking like a political scientist and acting as an engaged community member include *deliberation* and *discussion* and *debate,* various *changemaking strategies* (letter writing, boycotts, collective bargaining, marches, civil disobedience, campaigns, elections, etc.), *restorative justice,* and social science instruments like *surveys* and *observations. Critical media literacy* is increasingly important (Luft, 2016) as our capacity to care about each other and address social problems depends greatly on our ability to access and interpret credible information (Weber & Hagan, 2020). As social media and propagandist news sources make this harder—and students soak up literal hours of these messages every day—critical media literacy *must* be among the skills we are teaching children so they can thoughtfully engage with advertising (Gainer, Valdez-Gainer, & Kinard, 2009), memes (Elmore & Coleman, 2019), "fake" news (Journell, 2020), and partisan rhetoric (McArthur, 2019).

**TEACHING CRITICAL MEDIA LITERACY**

For resources on teaching critical media literacy, check out Renee Hobbs's (2020) book *Mind Over Media: Propaganda Education for a Digital Age* as well as the work of teacher educators Dan Krutka (2017) and Carolyn Weber and Heather Hagan (2020) who created powerful inquiries for upper-elementary classrooms that center student evaluation of media sources. The News Literacy Project (www.thenewsliteracyproject.org), Learning for Justice's Digital Literacy Framework (www.learningforjustice.org/frameworks/digital-literacy), Tom Jackson and Cristina Guitian's (2020) *Fake News* and Scheibe and Rogow's (2012) six key concepts in media analysis, are also quite helpful.

Does civics include teaching *elections* and the *branches and functions of local, state, and federal governments*? Yep. But it also involves learning about *social movements* and *activism* and *protest strategies* and *rights* and *responsibilities* and *citizenship*. Juicy stuff! Analyzing or involving students in civic engagement inevitably involves the concept of citizenship, which education professor Amanda Vickery (2015) powerfully reminds us has *always* been experienced differently by various marginalized groups—if they are included at all. The government affords some citizens wider options for civic engagement and exposes them to fewer or less damaging consequences for their actions, whereas others face greater constraints and risks due to oppression (transphobia, anti-Blackness, xenophobia). Of course, our communities have valuable members who the state does not and may never consider to be a citizen. Questions of who should be a citizen and what the rights and responsibilities of citizens should be are among the most important questions we must grapple with in a diverse democracy.

When applying a civics lens to our teaching, it is exceedingly important to keep these inequities in mind and do whatever we can to *not* reinforce students' vulnerabilities. For example, we know that school rules and teachers' classroom-management strategies communicate all sorts of messages about what kinds of civic engagement are good or bad. They often emphasize students' efforts to put their own self-interest over the common good or automatically obey authority without complaint. Education scholars Chris Busey and Irenea Walker (2017) call this "authoritarian patriotism" (p. 460); the ideology behind approaches prizing unquestioning loyalty and conformity or framing dissent as dangerous and un-American. Elementary schools are filled with models like this that actually work *against* children learning to build a better world.

Instead, we recommend a critically democratic (Busey & Walker, 2017), "justice-oriented" model that values rules and volunteerism but stresses consideration of the common good, questioning the status quo, examining root causes of social problems, and imagining and working to realize a better world (Westheimer & Kahne, 2004). Of course, we must explicitly describe what we mean by a "better world." If we don't, then protesters like the white nationalists at the 2017 Unite the Right rally in Charlottesville, Virginia, could qualify as "good" citizens in that they took action against what they perceived to be the root causes of social problems: Jewish people and People of Color. We would *never* consider our teaching a success if we saw one of our students applying what they had learned about social movements and inequality to participate in that rally. A vision of a "better" world that is hateful and dehumanizing has no place in public schools (or anywhere, for that matter).

In ways big and small, even the youngest of elementary students can absolutely learn about all sorts of different ways to organize and govern themselves to address community concerns in a justice-oriented, critically democratic way (Payne, 2020) from solving classroom problems like where kids should sit (Wheeler-Bell & Swalwell, 2021) to demanding that city officials address their school's crumbling infrastructure (Schultz, 2018). Check out general resources for youth-led activism like *The Kid's Guide to Social Action* by Barbara A. Lewis (1998), issue-specific resources like *Young Water Protectors: A Story About Standing Rock* by Aslan Tudor, Kelly Tudor, and Jason EagleSpeaker (2018), and specific campaigns like #1000blackgirlbooks launched by Marley Dias for additional examples of this.

To think that other people will do the hard work of solving social problems, to simply follow rules without question, to ignore the root causes of suffering, or to blame victims of oppression for the disparities that exist—none of that helps build a better world that is more just and sustainable.

### Geography

Last discipline! When you think of geography, are you picturing a map? While maps are incredibly important for geographers, it's not their only tool as they try to answer empirical questions like *What places matter to people, and why? How do people represent places? What makes places similar and different?* and *What connections do people and places have, and why?* Geographers' primary concepts include the five themes identified by the National Geographic Society (Boehm & Petersen, 1994): *physical* and *human characteristics of a place; absolute* and *relative location; human–environment interaction; movement;* and *regions* as well as related concepts like *distribution, orientation,* various *landforms* and *waterways*, the *global* relative to the *local*, and *sustainability*. Tools for spatial thinking include *cartography* with *globes*, *grids*, *graphs*, and a million different kinds of *maps* that include components like a *key*, a *scale*, *representations*, and *projections*.

Geography education professors Sarah Witham Bednarz, Gillian Acheson, and Robert S. Bednarz (2006) recommend teaching *about* maps so that students can interpret and produce maps themselves, teaching *with* maps so students learn specific content, and teaching *through* maps so students can think spatially as they solve problems (p. 399). All three approaches provide opportunities for interdisciplinary curriculum whether it's using a map to locate where an event took place (history), documenting important cultural sites in a community (behavioral sciences), assessing pros and cons of a spatial decision (economics), or understanding representation in a governing body (civics). As with the other disciplines, we cannot stress enough how important it is to engage even very young children in geographic thinking and spatial reasoning (see Strachan, Block, & Roberts, 2016).

Ultimately, a space is made into a place because humans have given it meaning. And if humans are involved, there are going to be power struggles. Normative geographic questions thus include *Who should get to access or claim a place? How should people represent places? What makes a place good or bad?* and *What are our obligations to particular places and the life that inhabits them, and why?* There are so many contentious issues related to these questions. Consider controversies over whether places ought to change their names to avoid commemorating enslavers or to restore Indigenous names of places. There are all sorts of debates about land use including right-wing militias declaring the federal government has no claim on grazing lands and environmentalists' protests against fracking. Gentrification, water disputes, the effects of climate change, gerrymandering, environmental racism, and restrictions on refugees' ability to seek asylum highlight the crucial role of spatial thinking in understanding and solving contemporary social problems.

Geography as a discipline can also help nurture students' love of a place. Ideally, this love translates into their willingness and ability to take actions to improve the well-being of the social and ecological places that are special to them. Professor David Gruenewald (2003) articulates the need for a "critical pedagogy of place" that teaches about struggles with oppression in relation to specific places to help students. Through Indigenous and Black feminist lenses, professor Fikile Nxumalo (2019) advocates for education that equips students to inherit an ecologically damaged planet without positioning them (especially those who are white and wealthy) as "future earth saviors and stewards" (p. 1). More-over, Nxumalo and her colleague Marleen Villanueva (2019) stress the need for children to "relate to the more-than-human world" (p. 41), to disrupt dominant narratives that view humans as superior to or separate from nonhumans, and reject valuing more-than-human others (cows, trees, mountains, rivers) in terms of how humans benefit from them. This is the kind of geographic thinking that will help us build a better world.

There are also important values-based dilemmas regarding spatial representation. In short, we must teach children that maps are not neu-tral (Kaiser & Wood, 2001). That doesn't mean they're not useful—it's simply a reminder that maps always construct a narrative, which means we need to be mindful of power and perspective. There are several exercises we have done with students to illuminate this. One involves exploring how many continents there are, a deceptively simple question that becomes more challenging as they examine criteria that depend on plate tectonics or the history of colonization and white supremacy (for example, identifying "Europe" as a continent makes little sense unless we are centering whiteness; many people in Latin America consider "America" to be a single continent).

As another example, our students create mental maps of the world in 5 minutes. There are groans and giggles as they sketch. Afterward, we compare their drawings with more formal projections, revealing how deeply internalized dominant narratives are. They often depict what we refer to as North America and Europe as oversized with lots of details while Africa, Central America, and South America are tiny, detail-less, and displaced. They often label Asia as "China," drawn as a rectangle with no Korean, Arabian, or Indian peninsulas. Their maps have no waterways, U.S. territories, or island nations except Australia. Students with deep connections to other parts of the world, however, provide important counter narratives that push back against the erasures and inaccuracies of the dominant perspective. In addition, we discuss the consequences of not having particular places on our minds. Will we care about the health of oceans if we don't think to label them? Will we pay attention to politicians' decisions about wars if we don't know where they are happening? Are we more likely to believe stereotypes about places that are skewed on our maps (Randolph & DeMulder, 2008)? Will we ignore pleas for help from fellow Americans if we do not even know what legally constitutes the United States? Will we recognize demands to respect sovereignty if we do not know Indigenous names for places or the history of how borders have been constructed and contested?

Thinking geographically is so much more than being able to read a map: it's questioning how we name and perceive the world and never taking for granted that the places or borders entrenched in our minds are natural or fixed or accurate. Thinking about the "where" of our world is *fundamental* to any attempt to make it better.

## Key Takeaways

We know this is a lot and invite you to revisit these sections as you move through the book. As a few key takeaways, remember the following points: *all* of the social studies disciplines are important and inform each other for a robust, interdisciplinary understanding of our social world. Each is organized around normative *and* empirical questions rather than fixed facts or figures to memorize (though facts and figures are, of course, important). None of them are static or acultural—the questions we ask are always intimately tied to who we are and what we care about. And, lastly, rather than teaching in ways that reinforce dominant narratives obscuring inequities or justifying them as "natural," we must center *counter* narratives that offer a more complex, accurate understanding of the world.

## Putting These Ideas Into Practice

### Find the Social Studies Everywhere

Pick any object at random and generate as many empirical and normative questions from each discipline as possible. We have our teacher education students select something from a basket of everyday objects. Our

favorite was, strangely enough, a tampon. It sparked a flurry of compelling questions: When was the tampon invented? Who invented it? How
did women get convinced to use it? What do people who are homeless do
if they need tampons? What are tampons made out of to be safe? Do people in other parts of the world use tampons? Students burst into intense
deliberation around normative questions like whether the government
should provide tampons for free or if people should hide tampons when
they walk to the bathroom. Whatever objects you use, students can and
will flood you with questions. Giving them regular space to do this will
help nurture their natural curiosity and critical thinking.

### Connect Disciplinary Questions to Your Life

As a way to critically reflect on your own lived experience in relation
to the disciplines, respond to the following questions. This activity
can be adapted for young learners to understand disciplinary thinking
and build community. While we do not want anyone to reexperience
trauma through these questions, we do encourage students to avoid
superficial answers. Meta-reflection on the patterns of responses can
help bring to the surface the ways in which our dominant or nondominant positions matter. A template for your responses (Table B.4 *Connect Disciplinary Questions to Your Life*) and a model of our responses
(Table B.5 *Connect Disciplinary Questions to Your Life: Noreen and
Katy's Sample Responses*) are shared in Appendix B.

- **History**: What historical event or figure is important to your
  family and why? (In other words, "My family wouldn't be the
  same if __ hadn't happened/lived.")
- **Geography**: Where is a place that you have felt like you
  belong(ed), and why? Where is a place that you *haven't* felt a sense
  of belonging, and why?
- **Economics**: What has been a pivotal choice in your life, and
  what shaped your decision?
- **Behavioral Sciences**: What social identity or combination of
  identities is most important in your life, and why?
- **Civics**: What community rules, levels of government, or social
  movements impact your life most?

## 2

# The Transformative Potential of Social Studies

This chapter outlines the various theoretical approaches and beliefs that inform our framework for anti-oppressive social studies in elementary schools. In it, we explain how we understand the world, why we want to make it better, and what we imagine a better world to look like. We will lay out our research and theory-driven philosophies by framing them with overarching questions.

## Why Do We Use the Term *Anti-Oppressive* Social Studies?

There are many labels for the kind of social studies education we describe in this book. While we use *anti-oppressive*, others may call similar approaches *anti-bias*, *anti-racist*, or *social justice*. Each of these terms has its limitations and may inspire some while alienating others. For us, *anti-bias* feels too focused on interpersonal prejudices with little acknowledgement of structural power differentials, and *anti-racist* does not necessarily attend to the ways that multiple oppressions may intersect with racism—a concept that legal scholar Kimberlé Crenshaw described as intersectionality, which we detail below. With regards to *social justice*, education scholar Gloria Ladson-Billings (2015) explains that the term is not expansive enough to help us confront the injustices that we aim to disrupt, largely because it depends too heavily on

Western conceptions of justice (which often focus on individuals) and is typically relegated to theory rather than practice. Instead, Ladson-Billings argues, "what we should be seeking and fighting for is justice . . . *just* justice." We agree with Ladson-Billings's concerns about the ways social justice has increasingly been taken up as a buzzword in ways that ultimately maintain the status quo. Thus, our goal is justice—*just* justice.

*Anti-oppressive*, then, draws our attention to long-standing structures and systems within which people learn and enact prejudices that reproduce unjust power relations. We recognize that oppression takes many forms, and it can be an insidious shapeshifter that is not always easy to identify. While it has historical roots that are important to understand, it is also crucial to recognize that oppression *still* exists in multiple forms in the world around us: racism, heterosexism, classism, ableism, transphobia, anti-Semitism, Islamophobia, xenophobia, capitalism, and many more forms of exploitation, marginalization, powerlessness, cultural domination, and violence (Young, 2014). In other words, not everyone in our world is able to live their lives freely. For people with multiple intersecting marginalized identities, oppression is especially pronounced and may be experienced in distinct ways that people without those identities may never understand. Oppression also extends beyond human life; for example, consider the ongoing acts of exploitation and decimation of the air, land, waterways, animals, and plants.

Some types of oppression are so deeply ingrained in our culture that they often go unrecognized or can easily be confused—with damaging consequences. For example, non-Native people regularly ignore entirely or misunderstand and mischaracterize Native or Indigenous Peoples as a racialized category. While some Native and Indigenous people do consider themselves to be Black or Brown, others consider themselves to be or are viewed by others as white. In addition to their ethnoracial identities, Native Peoples and Nations are distinctive because they have *sovereignty*. That is, nearly 400 treaties (contracts between two sovereign nations) recognize the sovereignty of Native Nations, which includes their rights to self-govern, sustain, and utilize their homelands as they see fit. Yet the U.S. government has threatened Native lands and lives—both in the past and present. These ongoing efforts toward erasure and domination are known as *settler colonialism*. However, while settler colonialism clearly inhibits Native sovereignty, it is not always recognized in PK–12 schools as an ongoing form of oppression.

---

### ANTI-OPPRESSIVE SOCIAL STUDIES IS FOR *EVERYONE*

Even the least diverse communities need anti-oppressive social studies. In fact, it may be even *more* important in homogeneous communities where students are likely to have few opportunities to learn firsthand about and across differences, especially in communities populated by people with *dominant* identities (white, wealthy) who render the forces and consequences of oppression invisible. Besides, no community is ever completely homogeneous, nor are any communities disconnected from the rest of the world.

---

We use the term *oppression* broadly and stand against its many forms in schools and society. As decades of social studies and literacy research have shown us, the curriculum shared from preschool through 12th grade often ignores or explains away oppression and centers the perspectives of white, middle- and upper-class, cisgender, heterosexual, able-bodied, settler, English-monolingual Christian men in the Global North. Despite many efforts to create more inclusive curricula, there remains little diverse representation in the literary canon, and the United States continues to be portrayed as an exceptional nation of ongoing progress and a land of opportunity where hardworking individuals thrive (VanSledright, 2008). In this dominant narrative, injustice either does not exist or is rationalized through bigotry or myths of meritocracy.

We use the term *anti-oppressive* to describe an education that explicitly addresses the functions and impacts of oppression as well as the courageous and inspiring struggles against it—*as a means of disrupting oppression*. For the record, there is no "non-oppressive" teaching. Because teaching entails making infinite choices about what to include and foreground, as well as what to exclude and background, there is no escaping it. As educators, our curriculum and instruction are either invested in reproducing oppression or committed to disrupting it. You have to pick a side.

## What Is the Better World We're Imagining, and How Do We Build It?

### Beyond Diversity and Inclusion

While we appreciate some curricular and pedagogical approaches that celebrate difference, we want to make clear that our idea of an education to build a better world is not one that is simply more diverse or inclusive. Of course, there is value in teaching students to appreciate differences and to develop a strong sense of self, but these are not sufficient for the goal of equipping them to identify and address a range of injustices. While *diversity* and *inclusivity* are popular buzzwords and initiatives, simply making room to celebrate a range of identities, cultures, languages, and traditions fails to explain why particular identities, cultures, languages, and traditions are centered and considered normal while others get pushed to the margins or attacked. Even the act of "being more inclusive" still implies that the dominant group has the power to decide what gets in and what stays out. As public school administrator Lauryn Mascareñaz tweeted, "The phrase 'INVITE marginalized people to the table' assumes a white, dominant culture as the hosts of the table/conversation. It implies that they are benevolent decision makers who so kindly invited 'others'" (2020). Simply adding seats to a table is *not* an anti-oppressive solution. What we support are efforts to rethink how people come to sit around the table in the first place—or even create another place to sit.

Higher education scholar D-L Stewart (2017) distinguishes among these ideas of diversity, inclusion, equity, and justice by the fundamentally different kinds of questions they ask. For example, a diversity focus might ask, "Who is in the room?" or "How many more of a minoritized group do we have this year than last year?" while an equity perspective would ask, "Who is trying to get in the room, but can't?" "Whose presence in the room is under constant threat of erasure?" or "What conditions have we created that maintain certain groups as the perpetual majority?" An inclusion approach might ask, "Have everyone's ideas been heard?" or "Is this environment safe for everyone to feel like they belong?" In contrast, a justice framing would ask, "Whose ideas aren't taken seriously because they aren't in the majority?" or "Whose safety is sacrificed or minimized for the sake of the people feeling comfortable to maintain dehumanizing views?" (para.7). While Stewart's (2017) examples are designed to examine postsecondary educational spaces and institutions, they certainly apply to PK–12 settings—both for students and for those who are charged with educating them. They also apply to the kind of social studies teaching and learning we urge educators to imagine in this book.

## Deeper Than Kindness or Tolerance

Similar to diversity and inclusion efforts, some educators subscribe to teaching "kindness" or "tolerance" as a way to disrupt oppression. But being kind or tolerating someone does not change or critique inequitable power structures. You can be kind to someone while ignoring the oppression that impacts their daily life. You can tolerate someone's presence without considering them to be an equal or addressing the power imbalance that positions you over them. While some conceptions of kindness focus on the importance of compassion, this is not inherent to the word, which is frequently considered a synonym for niceness. For example, we live in the Midwest, where niceness is considered a regional trait that folks often brag about. But for BIPOC communities, niceness often serves as a front for behavior that masks racism (Loga, 2020). Although acts of genuine kindness are certainly essential to the work we describe, in that we seek to make connections and be in community with others, we take pause whenever kindness is the sole guiding principle as it does not necessarily mean that efforts are in place to identify and disrupt inequity and injustice.

## Mutual Concern and Beloved Community

Rather than a focus on a "diverse," "inclusive," or "kind" community, our vision of a better world largely draws from the legacies of Indigenous and Black feminist scholars who have long emphasized the importance of deep relationships of mutual obligation and care for each other

(Collins, 2002; Simpson, 2017). As neither of us is Indigenous nor Black, we strive to honor these insights—not appropriate them. When we describe community, then, we are not solely thinking of those who surround us in the present. Rather, we view ourselves and everyone around us as part of the larger human experience within the context of nature and among other beings, and believe it is our responsibility to do right by all of them. We are obligated to care for each other and the world in which we live. To "care" means to seek to understand each other, to sacrifice for the community when appropriate, to use our unique gifts on behalf of others, and to value contributions that may be different than our own.

This emphasis on mutuality exists in many cultures and traditions, from the Nguni Bantu ubuntu ("I am because we are") to the Lakota mitákuye oyás'iŋ ("All my relations / we are all related") to the Mayan in lak'ech ala ki'n ("I am you and you are me") and to Zen Buddhist monk Thich Nhat Hanh's concept of interbeing. According to Nishnaabeg elder Edna Manitowabi (in Simpson, 2017), the Nishnaabeg word kobade refers to great-grandparents and great-grandchildren and means "a link in the chain between generations, between nations, between states of being, between individuals. I am a link in a chain. We are all links in a chain" (Simpson, 2017, p. 8). What affects one, affects all, past, present, and future. This interconnectedness is also reflected in many social and political organizations, including the Combahee River Collective, a Black lesbian socialist feminist organization that began meeting in 1974, which emphasized developing community through continual self-examination, inclusivity, and sharing ideas. To us, this mutuality is the essence of social studies, and a critical aspect of education.

This idea is echoed in Martin Luther King, Jr.'s vision of beloved community. Beloved community is one in which love and justice triumph over oppression, and is based on Christian teachings of love, peace, and self-sacrifice as well as the nonviolent activism of Mahatma Gandhi (Joseph, 2020). King's conception of love drew from the Greek New Testament agape, which means goodwill for all people. "*Agape* is love seeking to preserve and create community. It is insistence on community even when one seeks to break it. *Agape* is a willingness to sacrifice in the interest of mutuality" (M. L. King, 1960, p. 84). Ultimately, agape recognizes that all life is interrelated, and that we have a collective obligation to ensure that the most vulnerable are protected. This collective obligation is reflected in the words of poet Emma Lazarus (1883/1987), which were later paraphrased by King: "Until we are all free, none of us are free" (p. 30). In beloved community, the interests of the community—both human and more-than-human—are the priority over individual gains.

King considered beloved community to be an achievable goal that could be attained by a critical mass engaged in the "long and bitter—but beautiful—struggle for a new world" (Joseph, 2020). This long, bitter, beautiful struggle is the work of generations. Building a better world is not done quickly, nor is it done alone. The struggle is arduous because people in power are often deeply committed to preventing and squelching any efforts to change; it does not benefit them to create and maintain the conditions needed for justice and equity. So, rather than solely relying on convincing or pressuring leaders in positions of power to initiate the change we need, we understand our current world as one where social movements led by everyday people largely drive change both in and outside of existing systems and structures. This theory of change has implications for how and what we teach students, nurturing their "collective sensibilities" (Wheeler-Bell, 2014, p. 464), and exposing them to a variety of social movements' organizations and strategies as they develop their sense of justice.

## Dehumanization Is Not an Option

As we strive to help young people better understand the injustices in our world, we caution educators against presenting "both sides" of every issue. First, we want to stress that there are often more than two sides. Secondly, we agree with author Tayari Jones (2018) that this approach presents a "false equivalency of ideas" that can easily lead to what she calls the "'good people on both sides' phenomenon." "What is halfway between moral and immoral?" Jones powerfully asks. Similarly, middle school teacher Jonathan Gold (2017) describes arguments for teaching "both sides" as a trap that creates a false comparison between two or more contradictory sides while ignoring imbalances of power among them. Some issues, like enslavement, have only one "side" that values human life and liberation. A dehumanizing perspective defending slavery merits no defense in classrooms that are dedicated to beloved community. People's humanity is *never* up for debate, no matter their racialized identity, religion, sexuality, immigration status, and so forth. Additionally, the both sides approach often prioritizes intent while negating impact (Collins, 2019). Although intent matters, impact does too, and when impact leads to harm, that *must* be attended to in ways that strive to make things right for those who have been harmed.

The better world we imagine takes the firm stance that dehumanizing perspectives are *not* an option. We know that the line between dehumanizing language and differing perspectives may seem confusing. We view dehumanizing language as rhetoric that values *anyone* as less important or worthy based on some aspect of their identity. Some political stances or opinions overtly dehumanize, while others may be less obvious and may put educators in a tricky position.

Consider the example of Black Lives Matter and Blue Lives Matter. Black Lives Matter is a social movement that emerged from a hashtag created by Patrisse Cullors, Alicia Garza, and Opal Tometi in 2013 in response to the acquittal of Trayvon Martin's murderer, an event that made painfully clear how often Black people—even children—are targets of lethal violence, and how rarely those who perpetrate this violence face consequences or accountability. The hashtag Blue Lives Matter emerged in response, advocating for legislation that made the killing of law enforcement officers a hate crime. However, Black Lives Matter is about how society racializes Black bodies, presenting them as dangerous and disposable and treating them as if they *don't* matter. Being Black is not a choice, and not something that one can put on or take off. "Blue" references anyone who works in law enforcement, a profession that one *chooses* and goes unnoticed when not in uniform.

A perspective that defends the dehumanization of others is *not* anti-oppressive, and therefore does not represent the values of beloved community. We urge multiple perspectives and stories that add greater complexity and nuance to the dominant narrative, and even replace that narrative altogether, but the perspectives and stories must *always* make space for critiques related to power.

You want to teach students about Black Lives Matter and other local organizations that are working to end racial profiling. A colleague is upset that you would encourage such "divisive thinking" and demands that you instead teach children that "All Lives Matter." How would you respond?

## What Ideas Shape How We View Our Students and Our Work Together?

The centering of the collective is at the heart of what we want to achieve in social studies. Understanding the complexity of the collective is essential, particularly when it comes to those whose identities, experiences, and histories schools marginalize, sometimes in multiple ways. Here, we introduce you to three key theories that articulate how an anti-oppressive lens radically shifts how we view the students we work with and the content we engage in together: *intersectionality* (Crenshaw, 1988, 1991), *funds of knowledge* (Moll et al., 1992), and *transformative justice* (Winn, 2018).

### Intersectionality

When we discuss oppression, it is essential that we don't generalize the ways it is experienced. In particular, some people experience multiple oppressions, which manifest in unique and complex ways. Legal scholar Kimberlé Crenshaw (1988, 1991) used the term *intersectionality* to describe how multiple oppressions interact together, particularly regarding violence against women of color. Crenshaw (1991) argued that for Black women, racism and sexism factor into their lives in ways that cannot be fully captured by looking at racism or sexism separately. Many scholars and activists have taken up Crenshaw's notion of intersectionality to consider how members of the LGBTQIA+ and other marginalized communities are impacted by multiple oppressions. These multiple oppressions are not always obvious or experienced in the same way, so it is especially important that educators take the time to learn about identities and experiences that differ from their own. As scholar and spoken-word poet Jamila Lyiscott (2019) notes, "if you are an educator who has never faced their story as it intersects with the various social locations that shape how you show up in schools and in our world, then you are destined to do this work irresponsibly" (p. 13).

The social studies we teach, regardless of discipline, must reflect an intersectional approach that recognizes imbalances of power. If we choose to not intervene and avoid conversations about these issues, that sends children a clear signal: We do not think there is a problem with the way things are and we do not think these issues are worth talking about. Educator and activist Carla Shalaby (2017) explains this very poignantly:

> *Our children are learning that only some lives matter, that only some deaths are tragic, that only a precious few deserve relief from suffering. We need schools that offer young people a chance to grapple with these lessons—schools fueled by the imperative to imagine and to create a world in which there are no throwaway lives. Any of us invested in the rights of persons to be free have cause to care about the lives of children at school and to resurrect our imagination for schooling as a deeply human, wildly revolutionary site of possibility. (p. xviii)*

We believe social studies is a site of such possibility and provide many examples in this book. If we take up social studies as a space to make clear that, as Shalaby (2017) insists, "there are no throwaway lives" and that every human being is valuable and important, then we can truly begin to imagine the reality of liberty and justice for *all*.

### Funds of Knowledge

The myriad perspectives and voices missing from or marginalized in the curriculum can often be found in our own communities. Students should know that they, and the members of their communities, possess wisdom to be shared. Education scholars Luis Moll, Cathy Amanti, Deborah Neff, and Norma González (1992) use the term *funds of knowledge* to describe the knowledge and skills found in local households, particularly by working-class immigrant families and families of color. Given the ways that white, middle-class culture is normed in schools, Moll and colleagues (1992), along with the many scholars who have extended their work, urge educators to recognize and draw on students' and families' funds of knowledge and to find ways to bring these funds into the classroom.

The funds of knowledge approach rejects any reliance on negative assumptions and stereotypes that create a deficit lens in the classroom (Hogg & Volman, 2020). That being said, sometimes educators solely seek what professor Lew Zipin (2009) describes as "positive" funds of knowledge from their students, and actively avoid any funds of knowledge that might deal with "negative" topics like violence, abuse, and mental health struggles. However, these and other difficult issues are a part of many students' lived experiences that can and should be viewed as learning assets, too (Rodríguez & Salinas, 2019). When students share their funds of knowledge, they become producers of knowledge rather than simply consumers of knowledge created by others (González & Moll, 2002). This, in turn, fosters the kind of community and family involvement we encourage throughout this book.

## Transformative Justice

Our framework also relies on *transformative justice pedagogies* developed by Maisha Winn (2018) and the scholar practitioners affiliated with the Transformative Justice in Education (TJE) Center at the University at California–Davis (Winn & Winn, 2021). Transformative justice pedagogies disrupt educational and social inequities (Annamma & Winn, 2019) and apply *restorative justice theory* (Zehr, 2015) to schooling contexts. In restorative justice work, identifying harms and needs is central, as is holding people accountable and responsible for their actions. "Restorative" refers to the restoration of relationships, not the restoration of the unjust status quo. To be anti-oppressive or "transformative," educators must take up restorative justice pedagogical stances that change how they "conceptualize and administer punishment, shame, and guilt in order to reflect a more nuanced understanding of harm, the needs of those harmed, and those who have caused harm" (Winn, 2018, pp. 11–12).

A central component of transformative justice pedagogies involves attending to harm done. Winn (2018) argues that "many of the students who cause harm in schools have also experienced harm in schools, through miseducation, constant surveillance, isolation, and discrimination" (p. 19). Educators, too, have experienced harm through systemic issues including devaluation, low salaries, strained relationships with administrators, and pressure to prepare students for standardized testing instead of fostering learners' curiosities about the world—in addition to harmful treatment depending on their identities. Throughout the book, we offer ways to teach social studies that reflect a more nuanced understanding of harm and the needs of those harmed.

The figure below, created by Noreen with the TJE Center through the Transformative Justice in Teacher Education Spencer Learning Community illustrates how a transformative justice approach to social studies would be different from the existing curriculum if it responded to the question, *How and why might social studies educators affirm and*

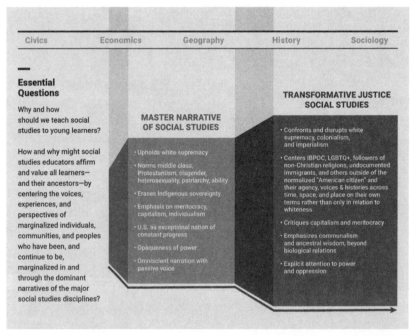

Transformative Justice in Social Studies Framework (CREATED BY THE TRANSFORMATIVE JUSTICE IN EDUCATION CENTER AND NOREEN NASEEM RODRÍGUEZ)

*value all learners—and their ancestors—by centering the voices, experiences, and perspectives of marginalized individuals, communities, and peoples who have been, and continue to be, marginalized in and through the dominant narratives of the major social studies disciplines?* (Rodríguez, 2020). In recognition of the harm that has occurred historically and continues today through the dominant narrative, a transformative justice approach to the social studies disrupts and decenters white supremacy and the norms upheld by dominant narratives, recognizes the erasure of Indigenous sovereignty, critiques capitalism and meritocracy, emphasizes communalism, and pays explicit attention to power and oppression.

## What Does This Mean for the Teacher?

It is possible to help children wrestle with the difficulties of an unjust society while also emphasizing hope and a vision for change that incorporates the theories we've laid out here. Next, we discuss two essential elements of anti-oppressive social studies education: addressing controversy and avoiding indoctrination.

### Addressing Controversy

While adults may feel shame or discomfort when discussing these issues, children are often open to engaging in dialogue as part of their natural sense of curiosity and wonder about the world around them. Civil rights activist Valarie Kaur (2020) describes wonder as our birthright, as something that comes easily in childhood and creates the capacity to learn and care about others:

> *If we are safe and nurtured enough to develop our capacity to wonder, we start to wonder about the people in our lives, too—their thoughts and experiences, their pain and joy, their wants and needs. We begin to sense that they are to themselves as vast and complex as we are to ourselves, their inner world as infinite as our own. In other words, we are seeing them as our equal. We are gaining information about how to love them. Wonder is the wellspring for love. . . . It is easy to wonder about the internal life of the people closest to us. It is*

*harder to wonder about people who seem like strangers or outsiders.*
*But when we choose to wonder about people we don't know, when we*
*imagine their lives and listen for their stories, we begin to expand the*
*circle of those we see as part of us. (p. 10)*

Adults, however, have often been taught that certain topics (race, sexuality, immigration status) are not polite or appropriate to discuss. Adults have also been taught that certain topics have no place in school, or should be better left to children's families and caretakers. Thus, they pass those lessons onto kids and start the cycle all over again, unwilling to do anything that may be considered controversial.

*Controversy* refers simply to legitimate, competing points of view about questions that matter to people (Hess, 2004). "Open" controversies are those that are currently up for debate while "closed" controversies are those that have shut—either because there are legal decisions, overwhelming evidence, or informal consensus among the general public. Questions open and close all the time. Consider the question of whether marijuana should be legal. For hundreds of years, the government encouraged farmers to grow hemp and permitted marijuana as a popular medicinal ingredient. In the early 20th century, however, anti-immigration activists denounced recreational marijuana as a menace brought into the United States by "criminal" Mexicans. Pseudoscience, racism, classism, and xenophobia fueled the criminalization of marijuana through the federal government's War on Drugs in the 1980s. Recently, this question has reopened and even begun closing on the side of legality as many states now permit medicinal and recreational use—increasing tax revenues and expanding health care options, yet lining the pockets of white businesspeople while disproportionately large numbers of Black and Brown Americans remain incarcerated for their entrepreneurship.

Note that controversies are questions and *not* topics. "Abortion" is not controversial. Under what conditions it should be legal *is*. And just because someone has an opinion does not make it a "legitimate" point of view. There are people who think that the Holocaust didn't happen or that the Earth is flat. Not legitimate. Of course, what counts as "legitimate" can itself be controversial. For example, scientists overwhelmingly agree that climate change is real and accelerated by human activity. Many politicians and their supporters, however, disagree. Do you teach the question of whether climate change is happening as an "open" question by presenting multiple points of view in a balanced way—or acknowledge all of the sides while teaching that one is better? Do you teach it as a "closed" question, only exposing students to the "right" answer? Do you avoid the question altogether, nervously laughing when a kid brings it up and changing the subject immediately? Not to stress you out, but it always depends.

Our methods students often think the right answer is always to teach in a "balanced" way—but there are *very* good reasons why this could be a terrible idea. There are all sorts of contextual factors that educators must carefully weigh (Hess & McAvoy, 2014) related to intersectionality, funds of knowledge, and transformative justice. As we emphasize throughout this book, knowing yourself, knowing your students, knowing your community, and having a clearly defined vision for social studies is what helps you weigh multiple factors in a professional, responsible way.

> **TEACHING ABOUT CONTROVERSIAL ISSUES**
> Education scholar Diana Hess (2004) identifies four approaches teachers must choose from when navigating controversial issues with students. These include *denial*, when the teacher refuses to frame a question as controversial and instead presents a "right" answer; *privilege*, when the teacher acknowledges multiple viewpoints, but indicates that one is better; *avoidance*, when the teacher acknowledges a controversy but does not feel comfortable or confident that they can responsibly teach it; and *balance*, when the teacher exposes students to multiple points of view in equal measure (p. 259). Of course, deciding which approach to take can itself be controversial.

Fortunately, many districts have policies to help guide educators, and some states even have standards *requiring* that students grapple with controversy. This is because navigating controversy in a constructive way is an *incredibly* important skill for members of a diverse democracy to practice—even our youngest community members. Educators are extraordinarily powerful forces in helping to shape what becomes "common sense" to youth given that how they decide to address a controversy communicates information *and* values to their students. They are not the only influence, of course; students' friends and families, the media, and other institutions play huge roles. But as educators spend dozens of waking hours with their students, the topics they allow for conversations and the topics they prohibit can be deeply influential.

Many educators we work with want to know when it is appropriate to address controversies with youth. At the very least, children bringing up controversies in the classroom through their questions and connections (even their teasing or bullying) is a clear indicator that they want and are ready to talk about them. When youth have the courage to ask educators about issues directly, they are looking to the educators for answers and clarification. That is our job! It is actually a form of educational malpractice to *not* honor children's questions or to refuse to make space for them to grapple with their curiosity in deep, thoughtful ways. Historian Hasan Kwame Jeffries reminds us, "As teachers, we are dutybound to provide students the unvarnished truth. And the times in which we live demand that we do so. To do anything less is to commit educational malpractice. Fortunately, the tools and techniques needed to teach . . . accurately and effectively are at our disposal. We just have to have the courage to use them" (Jeffries, 2019, p. xiv).

## Avoiding Indoctrination

We do not want our students to think just like us—to vote for our favorite candidate or prioritize issues as we might, to participate in all the same social actions, or to convey their opinions exactly as we do. That is indoctrination and is *not* anti-oppressive. That said, we can and *should* demand that students consider the impacts of their actions on the community, provide credible evidence to explain who and what they support, and to be considerate of how sharing of those ideas may impact others. There are always nonnegotiable values, or lines we will not cross—even refusing to take a stand is itself a stand. So the question is not *whether* we have "lines," it's how we determine where those lines will be and how we engage critiques that the lines should be drawn differently. Anti-oppressive classrooms shouldn't be indoctrinatory, but neither should they be spaces where anything goes.

The pedagogy we propose in this book clearly does not accept the current social order as either equitable or just, and requires educators to understand the legacies of cultural, linguistic, and economic oppression in our nation and beyond. Once you know more about these different histories of oppression, their impact on our world becomes painfully clear—you can't ignore them, and we don't want you to. Instead, we urge you to take up the challenge to take responsibility and commit to do better; this is how we engage in revolutionary teaching, and ultimately how we build a better world together. We are well aware that there will be some people who think anti-oppressive social studies is indoctrination, or that to insist on the good of the collective over the good of the individual is somehow unfair and unjust to them. We live in a society that has emphasized individualism and exceptionalism for centuries, so it makes sense that some folks have internalized those values and may consider any effort to care for the larger community to be a threat to their way of life. To us, however, the collective good, our beloved community, is what the *social* in social studies is all about. It is what makes a true democracy, which we have yet to achieve.

## Why Does Any of This Matter?

At the risk of sounding dramatic, the better world we are envisioning is at stake if we don't engage young people in a more rigorous, critical, social studies education. We live in an era when fake news and alternative facts abound, fueled by propaganda and misinformation pumped through social media. This is literally a life-and-death problem. While this may feel especially urgent to many of us right now, not one of the challenges we face is new and our general anti-oppressive approach is not novel. There is a long tradition of anti-oppressive education that we echo with the framework we present here: problem-posing critical pedagogy, various Indigenous pedagogical approaches, ecojustice pedagogies, feminist and womanist pedagogies, popular educational efforts, and more.

To alert our students to the ancestors on whose shoulders they stand and the duration of the social problems we highlight, we often assign "A Talk to Teachers," which is a speech that writer and activist James Baldwin gave in 1963 to an audience of educators. In it, Baldwin (1985) outlines the many threats facing Black children both in and out of schools and calls for an education very similar to what we describe here. After reading it, many of our teacher candidates guess it was written last year, not half a century ago. Baldwin declares:

> *To any citizen of this country who figures himself as responsible— and particularly those of you who deal with the minds and hearts of young people—must be prepared to "go for broke." Or to put it another way, you must understand that in the attempt to correct so many generations of bad faith and cruelty, when it is operating not only in the classroom but in society, you will meet the most fantastic, the most brutal, and the most determined resistance. There is no point in pretending that this won't happen. . . . [I]f I were a teacher in this school . . . I would try to make [the children] know that just as American history is longer, larger, more various, more beautiful and more terrible than anything anyone has ever said about it, so is the world larger, more daring, more beautiful and more terrible, but principally larger—and that it belongs to [them]. (p. 325)*

Our vision of transformative social studies is our attempt to "go for broke." It strives for equity and justice. Period. It is grounded in anti-oppression, with the hope that, someday, people might have the freedom to determine their own fates in consideration of their impact on others. It directly engages the question of how people work collectively, drawing from the experiences and knowledges of those who came before, to build better futures for all life in every place. As James Baldwin reminds us, "It is your responsibility to change society if you think of yourself as an educated person"(p. 325).

While at times we feel completely overwhelmed and full of despair, we remain hopeful that things can and will get better. This is what scholars have dubbed "critical hope," which recognizes the systems of inequality that surround us and holds us responsible for building relationships and solidarity with others in order to effect change (Boler,

2004; Freire, 1994; Zembylas, 2017). While we are certain that the teaching of powerful and purposeful social studies can offer the futures we dream of so our young children can build that better world, we know the work needed to achieve this goal is neither easy nor intuitive. It is often not what is taught in traditional teacher-preparation programs, or what is supported in PK–12 systems. But it *is* possible.

## Putting These Ideas Into Practice

### Your Manifesto

Draft a statement that you could share with students' caregivers identifying the guiding principles in your philosophy of teaching social studies, and how they influence what and how you teach. Use the subheading questions in this chapter as prompts. In your manifesto, be sure to explain what obligations you feel with regards to your social studies teaching—to whom do you feel them, and why? For those who are currently teaching, link your manifesto to what you learned in the survey we recommended conducting in Chapter 3 so that the children and families you serve are directly reflected.

### Memories

Think back to your own experiences as a student learning social studies, whether during formal school instruction or out-of-school time with your family, religious or cultural community, etc. Which experiences exemplified the philosophy we lay out here? Which experiences do *not* align with what we've shared? How do you think these collective experiences have shaped you and your teaching practices, and what do you want to commit yourself to doing moving forward?

### Open and Shut

Trace the history of a controversy that matters to you. How has it opened and closed over the years? How have educators influenced this opening and closing—especially with regards to establishing "common sense" around a question, and how do *you* plan to teach about it (e.g., avoid, privilege, deny, balance)?

## Part II

# Common Pitfalls
# and Creative Solutions

In the following four chapters, we introduce you to common ways that elementary social studies can be *problematic*. "Problematic" is a formal, academic way to say "toxic garbage" and is the opposite of anti-oppressive. Problematic teaching is harmful to youth, particularly those with marginalized identities, because it advances stereotypes, excludes students, centers dominant narratives, reproduces oppression, and/or advances misinformation. The four problematics of elementary social studies we explore in this section are: *normalization*, *idealization*, *heroification*, and *dramatization/gamification*.

In each chapter, we examine what one problematic looks like through specific classroom examples: holidays and families for normalization; rules, communities, and community helpers for idealization; "Founding Fathers," suffragists, and Civil Rights Movement leaders for heroification; and immigration, "Westward Expansion," and slavery for dramatization. This is not to say that these examples cannot and do not overlap with the other problematics—they can and do—but by specifying topics, we hope to touch on as many commonly taught activities and content as possible. As you can imagine, these examples are not comprehensive; unfortunately, there are *many* ways that each of these problematics exists far beyond what we outline here. As you read, we hope that you take the time to learn more about any content we mention that is unfamiliar to you in these examples. Please consult Appendix A ("Recommended Resources") and our website (www.ssfabw.com) for more resources to guide you.

In addition to describing each problem, we also explore some of the concerning ways that teachers may try to avoid problematic social studies, inadvertently making things even worse. We call these *common pitfalls*, and they are especially heartbreaking because they happen when teachers are trying to do right by students but haven't quite thought it all the way through. We don't want to see that happen to you! To prevent this, we suggest *creative solutions* to avoid the problematic parts of common elementary social studies curriculum while also steering clear of these pitfalls.

After reading the following four chapters, we recommend you come back to this introduction and the table below to reflect on how these general problems and pitfalls may exist in the curriculum and teaching you've observed or enacted in schools. Adaptations of the table for each general problem with an additional column for self-reflection are included in Appendix B (Table B.6 *Normalization Lesson/Unit Reflection Worksheet*, Table B.7 *Idealization Lesson/Unit Reflection Worksheet*, Table B.8 *Heroification Lesson/Unit Reflection Worksheet*, Table B.9 *Dramatization/Gamification Lesson/Unit Reflection Worksheet*). Consider what it might take for an educator (yourself or one you know) to overcome the problems and pitfalls to work toward solutions that would result in anti-oppressive social studies. What can you do to make these changes and adjustments come to life?

## General Problems, Pitfalls, and Solutions for the Four Problematics of Elementary Social Studies

| General Problems<br>Why it's bad | General Pitfalls<br>How teachers try to make it better but still go wrong | General Solutions<br>Our advice for addressing the problems while avoiding pitfalls |
|---|---|---|
| **Normalization**<br>Reinforces supremacy for some kids and deviance or inferiority for others | – Expansion of inclusion (e.g., multicultural, diverse curriculum) that is superficial or inaccurate<br>– Exoticization<br>– Tokenization | Contextualization<br>Expansion |
| **Idealization**<br>Ignores reality | – Compliance with authority<br>– Only focuses on what is real<br>– Doesn't question the ideal put forth | Realization<br>Co-construction |
| **Heroification**<br>Erases complexity of canonical figures<br><br>Fails to acknowledge other important figures | – Makes canonical figures more complex, but doesn't acknowledge other historically significant figures or social movements / everyday people<br>– Presents nondominant people as saints or whitewashes them | Diversification<br>Humanization<br>Mobilization |
| **Problematic Dramatization / Gamification**<br>Prioritizes an activity's entertainment value over education<br><br>Reinforces dominant narratives by decentering or erasing marginalized perspectives | – Confuses students by not explicitly linking their experiences to the learning objectives (which can reinforce dominant narratives)<br>– Trivializes trauma and/or retraumatizes kids by assigning problematic roles or tasks | Dramatization / Gamification that honors and transforms |

# 3

# Normalization: Families and Holidays

F amilies and holidays are foundational topics in early child-hood classrooms and are often among the first formal social studies lessons students learn. Despite the wide array of familial structures and holidays that exist, however, normalization of dominant traditions persist. *Normalization* refers to the messages in the curriculum (echoed in popular media and the larger structures and systems of society more broadly) that promote ideas about what is normal and good or strange and bad. Does this remind you of the dominant narrative? It should! When specific images and constructs surround us all of the time, they become expected and can be perceived as natural or normal and even as inherently good. Meanwhile, any imagery that disrupts what we expect often becomes deemed *ab*normal, unacceptable, bad, or wrong (Tschida, Ryan, & Ticknor, 2014).

These normalized understandings of what a family looks like represent what author Chimamanda Ngozi Adichie (2009) calls a "single story." In her famous TED Talk, Adichie explains that "the single story creates stereotypes, and the problem with stereotypes is not that they are untrue, but that they are incomplete." While we find her words powerful, we are saddened by Adichie's refusal to apply her own advice in response to criticism of her former students, Olu Timehin Adegbeye and Akwaeke Emezi. For us, her unwillingness to identify trans women as women, and alignment with trans exclusionary radical feminists like

J. K. Rowling, is an example of the danger of a single story. Whether in feminist circles or early childhood classrooms, normalization that demands adherence to tidy categorizations is not just harmful—it's also inaccurate.

We all have constructed single stories about people and places with which we are unfamiliar, and may not even realize we have done it until we offend or upset someone. In schools, this occurs when students are called weird (or worse) because they do not follow the expected norms, whether due to clothing or religious markers they wear, the way they speak, the foods they eat, their behavior, and so forth. Without intervention, students who already experience marginalization may become further alienated from their peers, while those in the dominant group may only find value in those who are similar to them and develop a dangerously exaggerated sense of self (Bishop, 1990) that ultimately disrupts efforts to appreciate and honor diverse ways of being (James, 2015). While normalization has the most immediate and direct effects on minoritized and marginalized youth, it is terrible for *everyone.*

In recent decades, educators have worked to disrupt normalization, particularly during those initial weeks of the school year as they work to build community with a new group of students. But some of these efforts still end up centering some students while alienating others. The most common pitfalls are when these attempts are only superficial or lead to inaccuracies with little nuance or complexity. For example, a teacher may note that all religions have symbols that people might wear, but still assume that all people are religious or that there is only one way to practice a particular religion. Another pitfall occurs when the teacher is trying to be inclusive but ends up exoticizing or tokenizing students with connections to those identities or communities, making them stand out from the crowd even more. This could look like a teacher spotlighting the lone Jewish student in class to speak on behalf of Judaism or going on and on about how interesting a student's hijab is. In this chapter, we propose two solutions to these pitfalls: *expansion* of ideas and definitions and greater *contextualization* of these topics as they relate to the teaching of families and holidays.

# Families

The influence of family on children's individual development and identity, which then shapes their emerging understanding of the world around them, is inarguable. In social studies lessons and children's literature, however, families are often defined and depicted in the "traditional" nuclear sense: a cisgender woman legally married to a cisgender man of the same race or ethnicity, with cisgender biological children of the same race or ethnicity (Buchanan, Tschida, Bellows, & Shear, 2020; Tschida & Buchanan, 2017; Van Horn & Hawkman, 2018). Thus, students who belong to families that do not match the traditional nuclear structure are positioned outside the norm (divorced families, families with LGBTQIA+ members, multigenerational families, multiracial and/or multiethnic families, adoptive families, blended families). Examples of cisgender heteronormativity in schools abound. Given how much elementary educators focus on learning about students' identities, we turn a critical gaze to some of the ways that popular activities about families sometimes go awry.

## Common Pitfalls

At the beginning of every school year, educators often teach about families through activities that encourage students to get to know each other (Tschida & Buchanan, 2017). In Noreen's primary classrooms, students wrote poems about themselves and brought "All About Me" bags filled with personal items to share with their classmates. Many teachers have students create "Star Student" posters and similar projects that allow students to describe favorite foods, activities, hobbies, and their family. Each of these examples is designed to encourage students to describe themselves for others in an effort to build relationships and ultimately develop a classroom community.

Yet many of these activities are grounded in white, middle-class norms that expect all households to be English-speaking and literate, composed of nuclear families in which any employed adults work traditional 9-to-5 jobs with disposable income. For example, "Star Student" and "All About Me" projects that are sent home presume that students will receive support outside of school from individuals who are literate in English; as these projects are often distributed in the early weeks of the academic year, teachers may not yet know which languages are spoken in students' homes nor what learning supports are available during the week. For children in families where older siblings, extended family, or community members might be their caretakers after school while guardians work evenings or at multiple jobs (and for children who themselves might be responsible for the care of younger siblings or children), completing such projects may be far more difficult for them than it is for peers who have nannies, tutors, or family members at their disposal after the school day ends.

Activities about families are typically structured for European-origin nuclear families that presume legal heteronormative marriage and biological children. Therefore they often do not account for, and may ultimately exclude, multiracial parents, step-parents and -siblings, same-sex parents, single parents, adoption, extended family networks, unsheltered families, and foster families (McCoy, Sabzalian, & Ender, 2021; Templeton, 2020; Tschida & Buchanan, 2017). Family-tree projects are a classic classroom example that uphold these norms, and rarely offer space for students to deviate from normative biological mother–father units. A family survey might inquire about biological parents and siblings; if extended family members also live in the home and play an important role in a child's daily life, there may not be an opportunity to share that information.

But it's not just projects and surveys that endorse expectations of traditional family structures; many school and classroom forms and newsletters that go home request information specific to "parents" or "Mom and Dad," and some schools continue to host events like "Donuts with Dad" (Vazquez, 2019). The phrasing and imagery used on these documents can clearly exclude other caregivers, and rely on conceptions of family that often fail to represent the diverse realities of modern U.S. society. Clip art is often steeped in incredibly normalizing imagery, but is frequently included in homebound fliers and forms for its cute factor. Long story short: Images and communications that *exclude* aren't "cute." They're damaging. Don't use them.

Speaking of images, when using children's literature to discuss diverse families, educators must be intentional about using *human* examples. Recent reports from the Cooperative Children's Book Center (2020) found that the total number of children's literature published about African Americans, Asian Americans, Latinxs, and Native Americans *together* in 2018 was lower than the number of books about white and nonhuman characters (dinosaurs, animals, trucks, etc.). Increasingly, recently published books with themes about diversity and acceptance feature animal protagonists; while these books can be useful in developing student understandings, they should not be used at the exclusion of texts spotlighting real people. We're not saying get rid of the books about dump trucks, porcupines, and Tyrannosaurus rexes. Just make sure you offer plenty of human examples so that children can see themselves, their families, and families that differ from theirs reflected, too. We'll get into this more in Chapter 7.

## Creative Solutions

First and foremost, countering single stories involves getting to know people; we hope that every educator understands how important it is for them to *know* their students. This is how you make learning meaningful and connect what is covered in school to what occurs in their lives outside the classroom walls. But you can't know your students if you don't know their families. And you have to do more than just make their acquaintance—as much as possible, recognize each other as stakeholders with a shared investment in the growth and learning of a young person. This is especially ideal for social studies given the content area's focus on identity and people, but it matters for *all* learning.

Second, we urge educators to define family in the most *expansive* way possible, so that it includes extended family, guardians, foster parents, and nonbiological friends and supporters. Then consider how you can *expand* the ways you learn about students' families, and for them to learn about you. The most common methods are offering surveys, hosting "Meet the Teacher" and other introductory events that aren't only available immediately after school or in the evening, engaging in community walks and other face-to-face interactions that allow for one-on-one conversations, and reimagining the types of projects that ask students to describe their families. We'll go through each of these methods and offer strategies that encourage greater *expansion* of who is included and *contextualization* of experiences.

Let's start with modes of direct communication, which help create the relationships needed to cultivate student success and inform educators' development of culturally relevant and sustaining pedagogy (Ladson-Billings, 1995; Paris, 2012). This includes the creation of lessons about family and self that recognize the unique and specific features of students' lived experiences. Surveys should go beyond basic contact information to include opportunities for families to share their student's strengths and interests as well as their concerns and issues that are important to them. Moreover, surveys should invite families to share about a wide range of topics in which they have expertise to share with the class, such as cultural celebrations and unique skills and talents. These topics should be clearly indicated as not solely limited to white-collar professional expertise and experience, and can include cooking, arts, construction, activism, and so forth (Moll, Amanti, Neff, et al., 1992; Yosso, 2005).

Keep in mind that many families may understandably be skeptical of teachers' intentions, given the historic abuse schools have inflicted on their communities—especially teachers who hold dominant identities. Trust must be earned, and this can take time. Take the family's lead, and do whatever you can to engage with them on their terms as you embark on a relationship of care. Teachers can build trust with families by following up on the information provided—especially with offers to help or expressions of concern. And surveys, along with all other communication, should be offered in languages other than English as needed and, as much as possible, should not require lengthy written responses that might limit who is able to complete them. Digital forms and polls that can be completed on phones as well as computers or printed for those without access to digital technology allow educators to organize results easily for quick reference throughout the school year, and consider what is accessible to all families.

## FAMILY COMMUNICATION AND
## LINGUISTIC HUMAN RIGHTS

One of the biggest norms in schools is the exclusive use of English. Although it's widely understood that civil rights are important to value and maintain, linguistic human rights receive little attention. *Linguistic human rights* are the right for people to speak whatever language they choose, in public and in private. The United States has no official national language, but English often serves as the default. It has been designated the official language in 32 states and is often associated with ideas of "Americanness." Many people who speak languages other than English in public have experienced, at one time or another, being told to "speak English" or "go back to where you came from!" This English-only attitude typically goes hand-in-hand with racism and/or xenophobia, yet it is disturbingly common in school settings, where translations may only be provided upon request and only in certain languages. Offering school communication in families' home languages (both in writing and orally) is an essential part of equitable schooling practices, but is often a low priority. Similarly, it is important to have children's literature available bilingually and in languages other than English.

Opportunities to meet the teacher should be organized in ways that do not exclude working families or those with family members who need care before or after the school day. If individuals cannot attend in person, how might materials be sent home with content that still acknowledges their important relationship to schools? For example, educators could include QR codes or links to videos that feature a short, recorded teacher introduction or classroom tour. Similarly, students could record such videos themselves in the classroom and school environment to share with family members who are unable to attend, either through smartphones or school-issued devices like tablets or laptops. Lastly, educators must engage the community outside of the schooling space, especially if they do not live in that community themselves. Whether organizing a neighborhood walk or meeting students and families at a local park on the weekend, it is important that educators demonstrate an interest in and understanding of students' communities beyond the school walls.

We realize that such extracurricular commitments are time consuming. Yet they have profound implications for building authentic and meaningful community and trust. Taking the time to explore your students' neighborhood may lead you to notice the soccer field students have referenced in class, or the frozen yogurt shop they visit on special occasions. These insights can lead to rich conversations about interests, hobbies, and sports that students and their families enjoy. They may also give you greater knowledge about challenges related to transportation, food access, and other needs; for instance, if a student has to cross railroad tracks or a busy intersection in order to reach the bus stop, a delayed train or heavy traffic may contribute to their tardiness. As poet Jesús Colón (1982) wrote, little things are big. These small details of students' lives add up, and are important for those who teach them to understand.

With this knowledge of students' families and their contexts in hand, educators can begin to explore family diversity with their students. This includes discussion of families beyond the traditional middle-class, heterosexual, single-race nuclear unit. To disrupt the white heteronormativity embedded in many family activities, educators should introduce the history of marriage equality (Van Horn & Hawkman, 2018). This is a great opportunity to apply civics thinking to the topic of families by considering questions like, *What laws have dictated what a family could be in the eyes of the government?* and *What benefits do couples receive when they are able to be legally married?*

Thinking interdisciplinarily, beyond civics, consider exploring the various global locations where students have family members and loved ones (without presuming everyone is in North America, if that's where your class is located), reflecting on what places are special to kids' families' traditions, describing routes and modes of transportation families use to get places, comparing families' ability to communicate and see each other in person in the past and present, or learning about the impacts of family separation policies for undocumented and/or mixed-status immigrant families. Of course, avoid making assumptions or pushing students to share. Educators should be especially sensitive when addressing this content with students who may be experiencing familial separation of any kind (death, deployment, incarceration, immigration), as it might be painful or traumatic for students to discuss in class.

Finally, there is a way to adjust those family trees and "All About Me" posters to make them more inclusive. Teacher educators Leilani Sabzalian (Alutiiq), Meredith McCoy (Métis/Anishinaabe), and Tommy Ender (in press) suggest asking students to create an image that reflects the important people in their lives. Or, rather than limiting family to bloodlines, students can create trees that list those who love and care for them. This offers space for greater inclusion and broadens the notion of family to that of kinship (McCoy, Sabzalian, & Ender, 2021). These changes demonstrate the expansive notions of family that allow all students, no matter what their family structure, to participate in ways that avoid potential irrelevance, shame, or exacerbation of existing traumas.

Ultimately, the way to disrupt the normalization rampant in the teaching of families is to interrupt limited definitions of family that reflect the dominant narrative. The key to avoiding the pitfalls of normalization is to expand the narratives available to young people and to fully contextualize the different ways that people live their lives. Deeply developing these ideas with young learners is essential to building a strong classroom community and support systems for students, and it's also the foundation for a pluralistic democracy.

### WHAT WOULD YOU DO?

At the beginning of the year, children bring in pictures of their families to hang in the room. When one of your students shares a picture of him with his brother and two moms, another student blurts out that his mom says that families should have a mommy and a daddy. Given your identity and your teaching context, what are your best options for an immediate response and in the longer term?

## Holidays

Another common example of normalization in elementary social studies is a focus on holidays. In addition to relying on irrelevant "cute" crafts that likely just get thrown away, the holidays discussed and celebrated in schools (or normalized through official school calendars) are overwhelmingly enacted through middle- and upper-class forms of celebration (wearing store-bought Halloween costumes for a school parade, morning meeting questions that presume students received Christmas gifts). In addition, many schools emphasize the religious traditions of the (perceived or real) majority in the community (James, 2015).

As the United States is a majority-Christian nation and the majority of the teaching force is composed of Christians, Christian holidays are those most often taught and celebrated in public schools. The academic calendar is structured around Judeo–Christian practices (Hartenstein, 1992), thereby normalizing these holidays. Social studies professor Jennifer Hauver James (2015) notes, "Even in classrooms where teachers make an occasional effort to read a book on Eid-al-Fitr or sing a dreidel song, students are quick to interpret the relative importance of differing religious and cultural practices. Democratic principles of tolerance, equity, and a common good are undermined when such imbalances go unchecked" (p. 27). This focus normalizes the dominant narrative of who is American/citizen and sets up a religious hierarchy with Christian religions at the top (Kleinrock, 2020). These messages are not lost on Christian students, whose dominance gets reinforced as schools constantly remind nonreligious and non-Christian students and families of their "otherness."

The First Amendment to the Constitution forbids the federal government from establishing a religion and protects the rights of individuals to worship however they choose. Yet, the practice and evangelization of religion has nonetheless managed to creep into public schools. Consider the Pledge of Allegiance, for which recitation is required in U.S. public schools in nearly every state. In 1954, the words "under God" were added after "one nation," purportedly to foster a stronger sense of patriotism (Kruse, 2015). This notion that love of country is attached to belief in God further normalizes the assumption that Americans are not only religious, but monotheistic.

So what is the difference between teaching *about* religion and teaching someone what they should believe? Teaching about religions, broadly, supports student engagement in our pluralistic democracy. It helps learners understand the role that religion plays in people's lives and how improved understanding of differences can improve civic life (James, 2015). But this can only be achieved if students learn about a multiplicity of religions and have opportunities to compare and contrast religious traditions and practices. When students are told what to believe, without the ability to dissent or consider different kinds of beliefs, this constitutes proselytizing, as such actions attempt to invite conversion to the religion of the teacher. Teaching *about* religions, plural, is fine and actually important to do in public schools; teaching one religion *only*, with an emphasis that it is inarguable truth, is indoctrination—oh, and unconstitutional.

## Common Pitfalls

To avoid reinforcing the normalization of Christianity, some educators have tried to include more "multicultural" holidays. But several common pitfalls occur when educators try to bring in holidays from other faiths and cultures without fully understanding their origins, traditions, or practices—all of which ultimately normalizes Christianity yet again. We'll examine how many schools have shifted away from traditional Christmas celebrations to generic winter celebrations or offer an array of winter holidays from multiple faiths and cultures, like Hanukkah, Diwali, Eid, and/or Kwanzaa. Unfortunately, "winter celebrations" still presuppose that Christmastime is considered *the holiday season* and other faiths can simply be folded into the mix, even if the holidays of other faiths that occur around December don't hold the same level of significance for those communities (Kleinrock, 2020). Once again, the dominant group problematically determines when marginalized groups are invited into the picture. Further, while we appreciate the effort to offer more religious and cultural diversity, these specific holidays don't necessarily make sense together. Let's explore several reasons why context is *so important* when making these kinds of decisions.

First of all, we need to get into technical issues about when holidays are celebrated in the first place. The Jewish, Hindu, Buddhist, and Jain calendars are lunisolar, and the Muslim calendar is lunar, meaning they all follow the cycles of the moon to varying extents. In contrast, the Gregorian calendar commonly used in schools and in Christianity is a solar calendar. These calendars are rarely in alignment, and the version of the lunar calendar used by Muslims actually cycles through all seasons of the solar year. Diwali, celebrated by Hindus, Jains, and Sikhs, occurs between October and November. This means that Hanukkah and Eid rarely coincide with Christmas; while Hanukkah tends to fall between late November and late December, Eid can occur in winter some years and in the middle of the summer in other years. Those familiar with Islam know that there are actually *two* Eids—Eid al-Adha and Eid al-Fitr. Of these two important Muslim holidays, Eid al-Adha is considered the most holy as it honors Abraham's willingness to sacrifice his son in the name of God. However, Eid al-Fitr is the subject of several widely available picture books and is often the Eid that is recognized in schools by those unfamiliar with Islam. So to call all of these celebrations winter holidays is a stretch.

Second, this combination of holidays conflates the religious with the secular. Kwanzaa is a uniquely African American holiday, created in 1966 by Black nationalist Maulana Karenga. Karenga drew from African harvest festivals to design a community-centered, 7-day holiday between December 26 and January 1; he intentionally scheduled Kwanzaa at the end of the Christmas shopping season to counter the commercialization of Christmas (Austin, 2004). Like Diwali, Hanukkah, and Advent traditions, the lighting of candles is part of Kwanzaa celebrations, which could lead to interesting comparisons and conversations about light as a symbol in rituals. But when educators inaccurately emphasize winter as the common thread across these holidays, this important connection is often lost. Further, as Kwanzaa is a community holiday rather than a religious one, someone might celebrate it in addition to one of the religious holidays typically taught during this time of year.

The third critique of these clustered "winter" holidays is that dominant Christmas traditions remain foregrounded, and it is often the holiday that educators feel the most knowledgeable about and teach with the greatest accuracy and cultural authenticity. Certain Christmas music and symbols (decorated evergreen trees with presents underneath, hanging lights on buildings, stockings for Santa Claus to fill) often infiltrate early childhood and elementary settings in ways that may detach the word *Christmas* but continue to normalize that holiday as representative of "the season." Consider how menorahs and kinaras may be absent from seasonal activities that occur throughout the month of December and only appear during specific lessons about Hanukkah and Kwanzaa, whereas certain Christmas symbols are ever-present as school decorations or seasonal clip art. Moreover, educators often draw from their own family and community traditions when describing Christmas but may rely solely on singular, outsider accounts when it comes to other holidays, ignoring that the one version of events they teach may not be an accurate or authentic representation. And even a Christian teacher may fail to recognize the wide diversity of Christmas traditions (decorated cacti, parols, shoes for the Three Kings to fill).

But the most harmful pitfall is when these holidays are directly *compared* to Christmas (or any normalized holiday celebrated by the dominant group). "Hanukkah is Jewish Christmas!" It. Is. Not. Christmas celebrates the birth of Jesus Christ, while Hanukkah celebrates the reclamation of the Second Temple by the Maccabees. Christmas is celebrated on December 25, while Hanukkah lasts eight nights. Christmas is often regarded as one of the most important Christian holidays, while Hanukkah is a holiday of less significance compared to the High Holy Days of Rosh Hashanah and Yom Kippur. The list of differences goes on, as does the list of other holidays subjected to such comparisons. Día de los Muertos (Day of the Dead) is *not* Mexican Halloween. Part of recognizing and celebrating holidays must include understanding them in their own right and in the context of their respective cultures—not as parallels or substitutes to dominant celebrations.

In summary, teaching holidays requires *context*. When teachers try to be more inclusive without putting in the time to fully understand the complexity and nuance of a holiday, that context can get lost and they can end up teaching a superficial, even offensive, version of the holiday to their students. A quick Pinterest search for teaching about any holiday will offer dozens of seemingly innocuous crafts, but many of these activities and projects fail to provide substance or history.

In the case of Cinco de Mayo, educators might choose to highlight the holiday in an effort to include Mexican American celebrations in the classroom. A quick internet search, however, shows results that are overwhelmingly stereotypical and even racist. Think sombreros, ponchos, and chili peppers. Making piñatas and playing bingo with beans (two popular Pinterest results) does not actually teach children anything valuable about the holiday, which commemorates Mexico's victory at the Battle of Puebla against the French. Moreover, because Mexico lost the war, this battle is not a prominent holiday in the country—except in the state of Puebla. Many people who aren't familiar with Mexican history or culture mistakenly believe that Cinco de Mayo is Mexican Independence Day, but that's actually on September 16. And those sombreros, ponchos, and piñata crafts and clip art have *nothing to do with this holiday.* Of greater Mexican American cultural significance are holidays like Día de los Muertos, 16 de septiembre, and las Posadas, which we'll describe in a moment.

### Creative Solutions

Let's look at ways that educators can be more purposeful about teaching holidays, both religious and secular, in ways that deeply attend to context as well as expanding students' knowledge about the holidays themselves. For many families, religion plays an important role in developing ethics and defining relationships with others. Holidays can be important aspects of one's religion or culture. We aren't saying that educators should outright avoid the teaching of all holidays—unless, of course, you're in a school that explicitly forbids their teaching. Instead, we offer some alternatives to Christian-centric and crafts-based approaches. We suggest including nonreligious holidays as well as teaching religiously homogeneous students about other traditions, while offering students of minoritized faiths opportunities to see their holidays reflected in the classroom.

Context is *so* important when deciding which holidays should be taught and celebrated in school. These choices *matter.* In Noreen's hometown of San Antonio, Texas, the tradition of Fiesta began in 1891 to honor those who fought in the Battle of the Alamo and the Battle of San Jacinto. It later grew into a 10-day celebration of the city's diverse cultures. To not acknowledge Fiesta in San Antonio classrooms would be blasphemous. Similarly, celebrations like Mardi Gras, Carnivale, and Juneteenth hold tremendous historical and cultural significance in specific locations. In places where the celebration of specific holidays is a local tradition, community members can offer rich histories and stories to students as a foundational part of their learning.

Tracing the origins of such holidays allows students to use a historical and geographic lens in their learning. Just remember to do so through a *critical* lens that doesn't shy away from complexity and controversy. Consider how Columbus Day has served as an important celebration for many Catholic Italian immigrants and their children who faced xenophobia and religious discrimination, but that it signifies the start of genocide and colonialism for many Indigenous Peoples. Contextualizing traditions and rituals rather than superficially celebrating them helps students grapple with tensions within and across minoritized and marginalized communities.

Context matters in terms of who your students are, too. When Noreen was a bilingual teacher in Austin, Texas, most of her students were Mexican American Catholics. Therefore, the winter holiday celebrations she and her first-grade teammates taught included las posadas—a ritual practiced by many Mexican Catholics that reenacts the holy family's search for refuge in Bethlehem (de los Ríos & Molina, 2020) and includes symbols like poinsettias and the Virgin Mary. In this case, teaching holidays was a means of culturally sustaining pedagogy (Paris, 2012), which "seeks to perpetuate and foster—to sustain—linguistic, literate, and cultural pluralism as part of the democratic project of schooling" (p. 95). Normalization presumes that traditional Protestant celebrations of Christmas are the "natural" approach, but the educators at Noreen's school knew that their students and their families celebrated Christmas through distinct bicultural and bilingual practices that needed to be recognized and affirmed in school. That being said, not *all* students and families were Catholic; remember not to essentialize or assume!

**TEACHING *ABOUT* CELEBRATIONS
VERSUS CELEBRATING**

Remember, there may be religious families whose beliefs prevent them from celebrating holidays (such as Jehovah's Witnesses) or families who may not be religious at all and don't want their children to participate in any religious celebrations (agnostic, atheist). Teaching *about* holidays is very different than actually celebrating holidays; learning about each other and our communities is an important part of public school. Equally important, however, is that we never ostracize students or make them opt in or out of celebrations because of their beliefs.

Expanding your approach to teaching holidays requires devoting time to understanding their histories. For example, Cinco de Mayo and St. Patrick's Day are holidays that have become emblematic of diasporic pride. In other words, these holidays allow Mexican Americans and Irish Americans to show pride in their heritage and pay homage to the traditional foods and libations of the motherland, while also serving as opportunities for people from other cultures to learn about them. But how they *became* mainstream reveals fascinating immigrant histories. In the case of Cinco de Mayo, it was due to the work of Chicano activists in the 1960s (Lovgren, 2010), while St. Patrick's Day, celebrated long before the founding of the United States, emerged on the national stage due to the combined efforts of immigrants and the Irish department of tourism (Cronin & Adair, 2004).

Exposing students to unfamiliar holidays is also an important aspect of the democratic project of schooling and social studies specifically. Returning to the example of winter holidays, how can educators do this well? First, you have to learn about holidays and celebrations yourself, and not just through a quick internet search or video. How do those who celebrate these events describe and experience them? As we will convey throughout this book, insider perspectives are essential but are often sorely lacking in traditional social studies curriculum. Quick caveat: If you have a student who might be an insider, don't *assume* they are or that they want to be the class expert. Ask them privately and consult with them before discussing the event in front of their peers; they may feel tokenized or exoticized in front of an audience. And, of course, remember that the way they celebrate is not the only way to do so.

Next, what is the learning objective you want to achieve? Do you want students to learn about diverse cultures or commemorations of historical events or about religious traditions? Perhaps you are hoping to integrate learning about the seasons in science with social studies and literacy. This is an excellent way to introduce a range of spring holidays and "new year" celebrations across cultures, from the Persian Nowruz to the Hindu celebration of Holi to the Thai Songkran and the Russian Maslenitsa. We've collected some of our favorite resources on our website (www.ssfabw.com) to help you gain knowledge about a range of celebrations, cultures, and histories.

Ultimately, any lesson or unit on holidays should avoid exoticization of cultures, food, or people. Those stereotypical Pinterest lessons we mentioned earlier? They are especially bad about associating "ethnic" food with BIPOC, which then denies the impact of globalization and the long histories of BIPOC foodways in the United States. Tacos are not unique to Mexico and sushi is not only found in Japan. Furthermore, situating foods or other traditions as *not* of the United States disregards everyone who takes part in that practice as a part of *their* respective American culture. Don't go down this road of continued marginalization! Instead of emphasizing nondominant holidays through a lens of difference, take these opportunities to teach and learn about our shared humanity and the multitude of ways people come together to celebrate milestones, traditions, and seasonal and religious events.

Lastly, in every culture there are particular customs and rites around birth and death that show reverence for life and love. While this is a clear behavioral science take on holidays, you can also use economics to consider how the scarcity of these events (most of which only occur once a year or even once in a lifetime) makes them all the more special and worth sharing with others. For a more critical take, economics can also be used to consider how holidays have become commodified. Who among us has not been tempted by retail chains' endless supply of tchotchkes for every holiday? But do we really need decor and gifts for *every* holiday? Students can consider the emphasis on *stuff*, both to decorate and to receive, for specific holidays and how such consumption distracts from the very purpose of the holiday.

## Takeaways for the Problematics of Normalization: Contextualization and Expansion

We live in a diverse country, in an immeasurably diverse world. Yet who is considered normal, and by extension, which behaviors, activities, and celebrations are deemed worthy of teaching and centering in the curriculum, largely remains limited to the dominant group. Educators have a responsibility to create learning spaces in which all students feel valued, and part of this work is getting to know students and their families and making frequent connections between school and home. This cannot happen if the tools offered for communication limit accessibility only to those who hold dominant identities, so educators must be willing to expand their tool kits to improve the ways they reach out to families and discuss families, notions of identity, and holidays in the classroom. We must also recognize the danger of teaching difference in ways that are superficial or inaccurate and that can tokenize or exoticize individuals. We find tremendous value in dedicating instructional time to the study of self, families, and holidays, but this instruction must be done in ways that are expansive and deeply contextualized to avoid doing harm. See Table B.6 *Normalization Lesson/Unit Reflection Worksheet* in the appendix to apply these ideas.

## Putting These Ideas Into Practice

### Family Survey

If you already use some kind of family survey, review it to see what could be added, modified, or deleted to make it more inclusive of diverse family structures. If you have not made one, create one! What specific prompts can you include that will allow you to learn about families' funds of knowledge? How can you circle back to this information throughout the year, and how might you draw from families' expertise to support the learning of all students?

## Rethinking Holidays

Check out calendars dedicated to highlighting a diverse range of holidays and events commemorating important struggles for justice and social issues like *Planning to Change the World* from the Education for Liberation Network Rethinking Schools or online lists from national organizations or state and regional groups. How might you teach about some of these holidays in a way that is culturally sustaining and allows your students to learn deeply about another culture or tradition?

# 4

# Idealization: Communities and Community Helpers

A distinguishing feature of elementary education is the emphasis on communities. Educators of young children address the notion of community in multiple ways, from developing interpersonal relationships and routines within the classroom to teaching explicitly about the school neighborhood, city, state, nation, and world. Yet how and why communities are created, how people interact within them, and the ways leaders and individuals wield and deny power to others is often presented in *idealized* form. Unsurprisingly, this idealization of communities forefronts individuals who reflect the norms we've discussed previously: white, cisgender, middle-class, abled, heterosexual Christians who are English-speaking U.S. citizens descended from European immigrants. But the curricular and classroom silence around oppression and inequity is what we want to really draw attention to in this chapter. Communities are not perfect but are often taught as if they *were* and *are*. Our democracy is not yet fully realized (just think about how deeply flawed the Electoral College is), but it's depicted as if it is an ideal to which other nations should aspire.

We begin our exploration with rules—an essential component of any learning community, but one that often centers compliance to adult figures. Two popular approaches that convey messages about community through how they remediate students' behavior and self-control are positive behavior interventions and support and social-emotional

learning. We explain pitfalls to these approaches that continue to reinforce compliance to authority figures, particularly when it comes to students with minoritized and marginalized identities. Then we consider
how communities beyond the classroom walls are often represented as
idyllic and focus solely on how they are perceived by the dominant
group, without always considering difficult histories behind how things
came to be. Lastly, we examine challenges with the teaching of community helpers, who are also depicted idyllically and in ways that demand
compliance and deference, despite the very real ways some of these helpers have harmed and continue to harm marginalized populations.

Our solutions to this set of issues are twofold: First, we urge *realization*, in which educators focus on real, lived experiences that include
successes and struggles. The second solution is *co-construction*; rather
than resigning students to accepting communities as they are, how
might we co-construct ideals that allow for greater imagination and
self-determination in our communities? If we recognize that our reality
is unequal and unjust, shouldn't we strive for better? And more importantly, shouldn't we give youth opportunities to imagine the world *they*
want?

## Rules

Creating a classroom community is often a central theme in any elementary learning space and one of the most powerful ways to teach
basic civics skills and concepts. There are many reasons why classroom
communities are important: They foster a sense of belonging and interdependence among students, they play a significant role in developing an array of social skills, and they create structure and routine that
should lead to a more effective learning environment. And most of
all, classroom communities develop the skills students need to become
active civic agents outside the school walls and to contribute to our
democracy. Rules guide people in understanding what is and is not
acceptable behavior within a given context, so they are understandably
critical to the function of classroom communities and beyond.

Rules exist from the moment students set foot on school property,
and much of a child's school day revolves around them. Sometimes

these rules are written and explicit, emblazoned on walls and listed in student conduct handbooks; others may be unwritten and hidden, yet expected and enforced nonetheless. Rules govern the spaces and places where students are allowed, the behaviors that are deemed appropriate and inappropriate in them, and the interactions with peers and adults; they can be attached to classwork, behavior, clothing, and even to the tone with which a student speaks. While rules may be designed to maintain order and behavior expectations, they can also be used to control students and maintain power in ways that are harmful, traumatizing, and ultimately prevent them from learning.

A 2018 report by the U.S. Government Accountability Office (GAO) found that Black students, boys, and students with disabilities were disproportionately disciplined in public schools across the country. Lesbian, gay, bisexual, and transgender students are also at higher disciplinary risk (Gregory, Skiba, & Mediratta, 2017). Scholars have confirmed these findings in a vast range of settings, and their research demonstrates an important pitfall in the creation of rules in classroom and school spaces: despite best intentions, rules are *not* created and enforced equitably. Often, rules are composed from an adult perspective, based on that adult's personal experience and perception of how a "good" student behaves. The GAO report suggests that teachers' implicit bias plays a significant role in disciplinary decisions.

Implicit bias is how stereotypes and unconscious associations impact social interactions. As evidenced by the GAO report and many other studies, in a society rife with oppression, educators who hold dominant identities often have greater implicit bias against students with marginalized identities—and the ways they treat and teach children with marginalized identities does *not* mirror the care and attention given to children of the dominant group. Educators' implicit bias may lead to disproportionate disciplinary actions based on how students' misbehaviors are attributed. For instance, some students are viewed as inherent "troublemakers" when they disrupt class, whereas others are given more grace and chances to self-correct as teachers consider external factors that might have led to the disruption (Okonofua, Walton, & Eberhardt, 2016; Shalaby, 2017).

Scholars like Anne Gregory, Russell Skiba, and Pedro Noguera

(2010) have found that the common disciplinary practice of classroom exclusion (whether sending a child to another classroom, to the counselor or administrator, or more-severe consequences like suspension or expulsion) contributes to racial gaps in academic achievement. Thus, if the rules that exist in a learning space are disproportionately applied to and broken by a certain population of students, who then are punished in ways that negatively impact their opportunities to learn, then the rule is not serving *all* students' educational needs and needs to be reconsidered or eliminated. We must remember that institutional rules are rarely created democratically; instead, they are created by and for those in power. Public schools were established by and for the dominant group, and the rules that exist in them are based on the dominant group's cultural norms. In order to create anti-oppressive conditions in schools, we must reevaluate the rules that govern these spaces with a particular focus on who is harmed by them.

## Common Pitfalls

In an effort to remediate the disproportionate ways teachers administer school discipline, two "idealistic" approaches are especially popular across the United States: positive behavior interventions and support (PBIS) and social-emotional learning (SEL). PBIS is typically implemented school- and/or district-wide as a means to clearly articulate desired student behaviors through positive reinforcement, such as incentives, and is intended to provide a consistent approach to behavior management (Bradshaw et al., 2008). SEL aims to teach students emotional regulation and develop empathy, and consists of five competency areas: self-awareness, self-management, social awareness, relationship skills, and responsible decision-making (Collaborative for Academic, Social, and Emotional Learning, 2020). Some programs center cultural competency and students' diverse identities, while others include scripted lessons with little room for flexibility and personalization. Both PBIS and SEL often involve substantial professional development as they are expected to be implemented consistently across staff, teachers, and administration, and subsequently require significant financial investment.

While these two methods may be motivated by a desire to disrupt class, gender, and ethnoracial disparities, they are not without serious flaws. We'll start with PBIS systems, which reinforce desired behaviors. The constant tracking of student behaviors often becomes so time intensive that it ends up distracting from or even preventing students' engagement with meaningful curriculum. While classroom management apps are a convenient way for educators to hold students accountable throughout the day, these behavior monitoring systems are still rooted in shame and fear—especially when used to *publicly* compare students' gains and losses like traditional behavior charts with clothespins or colors. These systems send mixed messages to students: Are we a beloved community engaged in genuine inquiry, or are we performing under constant surveillance? We can't be both.

Even more insidious is when teachers' implicit biases go unchecked—especially given the overwhelming homogeneity of dominant identities among the U.S. teaching force, which further entrench disparities and reinforce harmful stereotypes. In PBIS systems, this might look like students with marginalized identities being reprimanded more often for "bad" behavior whereas those with dominant identities get noticed for "good" behavior (Chin et al., 2020). Moreover, these systems normalize what counts as "appropriate" or "inappropriate" behavior (including classroom talk, dress codes, and conflict resolution)—even though all of this is cultural and based on the dominant group (Morris, 2005).

Lastly, PBIS prioritizes *extrinsic* motivation and individualism at the expense of *intrinsic* motivation and a concern for the collective. Classroom token economies are common PBIS systems where students gain currency through desired, "positive" behaviors as determined and observed by the teacher. Token economies range from small privileges and prizes like sitting in the teacher's chair to class stores and recognition at school-wide assemblies. Across this spectrum, perceived "good behavior" is the sole currency. These systems reinforce capitalism and consumerism while also encouraging teacher and student surveillance and policing, as currency is only available to those who the teacher observes and perceives as compliant and docile (Adams, 2020a). Instead of restoring relationships when harm is done or celebrating the health of the community in authentic ways, the classroom becomes a space where rewards or punishments are meted out by the adult authority figure.

What about SEL? Educator Dena Simmons (2019) says that SEL "can help us build communities that foster courageous conversations across difference so that our students can confront injustice, hate, and inequity" (para. 3). But in order to achieve this, SEL must be woven throughout the school day—not simply relegated to weekly 15-minute scripted lessons with no clear connection to students' lives or concerns. Children must have opportunities to communicate their needs and concerns to each other and their teachers as they arise, and have a voice in constructing solutions to their problems and concerns (Wheeler-Bell & Swalwell, 2021).

Additionally, SEL that is anti-oppressive *must* attend to power and privilege in the larger sociopolitical context. The SEL competencies of self-management and responsible decision-making are often connected to the notion of grit popularized by psychologist Angela Duckworth (2016). Yet common conceptions of grit fail to recognize the impact of trauma on students' behavior or the inequitable systems that surround them. We highly recommend scholar and activist Bettina Love's (2019) book *We Want to Do More Than Survive: Abolitionist Teaching and the Pursuit of Educational Freedom,* which explains why such SEL approaches are particularly harmful to BIPOC youth. Instead of decontextualized, idealized approaches like grit, the Communities for Just Schools Fund (2020) emphasizes that *true* SEL is culturally affirming. It is about understanding our relationships with ourselves and others, and being "able to see the humanity in others to fight, together, for the world we deserve, which is rooted in equity and justice" (para. 7). This is not work that can be read from a script or condensed into a short lesson, and it is not possible without serious and ongoing critical self-reflection on behalf of the educator.

We want to recognize that we completely understand the need for routines and behavior expectations in a classroom, no matter the age of the students. Our argument here is not NO RULES EVER, but rather that teachers and school leaders should consider the function and messaging of various rules and procedures and how they contribute to the learning environment and social development of young children. Are rules simply there to ensure constant compliance to adult authorities, or are they designed to promote safety and understanding of others? Do these rules and expectations allow for cultural and linguistic difference? Are they genuinely co-constructed with students—or are they imposed? And are rules *and* consequences fair and just? We are heartbroken and enraged by the case of 6-year-old Kaia Rolle, who was arrested by police officers and bound at the wrist with zip ties for throwing a tantrum in school. Rolle lives in Florida, where there is no minimum legal age for arrest. Such punitive and traumatic measures *cannot* be acceptable. If PBIS and SEL are used for the purposes of controlling youth, then they become tools of oppression—not liberation—even if applied under the guise of equity.

### Creative Solutions

If we recognize that traditional classroom rules and approaches to "management" are not in alignment with an anti-oppressive approach to teaching, then what are some alternatives? First, start with a self-assessment: What rules do you normally put in place, and why *those* rules? Which rules tend to get broken most often, why, and by whom? This can be applied to a single classroom, a grade level, or an entire campus. If we *first* consider who rules are harming, then the very purpose of the rules comes into question. If they are not effective, why keep them? If they do not serve the larger goal of learning, why do they exist? This is what we mean by *realization*—recognizing what is in place and reflecting on who is harmed, benefitted, and protected by those structures.

Second, consider class-created rules, in which students propose rules and use a democratic process to determine which rules are most important and how the class will uphold them. Not only does this more intentionally teach them social studies skills, but it will lead to better rules. Noreen used a "snowball fight" to both solicit ideas and discuss the function of rules. Students wrote down some rules they thought might lead to a safe learning environment, then wadded up their papers into balls and had 20 seconds to have a paper snowball fight. After the snowball fight was over, students were asked to grab the ball nearest to them and take a moment to think about what rules were needed to have a safe but fun snowball fight. Suggestions like "Don't throw balls in people's faces" and "Don't run across the classroom" were common examples that demonstrated shared concern for each other, which Noreen highlighted as they were proposed. Then, with ideas of caring for each other fresh on their minds, students opened the wadded papers and read through the list of anonymously written rules and made additions and suggestions. The fight resumed anew and continued for several rotations, then students came together on the carpet to discuss what they had written and read, and created rules based on what they agreed was most important.

A third approach is to start with what students want and need so you can help create an ideal learning opportunity. That might mean they want to go to the bathroom or get a drink of water without asking permission. Is there a way they could do this without interruption or losing significant learning time? Putting the onus of responsibility and process on students empowers them to think about the rules with which they are already familiar and may have already thought about a great deal. Compared to taking a quick bathroom or water break, sharpening a pencil in the middle of class might be more disruptive to the group. How might students devise a way to address this problem? Teachers can offer students different scenarios or have students come up with scenarios to pose to their classmates. This approach engages critical thinking and persuasive arguments alongside the development of civic ideals and considering multiple perspectives—it's a content integration dream!

On a final note, do youth have any voice in the *co-construction* or modification of rules? Noreen's fifth-grade students complained to her about the physical education teacher's no-bathroom rule. While in the gym for their weekly 50-minute class, students were not allowed to use the bathroom. This did not take into consideration bodily needs and differences, the fact that some classes had physical education immediately after lunch, or the menstruation needs of some students. In short, this rule was not fair. As a fellow teacher, Noreen understood the logic behind its implementation: the bathrooms were located outside of the gym, where students could not be easily supervised, and if students were constantly in and out of the gym, they could miss crucial instructions and participation that were packed into the short time frame provided by the daily schedule. But, as someone who spent all day with her students and knew that they were honest and responsible about going to the bathroom when needed, she understood their concern and advocated for them to let the physical education teacher know why *that rule in particular* was more harmful than helpful. If we think about rules in our city, state, or nation as embodied by laws and statutes, those *can* be changed if people work to make it so—we should offer young people similar opportunities for civic agency.

## Communities

Next, let's consider communities beyond the classroom walls. In the primary grades, educators often present communities as the neighborhood where the school is located; for older students, the notion of communities expands to include city, region, state, nation, and the world. Regardless of scope, communities are rarely presented as places where conflict or oppression occurs—even when histories of oppression like redlining abound or gentrification is occurring in real time—and the names of places and locations of borders are assigned for memorization with little attention to how they came to be or how they might be contested. This idealization of spaces and places fails to illustrate the full complexity of human environment interaction and movement.

### Common Pitfalls

In conversations about local, state, national, and global communities, teachers frequently rely on tools like maps to help students understand geographic themes of location, place, regions, movement, and human–environment interaction. Often, the labels and location of places centered on maps are taken for granted. In these cases, idealization obscures any controversy or contestation about these places, as Indigenous names go unacknowledged and popular maps distort the proportions of specific countries and continents. Sometimes these labels are clearly political and ideological in nature: Google and Apple Maps sparked global controversy when Palestine was removed from their services and when it was discovered that the border of the contested state of Kashmir varied whether one was looking at a map while in Pakistan or India. Other times, names drawn from histories of racism remain unproblematized, such as the town of White Settlement in Texas, or places and monuments that include racial slurs. Rather than list these place-slurs here, we encourage interested readers to do a quick web search for "racist place names" and prepare for your jaw to drop.

Sometimes the very trade books that teachers use to teach geography concepts contain stereotypical and offensive portrayals. A widely used example is *Me on the Map* (Sweeney, 1996/2018), which features a white girl spread across images of North America and Europe. Illustrations of other continents, however, feature stereotypically exotic Black and Brown children. Similarly, *Maps* (Mizielinska & Mizielinski, 2013) includes hand-drawn maps of an array of nations, with children and symbols splayed across each one. Yet upon closer inspection, the book is Eurocentric in coverage and contains many stereotypical representations of women and BIPOC. While these books may be marketed as ideal texts to introduce maps, they reiterate normative Eurocentrism and whiteness.

Our final pitfall is the teaching of borders. Students are introduced to borders as simple, clean lines on a map. They are presented as fact, neutral, innocent in their descriptive function, and fixed. But the location of borders, like the assignment of names to places, is determined by those in power. Also, borders do not all function in the same way: Some are built deliberately to exclude, others are crossed regularly, and still others are broken down and transcended (Menon & Saleh, 2018).

## Creative Solutions

How can you teach students about the complexities and injustices of the environment around them in ways that are both powerful and age appropriate? There are many potential activities that link economics and geography as students start to consider how their lives are impacted by nearby places, landmarks, and businesses. Where do they get food? Health care? School supplies? Gas? Books? Students' early mapping activities often involve places that are personally important to them, but such activities tend to remain hyper-focused on individuals. If the focus is on community as it *really* exists, students must consider their connections to others and places beyond their immediate locales.

For example, when second-grade teacher Jen Oliva's students asked her what happens if people can't afford food, she created a unit about food deserts in their city (Swalwell, Lambert, & Oliva, 2019). Her students brainstormed several ways to improve access to healthy food, considering the perspectives of different stakeholders like grocery-store owners. They ultimately decided that people who had less money should be entitled to discounted prices, which facilitated a conversation about real-world programs like the Supplemental Nutrition Assistance Program (SNAP). In another example, Katy is working with second-grade teachers Carli Jaff and Vincent DiGeronimo whose students shared that their parents wouldn't let them go to the homes of students who lived in "bad" (i.e., predominantly Black, lower-income) neighborhoods. As a result, the teachers constructed an entire unit around the question, *What makes a neighborhood "good"?* to challenge these misconceptions.

Students can directly connect with those who live and work in the surrounding neighborhood and members of local organizations to learn how various people contribute to the community. A simple walk around the block or to the corner store can be ripe with rich learning opportunities, particularly if you can find community members and business owners who can engage students' questions and curiosities about the places visited. For educators who do not live in the communities they teach in, becoming personally familiar with school neighborhoods is especially important. The Wisconsin Teachers of Local Culture website has a helpful set of resources for teachers and students to support their "local learning" in the tradition of place-based education. The Native Land website (www.native-land.ca) includes a teacher's guide with exercises for children to center Indigenous treaties, territories, and languages as they learn more about specific places.

### COMMUNITY WALKS/CAMINATAS

Noreen first learned about community walks as an undergraduate student in the College of Education at the University of Texas at Austin. As future Spanish/English bilingual educators, she and her classmates referred to community walks as caminatas. Noreen's professor, Haydée

Rodríguez, organized a tour featuring important people and places in the neighborhood surrounding one of the elementary schools where Noreen and her classmates interned. For example, the undergrads visited the home of a neighborhood baker and many elderly residents greeted them during their weekday walk. The undergrads realized these residents were likely very familiar to their students, and that the neighborhood was filled with rich histories and fascinating individuals who would have been completely unknown to them without their caminata. When Noreen became a classroom teacher, she began each school year with a similar walk: Teachers would leave Back to School Night flyers and school supply info on students' doorsteps. Kids would wave to them from windows and, if they were lucky, former students would emerge from their homes to bestow hugs. We highly recommend community walks for educators who do not live in the communities where they teach, but remember—be respectful, listen and learn, avoid judgment, and pass the mic to community members so they speak for themselves. Importantly, consider partnering with guides who offer perspectives and histories that help students (and teachers!) see the community through different perspectives, which might help everyone better understand whose histories, languages, cultures, and traditions are recognized through naming of places, style of architecture, placement of buildings, accessibility, and so forth—and how all of these change over time.

Another way for students to learn about local communities in a real rather than an idealized way is through a project that Katy developed at the University of Wisconsin–Madison called "Right Under Our Noses." This project asks students to find a person, place, or thing in their local environment that they've always wondered about and to conduct research to learn more about it. Students have investigated businesses, artwork, landforms, parks, plaques—even an empty lot and a memorable street performer. Katy and her methods students went on a tour of Washington, D.C. with muralist Joel Bergner to learn the background of murals throughout the city and her colleague Aaron Bird Bear (Mandan, Hidatsa and Diné) offered an Indigenous perspective of familiar campus spots including a magnificent tree, a memorial statue, and the union. Noreen modeled this project for her students by selecting a painting of an ivy-covered heart on an underpass that she drove by every day. Her research revealed that it was a memorial to Ivan Garth Johnson, a 17-year-old boy who was killed by a drunk driver (Largey, 2016). As local histories like this are unearthed, they deepen the connections we have to each other while increasing shared knowledge about community members, places, and spaces that came before us.

But what about those map problems we mentioned earlier? Consider the flaws in the map most commonly found in U.S. classrooms, the Mercator projection. This map was invented in 1569 by Flemish cartographer Gerardus Mercator. As it is understandably difficult to represent a 3-D world on a 2-D map, the Mercator projection substantially distorts sizes and distances at the poles, such that the entire continent of Africa looks smaller than Greenland even though Africa is 14.5 times as big as Greenland (Taylor, 2015), and typically centers North America and Europe. Teachers can disrupt these North American–centric distortions in a few different ways.

One approach is to take a Mercator projection and cut it so that fits onto a sphere, then color all the visible parts before taking the map off the sphere and examining how much of the map is left uncolored. If technology is available, the True Size tool (www.thetruesize.com) allows users to search for countries and drag outlines across a map to compare actual sizes without distortion. Students can also compare the Mercator projection to the Peters projection. The Peters world map, created by German historian Arno Peters, is a cylindrical, equal-area projection that has a notably less Eurocentric focus (Crampton, 1994). When laid side-by-side, the contrasts between the two maps make clear that cartography is not neutral. Students can debate which map is a better representation and why.

Names and borders are not neutral either. We encourage readers to begin with an investigation into naming. For example, the Native Land website mentioned above maps out Indigenous territories, treaties, and languages. A quick glimpse at the richness of colors on the website will blow students away; many likely never learned about such diversity among Native Peoples. Importantly, this resource represents

Native Peoples on their own terms, using the names they call themselves rather than names imposed upon them by colonial outsiders, and disrupts idyllic notions of an "empty" continent available for settlement. Analyzing the historical roots of colonization in the languages used for naming places, unpacking nicknames for places used by insiders and outsiders, and exploring controversies around namesakes provide additional rich opportunities for thinking critically about place.

Finally, we return to borders, which are often presented as ideal and fixed, with no need to question how they were decided upon or who might be harmed by them. Teacher educators Sajani Menon and Muna Saleh (2018) challenge educators to go beyond the singular view of borders as a means to separate geographic spaces, people, and ideas. Borders can also position spaces, people, and ideas in proximity to each other, and "can be molded, shifted, and shaped by experiences—internal and external, personal and social—over time and in relation with one another" (Menon & Saleh, 2018, p. 55). For a clear example of how to engage young children in the messiness and power present in borders, think about areas in a classroom or playground where certain students are encouraged to play yet others are not allowed nor welcomed. Not all of these boundaries are visible or spoken but are present nonetheless. Similarly, there are often constructed borders around homes, places that children recognize as safe, and places they have been instructed never to go without an adult. Children's lived experiences can offer a wealth of these examples that can then be applied to other contexts. Why wouldn't we take advantage of such vibrant learning opportunities?

## Community Helpers

Firefighters. Police. Mail carriers. These are the workers who are frequently cited as "community helpers" in early childhood classrooms. Doctors. Nurses. Veterinarians. Waste collectors. People who provide vital services that allow us to live our daily lives in safe and clean environments. These individuals are often idealized, depicted as happy and friendly helpers to anyone in need, people on whom students can rely. But these workers, and the ways they conduct their jobs, are complex and can't be expressed through a single story.

For example, in many rural areas, emergency workers may have other jobs or serve on a volunteer basis. The state of California has relied on incarcerated "hand crews" to fight fires for decades; during the wildfires of 2020, inmates made up nearly 1 out of every 4 of the state's wildfire firefighters and did some of the most hazardous work (Carber, 2020). In some parts of the country, doctors and nurses are recruited from abroad to fulfill crucial medical positions that would otherwise be understaffed. Some towns and cities include garbage disposal and recycling services as basic public utilities, while others rely on private companies. In other words, not all community helpers come to their important work in the same way, nor do all community helpers offer care and support equitably. These truths are messy and may be uncomfortable, but your students may be well aware of them, particularly if they have helpers in their families or they belong to communities that experience harm from those who are supposed to help.

## Common Pitfalls

Units about community helpers overwhelmingly idealize a world where adults justly wield power and students are expected to trust their authority without question. Rarely do these lessons attend to the realities of injustice like the disproportionate impact on communities of color of police-involved shootings and racial profiling (Love & Bradley, 2015). Earlier, we mentioned Kaia Rolle, the 6-year-old who threw a tantrum at school. One can only imagine the terror Rolle must have felt when police officers arrived after she had already calmed down. These community helpers were not there to help her, but to restrain her and take her away. For those in power, the police are the ones who will be believed and trusted, even if they are more likely a threat than a source of safety and protection for others in the community. Thus, many families who are targets of oppression must, very reasonably, teach their children to be cautious and careful when encountering traditional community helpers for their survival.

A recent police shooting that killed an unarmed Black teenager is dominating headlines in your community and inspiring protests and counter protests. You're about to teach the standard curriculum about police officers being community helpers. Given your teaching context, how should you address this event and what would be your goals for doing so? What responses from students, families, and colleagues would you anticipate, and how would you plan to address them?

It is important to recognize that the inequities and injustices that often make headlines with regards to law enforcement are not limited to those institutions; the educational systems where we have dedicated so much of our work, energy, time, and passion are absolutely responsible for disproportionately harming and mistreating marginalized youth. These harms similarly exist in the health care system, which people in the United States have yet to access in ways that are equal and without discrimination on the basis of race, gender, sexuality, class, ability, language, and religion. Across these systems, we teach children to defer to and obey adults, but we offer them little agency in the event that those community members harm them emotionally or physically.

While some educators have expanded *helpers* to include custodial staff and other service workers whose labor is vital to the health of our communities, another pitfall is when educators simply add on more community members without actually interrogating why their roles matter. In another problematic attempt to be more inclusive, teachers may present idyllic diversity without attending to how these positions are often raced, classed, and gendered. Educator Bill Ayers (2004) remembers such a moment while working at a school that prided itself on anti-bias materials for students, like dolls that included a white male nurse and a Black female firefighter. During a field trip to the fire station, a 5-year-old girl asked the firefighter giving them a tour when a woman would work there. The man laughed and said, "Never, I hope!" Ayers recognized that the school's anti-bias materials were "in combat with some hard facts . . . [and that] changing language did not in itself change worlds." Instead, he reflected on how powerful teaching *reality* is for children, and the obligation educators have "to present the concrete situations they encounter as problems that challenge them and call for our response" (Ayers, 2004, p. 69). In this instance, students wrote letters to city officials alerting them to their belief that women could be firefighters, too.

There is a delicate balance here. While we want to keep it real with students, we also want to nurture their imagination to dream up ideals. That young girl's question and desire to speak out when she didn't like the answer was fueled by the ideal her teacher helped cultivate. Educator and activist Carla Shalaby maintains that if we "prepare children for the world we have now, we will necessarily reflect and reinforce the everyday harms and assaults of punishment, confinement, and exclusion. Instead, we have to begin to prepare children for the world we want" (2017, p. 174). In our shared effort to build a better world, what might a more honest unit about the community helpers we *want* look like?

## Creative Solutions

Supporting students in understanding the many moving parts of an ecosystem is an excellent starting point for imagining the world we want. Who are the individuals who contribute to students' care, health, and safety during the school day? What would happen if one of those individuals no longer supported the classroom community or the larger school community? Once students identify the important roles that each person plays in contributing to the larger group, then they can consider ways to show appreciation and gratitude—not just once, but consistently. *The Kid Who Changed the World* (Andrews, 2014) is a picture book that illustrates how the actions of a single person can extend in multiple directions and impact many others. Ideally, the recognition of shared labor and energies will lead to increased respect and value for everyone involved. That's our dream!

The next solution is thinking beyond what currently exists—what we describe as *co-construction*, because it's about coming together to imagine what could be if we worked together to create something different and better. One example of co-construction is the movement for prison abolition. Geography professor and prison-abolition activist

Ruth Wilson Gilmore describes abolition as the development of multiple support systems, like providing jobs, education, health care, and housing, so people have the resources they need long before they have an opportunity to cause harm to themselves or others (Kushner, 2019). Abolition does *not* mean promoting an unsafe world with no consequences. In fact, it promotes the contrary. In schools, school resource officers would be replaced by counselors, all in the name of reducing harm to *everyone*. Abolitionist teachers would refuse to take part in zero-tolerance policies and the school-to-prison pipeline, and would reimagine and rewrite curricula with local and national activists to offer students examples and strategies of resistance (Love, 2019). Co-construction is about recognizing injustice and oppression and actively working in solidarity against the many ways these evils manifest in society, so that everyone does not just survive but *thrives*.

In the meantime, we must confront the differential and often discriminatory treatment of marginalized people and communities by the very individuals who are supposed to serve and protect them. Picture books like *For Beautiful Black Boys Who Believe in a Better World* (Waters, 2020), *Todos Iguales/All Equal: Un Corrido de Lemon Grove/A Ballad of Lemon Grove* (Hale, 2019), and *Voice of Freedom: Fannie Lou Hamer* (Weatherford, 2016) attend directly to these issues in the past and present. Injustice has never happened by accident, and while such realizations can be painful for children, it is also important that they have opportunities to process why injustice occurs and what they can do to confront and disrupt it. Models for this work are all around us, and community exemplars can be welcomed into the classroom so that students can learn more about how people solve problems in their communities. Students can learn about a range of injustices that directly impact community members *and* how members within the same community are taking action like organizing voter registration drives, stocking food pantries, establishing bail funds, generating rent relief, and more. Better yet, fostering these kinds of connections and building relationships with a range of people in the community who help make it run (especially in times of crisis) may offer students opportunities to become involved in solving problems themselves.

## Takeaways for the Problematics of Idealization: Realization and Co-Construction

The societies in which we live are rampant with oppressive forces and structures. Yet communities are taught to young learners as if the challenges and inequities that surround us don't exist. Educators can't proclaim to stand for equity if they don't address *in*equity, and this philosophy must be reflected in and outside of the classroom, from the rules that govern students' behavior in learning spaces to reckoning with the harsh injustices that are found in the neighborhoods that form school communities and the abuses of power that occur among community helpers. Rather than relying on approaches that depict ideals that don't or shouldn't exist, educators and students can work together to see things as they actually are, to understand how they came to be in often contested ways, *and* imagine how they could be better—a world where justice leads to self-determination and liberation. See Table B.7 *Idealization Lesson/Unit Reflection Worksheet* in the appendix to apply these ideas.

## Putting These Ideas Into Practice

### Algorithmic Caminata

Take a walk around the neighborhood that surrounds your school. To explore places you might otherwise not visit, try following the pattern of an "algorithmic walk" (www.brokencitylab.org/blog/algorithmic-walk/) (for instance, take the second block on the left, third block on the right, first block on the right, then second block on the right for 20 minutes). Couple this with Noreen's advice about caminatas to take notes, sketches, or photos about what you notice that you could connect to your curriculum. This could also be paired with the "Right Under Our Noses" activity described in the chapter.

### Community Organizations

Review your curriculum and see if you can find at least one local organization that may have resources or be interested in partnering in some way with your students for sustained collaboration. Keep in mind those identities, cultures, languages, and histories that are most marginalized in your educational context as you reach out to a range of ethnic and cultural associations, art organizations, museums, and civic and advocacy groups. Families can help with these connections, too!

# 5

# Heroification: The "Founding Fathers," Suffragists, and Civil Rights Movement Leaders

There is always a need to teach youth about important individuals to develop content knowledge as well as to provide models for how to live our lives. That said, the problem with focusing on famous people is that we easily *heroify* these figures. Historian James Loewen (2008) defines heroification as a process through which individuals are turned into "pious, perfect creatures without conflicts, pain, credibility, or human interest" (p. 11). This approach can bore, mislead, and even alienate youth (Woodson, 2016). We hope it is obvious—that's not anti-oppressive teaching. Students need to know that they don't have to be a perfect, legendary national figure to build a better world.

Although the specifics may differ, educators' attempts to avoid heroification can lead to common pitfalls like whitewashing nondominant individuals and obscuring the importance of organized groups, systems, and structures that both fight against and defend oppression. In response, we encourage educators to lean into the complexity of a *diversified* range of significant individuals' lives by *humanizing* rather than heroifying them. In addition, we recommend shifting away from focusing exclusively on individuals to recognize the power of grassroots *mobilization*—not only famous figures' relationships to people-powered organizations, but an acknowledgment of how generations of "ordinary" people and mass movements are critical for social change.

We are not arguing for the end of stories about famous individuals, but instead urge readers to present them as complex humans rather than saints or sinners (Kent, 1999), and consider the significance of who we teach about in relation to others. Who influenced these figures? And who did they influence? How did the struggles and accomplishments of one community impact another? Below, we examine these issues with three commonly taught sets of "heroes": the "Founding Fathers," suffragists, and Civil Rights Movement leaders.

## The "Founding Fathers"

When discussing politicians such as the "Founding Fathers," elementary educators often gloss over problematic aspects of the individuals' lives in favor of nationalistic narratives that treat them like saviors— "great American heroes who brought democracy to the world and are consequently celebrated as the founders of the United States of America" (L. J. King & Womac, 2014, p. 36). Landowning white men were individuals with tremendous wealth and institutional power, but their stories and perspectives are insufficient for understanding our histories and current situations. Rather than investigating who else helped shape the founding of the nation, which would expand the individuals and groups under consideration, or examining the tensions in the complicated lives of these significant figures, educators often present the canonical signers of the Declaration of Independence and the U.S. Constitution on pedestals through biographies with a focus on trivia. To reinforce this, we refer to the "Founding Fathers" in quotation marks because we want to remind readers that this moniker is something to question and complicate.

Take, for example, elementary student Asha Jeffries's assignment to learn "fun facts about George Washington" as a precursor to writing a list of fun facts about herself. George Washington loved his pet rabbits and only had one of his own teeth when he became president! Because Asha is the daughter of historian Hasan Kwame Jeffries, she learned much more from this homework than the teacher likely intended. Jeffries informed his daughter that Washington also owned people in

addition to his beloved rabbits and had his false teeth made by extract-
ing those of the people he enslaved. Says Jeffries (2019),

> *[T]he idea that so-called fun facts about early American presidents is*
> *how our children are introduced to enslavers troubled me then and*
> *troubles me now. Because when students are finally taught about*
> *slavery . . . they have already been conditioned to believe that those*
> *who held others in bondage were good people, the kind of people who*
> *owned pets and bunny rabbits no less.*

Maybe educators don't want to teach students about the actions or
beliefs of the "Founding Fathers" that they do not want to model (their
misogyny, racism, etc.)—or maybe they themselves simply don't know
this information. Either way, *it has to stop.*

## Common Pitfalls

An obvious solution to the problem of heroification is to present the
"Founding Fathers" as more complicated figures. A potential pitfall,
however, is to swing too far in the other direction and write them off
entirely or to simplistically demonize them. We know our approach to
teaching social studies raises concerns about real or perceived "cancel
culture" where students would no longer learn about George Washington at all or learn he's some sort of evil genius. Let's be clear: That's
absurd. We are simply explaining why presenting superficial accounts
of these figures as *either* sacred heroes or villains is bad pedagogy. These
are important figures whose significance is tied up with how they
wielded power in damaging ways.

In thinking about how to both appreciate Washington and the contributions of other enslaver "Founders" while honoring the people they
harmed, historian Roger Wilkins (2002) writes,

> *[H]owever noble their accomplishments . . . [the Founders] lived*
> *lives cushioned by slavery . . . They created a nation conceived in lib-*
> *erty and dedicated to the proposition that whites were and should*
> *be supreme. They celebrated freedom while stealing the substance of*

*life from the people they 'owned.'. . . . And they created the country that gives me, the descendant of slaves and slave owners, much of the context for my existence, the freedom that I cherish and the democratic citizenship that I have used relentlessly for the past half century. How is one to understand a country whose dreams the slave owners despoiled even as they were creating it? How is a black person to regard a land where his ancestors were meant to serve but not to grow? (p. 5)*

We owe youth of any racialized background a more honest engagement with these legacies. It's complicated, and that's a good thing—and something even young children can handle.

The canonical figures from the founding of the republic are worthy of study because they were unquestionably significant. Teaching students that they are *the only* consequential figures, even if done in more nuanced and honest ways, paints a deeply dishonest picture of the past. We must be mindful to go beyond "just white people bravely and busily creating a country" (Wilkins, 2002, p. 5) to include a much more diverse cast of characters. This quick fix of simply expanding who counts as "Founding Fathers" can still backfire, however, if the fundamental problem of heroification has not been addressed. For example, when teaching about Black "Founding Fathers," history education scholars LaGarrett King and Patrick Womac (2014) caution that a "bundle of silences" (Trouillot, 1995) may still exist if these men are presented without any mention of the racial conflict and institutional racism they faced or the radical ways they challenged white supremacy. King and Womac (2014) remind us that the illusions of inclusions through a few tokenized individuals in history "are 'red herrings' that ignore the totality and complexity" of how various cultural groups "contributed to the social, economic, and political aspects of U.S. society" (p. 41).

We also want to make sure we avoid slapdash inclusion of nondominant figures whose actual historical significance is questionable at best. Take the story of Betsy Ross—one of the few "Founding Mothers" who most American children can name. Her supposed creation of the "Stars and Stripes" flag is not well-documented nor was she influential at the time. According to historian Lauren Thatcher Ulrich (2007), were it not for Betsy Ross's descendants who popularized her life nearly a century after the Revolutionary War as part of a movement to venerate the flag, she would be "indistinguishable from the mass of American women who lived through a war, survived widowhood, raised families, and sustained communities." The story of Ross persists "not because of what she did or did not do in the 1770s, but because her story embodied nineteenth-century ideas about the place of women" (Ulrich, 2007, para. 42).

Compare that to Mercy Otis Warren, a white woman playwright and historian who was one of the leading Patriots of the Revolution. Or poet Phillis Wheatley, an enslaved woman, who was one of the first women *and* the first Black woman in the colonies to become a published writer—as a teenager! Or Deborah Sampson, a white woman and former indentured servant who disguised herself as a man to fight in the Revolutionary War and fought to receive her military pension, securing it only after Congress passed an act to extend her benefits. Ross still may be a useful figure to learn about as a way to understand how "everyday" older women made important contributions to the war effort, but she was *not* a significant figure during her time.

### Creative Solutions

First and foremost, let's keep in mind that we can't desecrate the "Founding Fathers" as some critics may contend, because they *weren't ever sacred figures to begin with*. We're simply de-heroifying them to humanize them and contextualize their accomplishments. This means learning about their interactions with Indigenous people (Dunbar-Ortiz, 2014), relationships with women of all backgrounds (Kann, 1999), and connections to enslavement (Finkelman, 2014). In addition, thinking geographically would expand our understanding of "Founders" beyond British colonists to include Indigenous leaders who helped shape ideas about a confederation of states (Johansen, 1990) as well as influential people in other parts of what would become the United States (Saunt, 2014) including the territories (Immerwahr, 2019). And, of course, we should go beyond individual figures to include organizations that were crucial to the founding, like the Daughters of Liberty, women who organized many boycotts of British goods and produced substitute goods to serve in their place.

There are many appropriate and engaging ways to do this with young people. Education professors Scott Roberts, Stephanie Strachan, and Meghan Block (2019) use the example of Alexander Hamilton to demonstrate their "Great/Not So Great" framework helping primary-grade students "rate" historical figures. After engaging with multiple sources, students must identify what is great about a person, what is not-so-great, and what is not great at all with a final rating and evidence to support their claim. This same framework should be applied to a diverse range of figures who helped found the nation beyond simply white, landowning men—not in the spirit of "Look! Everything was awesome! Other people did great things, too!" but as a way to center their counter stories, highlight the unique experiences of their intersecting identities, and understand that gains for them only happened when their interests converged with those of powerful white people (L. J. King & Womac, 2014).

A straightforward way to do this could be to use a graphic organizer that keeps track of each figure's structural advantages and disadvantages, or preparing biographies and portraits of each figure in relation to the identity chart figure introduced in Chapter 1. If students are writing biographies, provide them with questions about these complexities to incorporate into their writing or presentations. Rather than traditional reports or research projects that list "great accomplishments" and "fun facts," require students to consider complex, humanizing details about these figures. Another idea is to engage students in an inquiry into how the canonical "Founders" are and ought to be commemorated, linking the construction of "heroic" narratives to current debates about whether statues and namesakes should be removed or who should be depicted in the first place (Saylor & Schmeichel, 2020). Perhaps a local school, street, park, or nearby town is named for one of these "Founders"? Education professor Meir Muller (2018) describes just such a unit with primary-grade students that started with a field trip to examine bias in monuments and culminated in writing letters to legislators demanding a change.

When highlighting the roles of canonical "Founders," we must also attend to *why* only white, landowning men signed those important documents, and help students understand that the homogeneity of the Constitutional Convention wasn't just a coincidence or the result of people with other identities opting out. This involves naming the "Founders'" identities (use that identity chart in Chapter 1!) and asking about who was at the proverbial table and who wasn't—and *why*. Examining works of art through the lenses of race and gender is an especially powerful approach and is accessible for emergent readers. Take for example the famous *Declaration of Independence* painting by John Trumbull. Filmmaker Arlen Parsa modified the painting by putting red circles on the faces of each man who enslaved people. Thirty-four of the 47 figures were enslavers (De Liscia, 2020). Students could examine Parsa's mark-ups in relation to their rhetoric of freedom and liberty in the Declaration of Independence. Ultimately, helping students practice posing questions about whose stories are included and excluded develops valuable critical media literacy skills that will serve them beyond any single unit.

---

**WHAT WOULD YOU DO?**

After finishing your unit about the founding of the nation, a student's father angrily confronts you after school. "Why are you teaching my kid to be anti-American? He refuses to stand up for the anthem or say the pledge because you've taught them that the presidents were all evil men." How do you respond?

---

## Suffragists

Another great case to explore heroification is teaching about suffragists—the people who fought for women's right to vote in the United States. Because this topic inherently centers women, it may be easy for educators to think, "Aha! Counter narratives!" without recognizing the ways they may still be erasing, marginalizing, and decentering important stories—what L. J. King and Womac (2014) call "seemingly inclusive curriculum that is in fact anything but" (p. 38). Most notably, teaching about suffragists tends to focus almost exclusively on *white* women.

White suffragists are often idolized, single-handedly given credit for winning the right to vote for *all* women in the United States. Needless to say, it's a lot more complicated than that.

## Common Pitfalls

It is not uncommon for children's books and other educational resources to gloss over the classism, xenophobia, and racism many of the canonical white suffragists deployed in their fight for the vote. Take Carrie Chapman Catt, the founder of the League of Women Voters and one of the most important white leaders in the suffrage movement. In a book she wrote to counter objections to women's suffrage (1917), Catt reassures white Southern men that they will still be able to prevent Black people from voting through state voting laws, saying explicitly that "White supremacy will be strengthened, not weakened by women suffrage" (p. 76). In an 1888 speech, she further argued that the United States should extend suffrage to "pure," "virtuous," "intelligent," "patriotic" women like her if it allowed "uncivilized Indians," "barbarous Mexicans," and "idle, ignorant, and unworthy" men to vote (C. Catt, 1888). These are but two of many, many moments when white suffragists demonstrated a *serious* lack of intersectional solidarity (Hoganson, 2001; McDaneld, 2013). Including this gross part of Catt's legacy doesn't deny her influence—it simply helps students better understand her complexity and gives them the opportunity to interrogate the tactics many white suffragists employed that undermined their fellow women and reproduced harmful stereotypes about many different groups of men. For the record, this is especially important given that these are tactics *still* used by many white feminists today.

Even when educators lift up a more diverse cast of characters like African American Mary Church Terrell, Mexican American Adelina "Nina" Otero-Warren, Chinese American Mabel Ping-Hua Lee, and Yankton Sioux Zitkála-Šá, they may decontextualize their accomplishments by downplaying the intersectional oppression these women were fighting. Other pitfalls include underemphasizing many suffragists' radical tactics, particularly their acts of civil disobedience while in jail for the "crime" of picketing (Library of Congress, n.d.). In the typical narrative told to children, the fact that prison guards force-fed the imprisoned suffragists on hunger strike often goes untold. And, of course, any attention to historical figures should foreground the importance of "ordinary" women organizing for change and the organizations that lifted individual leaders to visibility with many members working behind the scenes in meaningful ways to make their movement effective (the National Association of Colored Women, the League of Women Voters, etc.).

The final pitfall we have seen is when educators conflate the passage of the Nineteenth Amendment with a full realization of women's suffrage. Not all women could vote after its passage—some Native women could not vote until 1962; the U.S. government did not allow all Asian American women to naturalize until 1952; and many Black women only secured access to the polls through the Civil Rights Act of 1965 (North, 2020). The influence of BIPOC women goes back much further than the Seneca Falls Convention, including inspiration from Haudenosaunee and Cherokee societies where women had important public leadership roles, and suffragist organizations for BIPOC women who were not welcomed in white suffragist spaces. The expansion of voting rights beyond the Nineteenth Amendment is thanks to activists who have and continue to fight for women's suffrage long after 1920 (namely, historical figures like Fannie Lou Hamer and organizations like Voto Latino). Again, it's not to deny the significance of individual suffragists or the Nineteenth Amendment—just to contextualize these narratives, make them more fully realized by complicating them, and connect them to ongoing voter suppression that disproportionately affects BIPOC women.

### Creative Solutions

To address these pitfalls, educators must first be sure to include a more diverse cast of influential figures. This is not simply to shove figures like Catt off a pedestal to make way for new heroification, as these women have complicated histories of their own. Rather, it acknowledges the broader contributions of women fighting against racism, xenophobia, and settler colonialism *in addition to sexism* in their struggle for the vote. Nor is it an attempt to slap on some superficial diversity—women like Terrell, Otero-Warren, Lee, and Zitkála-Šá were historically significant by any measure, and the fact that their white counterparts often denied them membership to or leadership roles in organizations and social actions is important to include in historical accounts. Learning about pro-suffrage activists who were *men*, like Frederick Douglass, and organizations like the Men's League for Women's Suffrage, also provides important cases in allyship. See our website (www.ssfabw.com) for recommendations of children's literature to support your teaching of these and other figures.

Remember, counter narratives are more inclusive and therefore more accurate than dominant narratives—they are *not* just a replacement dominant narrative that eschews nuance or critical thinking. There are many ways to incorporate this more humanized history into classroom activities, including adapting the suggestions from the earlier section (such as the "Great/Not So Great" report cards, and the identity chart analyses). When Noreen was teaching, her students used empty cereal boxes to create story box biographies that looked like books, which were then added to their classroom library in the absence of published books about lesser-known historical figures.

In addition, the use of primary sources can introduce the complexity described here with students—even very young learners. There are dozens of rich primary source sets available online to teach about suffragists, including letters, political cartoons, newspaper articles, flyers, and other documents and artifacts to spark students' curiosity. For example, students could examine a photograph of a chapter of the Colored Women Voters to raise questions about why such a group existed. Studying one of the "jailhouse door pins" women earned after being imprisoned for their suffrage activism can spark questions about why they were jailed and what happened to them as a result. Replicas or printed versions of these sources can be assembled in a journey box (Salinas, Fránquiz, & Rodríguez, 2016) with specific questions and tasks for students to engage in as they encounter each primary source. Or students could apply their language arts skills to paraphrase quotes from suffragists' writing and speeches into more kid-friendly language. All of this can be paired with children's literature to complicate and extend students' learning.

It is also worth including primary sources that introduce students to historical figures who fought *against* women's suffrage—not to hold them up as alternative heroes (remember our argument against "both sides"), but to better understand suffragists' struggles and to recognize how oppression, such as intersectional sexism, depends upon the active organizing of people who support oppression. In the case of women voting, that would include organizations like the National Association Opposed to Women's Suffrage and anti-suffragists like Josephine Jewell Dodge and Kate Douglas Wiggin, women privileged by their wealth and whiteness who did what they could to protect that advantage (Weeks, 2015). Looking at political cartoons, photographs, or reading excerpts of their speeches or letters can help foster students' awareness of these activists' efforts.

Another creative solution to these pitfalls is to apply disciplinary questions beyond history to dislodge dominant narratives of U.S. exceptionalism. Thinking geographically could spark inquiries into women's suffrage around the world, including how many Indigenous women participate in governance of their tribal nations (Sayers & MacDonald, 2001) and how countries like New Zealand permitted women to vote in national elections before the United States (Schaeffer, 2020). Thinking through a civics lens could help students examine current news stories about voter suppression and learn about contemporary efforts to ensure voting rights through leaders like Stacey Abrams. A graphic organizer like a Venn diagram allows students to compare what is happening today with voting rights to what happened 100 years ago. And thinking through a behavioral science lens could allow students to make connections to how many of the 19th-century tensions *still* exist in debates about women's rights and feminism today (Schmidt, 2020).

## Civil Rights Movement Leaders

Last, but not least, let's get into the heroification of leaders in the U.S. Civil Rights Movement. This historical era, often narrowly defined as struggles against Jim Crow segregation between the early 1950s to late 1960s, is perhaps the most frequently taught social studies content in U.S. elementary schools. It is also one that educators may think is a great example of their anti-oppressive practice—while actually doing more harm than good. "It's about Black people and activism, right? How could I *not* be teaching anti-oppressive social studies?" Oh, there's always a way. While the cast of characters do not represent the rich white men of the "Founding Fathers" or the white women suffragists, the same pitfalls of erasing complexity, marginalizing and whitewashing folks, and obscuring the role of social movements can still happen. Famed activists' connection to mass movements and truly revolutionary tactics are often obscured to favor a selective focus on individuals while watering down their tactics to appear less controversial.

## Common Pitfalls

If we say "list the names of Civil Rights Movement leaders taught in elementary schools," who comes to mind? The most common responses are Rosa Parks and Martin Luther King, Jr. Few people are heroified in the elementary curriculum as much as these two inarguably important figures. Their contributions and the magnitude of the problems they addressed, however, tend to be grossly oversimplified, such that students generally believe that King's "I Have a Dream" speech (often reduced to the single line about his children) and Parks's refusal to leave her bus seat were the only actions needed to end decades of Jim Crow and injustice (Busey & Walker, 2017).

It's worth noting that Parks did not remain seated because she was tired nor was her choice spontaneous—her actions were part of a highly strategic operation of which she was a longtime leader. In fact, she was *chosen* for this refusal—knowing she would get arrested—because her appearance as a "tired seamstress" would garner sympathy among the white public (Kohl, 2005). While King is now depicted as a peaceful leader who dreamt of a kumbaya moment of multiracial children holding hands, he was often a source of controversy. He was outspoken about not only racism but also militarism and poverty, which he dubbed the three evils of society. These governmental critiques led the FBI to surveil him through a program called COINTELPRO, which targeted many activists including Rosa Parks. Additionally, despite his saintly stature today, King was not a popular figure at the time of his murder (Cobb, 2018).

When educators offer students a heroified presentation of King and Parks, they promote what professor Derrick Alridge (2006) calls "messianic narratives" that frame such individuals as exceptionally flawless saviors of the oppressed, while demonizing or ignoring others within the community who disagreed or favored different approaches (armed self-defense, indirect action). Scholar Ashley Woodson (2016) notes how messianic narratives can actually reinforce dominant narratives through an overreliance on individualism and Judeo–Christian norms. Similarly, education professors Chris Busey and Irenea Walker (2017) found that elementary social studies standards often adapt Black acts of resistance to fit dominant narratives. Consider how many educators extol nonviolent disobedience for Black liberation while downplaying or critiquing other strategies—yet hold up white Revolutionary War era violent acts of resistance against England as "true Patriots." What accounts for violence employed for Black liberation being framed as dangerous or immoral while violence on behalf of freedom struggles that largely benefit white people is deemed as heroic? Bringing these ideas to the present, consider the vitriol and professional consequences for football quarterback Colin Kaepernick when he took up nonviolent protest during the national anthem. This contradictory critique continues today.

When centering individuals like King and Parks as those solely responsible for any gains of the Civil Rights Movement, even through a more accurate and complex account of their lives, educators overlook other figures who were influential in the movement but whose intersecting identities marginalized them both then and now. A focus on individual leaders also erases the importance of organizations, the power of dedicated, constant collective grassroots agitation, and the need for strategic mobilization of individuals in local communities and contexts *every day* (Vasquez Heilig, Brown, & Brown, 2012). This approach also disconnects struggles against Jim Crow from other related civil rights movements like those for migrant workers and people with disabilities. An exclusive focus on King and Parks to teach about struggles for racial justice can also lead to avoiding or downplaying the figures fighting *against* the expansion of civil rights to present sanitized narratives that avoid "robust attention to racism and White supremacy" (Swalwell, Pellegrino, & View, 2015, p. 80). And when leaders like Parks and King are heroified as having "won," educators obscure that their victories were partial—and that many of their struggles continue today.

Lastly, it is important to recognize the sneaky ways that phrasing can hide who is responsible for causing harm and oppression (Jordan, 2002). This happens all over the place in social studies, but is especially pervasive and pernicious in resources about the civil rights movement. Let's say we're teaching about the Children's March in Birmingham in 1963. Compare these two sentences:

**A)** *Black children demonstrators were attacked by dogs and fire hoses.*

**B)** *White police chief Bull Connor ordered his men to unleash dogs and use fire hoses to attack the Black children demonstrators.*

In the first sentence, it is unclear *who* was responsible for attacking the children. Did the dogs come out of nowhere? Who turned on the hoses? The first sentence is an example of passive voice, a grammatical device that obscures the person or thing responsible for the action and focuses on the person or object that experiences the action (Thomson, 2017). In contrast, the second sentence makes clear who perpetrated the violence against Black children—this is active voice, where the agent is named and present rather than invisible. Very different vibe, right? And guess who the passive voice protects in historical narratives?

Education theorist Zeus Leonardo (2004) explains the cost of "downplaying the active role of whites who take resources from people of color all over the world, appropriate their labor, and construct policies that deny minorities' full participation in society" (p. 138). The passive voice preserves the "innocence of whiteness" by describing racism "as happening almost without the knowledge of whites" or behind their backs rather than "on the backs of people of color" (p. 138). Whenever we are describing actions, we thus need to remember to name the agents of action. Saying explicitly that *white people* enacted harm, and naming specific historically significant people who used their agency to deny rights to others is critical to understanding how white supremacy works.

## Creative Solutions

Readers, you may be reflecting on your own background knowledge and thinking, "Oh no! I thought Rosa Parks sat down because she was tired! What else am I getting wrong?" If you're like us, you learned a heroified version of these histories growing up—*probably a lot*. Doing a better job of teaching the next generation can channel that shame and frustration into something constructive. The first step with any of our suggestions is to beef up your own understanding of these histories—we don't need to know *everything* before we teach (and we will never "know everything," of course), but be intentional about seeking out diverse perspectives. In particular, we appreciate Woodson's (2016) advice to "disrupt messianic master narratives by including activists from various racial, ethnic, gender, sexual, and ideological backgrounds" (p. 206). Here are a few counter narratives of civil rights movement leaders to get you started.

> ### LEARNING MORE ABOUT THE MOVEMENT
> We recommend political science professor Jean Theoharis's (2018) book *A More Beautiful and Terrible History: The Uses and Misuses of Civil Rights History*; historian Hasan Kwame Jeffries's (2019) *Understanding and Teaching the Civil Rights Movement*; *Putting the Movement Back Into Civil Rights Teaching* by Deborah Menkart, Alana Murray, and Jenice View (2014); *Teaching for Black Lives* (2018) edited by Dyan Watson, Jesse Hagopian, and Wayne Au; and *Black Lives Matter At Schools* by Denisha Jones and Jesse Hagopian (2020) to expand your knowledge of Civil Rights Movement histories and how to connect them to the work of social movements in the present.

Bayard Rustin was one of the lead organizers for the March on Washington for Jobs and Freedom where King gave his famous "I Have A Dream Speech." Homophobia related to Rustin's identity as a gay Black man has led to his omission from many civil rights narratives, even though it was Rustin who introduced King to Gandhi's nonviolent resistance strategies. Claudette Colvin refused to give up her seat on a Montgomery bus nine months before Parks. Because she was a teenager, working class, and known to speak back to white authority, the organizers of the boycott chose middle-aged, middle-class, "respectable" Parks to launch their campaign instead. Despite this strategic snub, Colvin stayed committed to the movement, even serving as one of the plaintiffs in the lawsuit that abolished segregated busing in Alabama. Both figures are the subject of children's literature that helps bring their stories to life for young readers.

Thinking like a geographer would help students expand their understanding of figures beyond the Deep South and large urban centers on the coasts who fought against anti-Blackness. Connecting national narratives to local examples of activists in your community is also a great hook for engaging students. Many educational resources focus on the Deep South or coastal urban centers, but even if you're teaching in these areas, it's important to highlight examples of segregation and activism in other regions (the Midwest, the U.S. territories) and contexts (rural communities, suburbs) to convey the depth of white supremacy—*and* the reach of the movement.

For us, this means examining legal and extralegal anti-Blackness in Iowa and highlighting figures like Edna Griffin who, like Parks, was a COINTELPRO-surveilled, longtime activist who leveraged her "nonthreatening" image as an affluent, formally educated woman to fight against various injustices through multiracial coalitions (see Swalwell & Gallagher, n.d.). In Washington, D.C., scholar Brigitte Emmanuelle Dubois (2011) featured a nationally renowned figure with deep roots in her students' neighborhood: Marian Wright Edelman, a lead organizer in King's Poor People's Campaign and founder of the Children's Defense Fund. Teaching and learning about less mainstream figures like Griffin or underappreciated leaders like Edelman is another way to understand the magnitude and diversity of the movement (Wills, 2001).

More nuanced attention to a diverse array of significant figures should situate them amidst the networks that made their actions possible. Rosa Parks's significance cannot be understood outside of multiple networks, like her training in civil disobedience at the Highlander Folk School and her longtime membership in the NAACP. The Montgomery Bus Boycott launched after Parks's arrest was effective because "ordinary" Black people sacrificed a great deal for over a year. And there are many important examples of grassroots organizing and strategies that diverged from the civil disobedience of Parks and King, like the Black Panther Party for Self Defense—a group many educators overlook or malign when teaching about the Civil Rights Movement (Sanchez & Hagopian, 2016). Primary sources and children's books can weave together stories of different people who took part in different ways for a fuller version of these histories.

A unit about the Civil Rights Movement should also acknowledge related struggles for justice like the American Indian Movement, the Chicano Movement, the Asian American Movement, the Third World Liberation Front fight for ethnic studies programs, the disabilities rights movement, LGBTQIA+ rights, and the Gray Panthers fighting against ageism, as well as struggles for human rights in other countries, like the anti-apartheid movement in South Africa. This opens up opportunities for including an even more diverse, nuanced, contextualized range of leaders and to emphasize the phenomenon of *long* struggle.

Let's review a few examples. When teaching the Gay Rights Movement and the 1969 Stonewall riots as resistance against police brutality of LGBTIA+ people, some educators neglect to center the stories of Marsha P. Johnson, Sylvia Rivera, and other transgender women of color who led the resistance—leaders who white, cisgender men and women pushed aside. Additionally, Compton's Cafeteria riot in San Francisco occurred three years *before* Stonewall and is now in a first-of-its-kind protected historic district thanks to organizing led by Black trans women (Levin, 2019). See educators Bárbara Cruz and Robert Bailey's (2017) article for more ideas about LGBTQ+ inclusive social studies. Or consider the activism of migrant agricultural workers, from the Filipino American– and Mexican American–led United Farm Workers to the multiethnic coalition that led the 1946 sugar strike in Hawai'i. Many of these organizers intentionally engaged in cross-racial solidarity and cross-issue collaborations. Activists like Yuri Kochiyama fought alongside Malcolm X in the struggle for Black liberation *and* organized against the Vietnam War *and* anti–Asian American discrimination. Highlighting the connections between issues and communities as well as the importance of being in solidarity together are important lessons for youth as they learn how to take action today.

With regards to avoiding the pitfall of using the passive voice and obscuring white supremacy: Use the active voice and make white supremacy clear. Take the story of Ruby Bridges, which has become a standard part of teaching about the Civil Rights Movement in many elementary schools, in large part because it involves a young girl who children can immediately empathize with. Many teaching materials depict the classic photograph of 6-year-old Ruby Bridges leaving school flanked by white federal agents, or the Norman Rockwell painting *The Problem We All Live With* dramatizing this moment. Both are used to celebrate her courage—but the only white people shown in either image are ostensibly protecting Bridges, so it's unclear to viewers *why* she has to be so brave. If we "zoom out" to include what was happening just across the street—a mob of white women known as the "cheerleaders" furiously shouting at this tiny girl with a sign that says "All I Want For Christmas is a Clean White School"—then Bridges's courage is brought into much sharper relief. This "zoom in/out" strategy is a common visual thinking approach with works of art and primary sources, and is useful to prompt student questions and considerations about agents of action.

### #NOTALLWHITEPEOPLE

At this point, you may be wondering if and how it is possible to talk about white people who supported the Civil Rights Movement. Thankfully, there have been and are people with dominant identities who have risked everything to be in solidarity with others. These figures are important for all students to learn about, but especially as models for those who share their identities. With regards to the Civil Rights Movement, this could mean teaching about Viola Liuzzo, a stay-at-home mom turned activist who left her family in Detroit, Michigan to help Black people registering voters in Selma, Alabama—an act of courage that ended in her murder at the hands of the Ku Klux Klan. Or Freedom Rider Joan Trumpeter Mulholland, a longtime civil rights activist who endured beatings and jail time. Mulholland's son Loki and author Angela Fairwell describe her story in the picture book *She Stood for Freedom* (2016).

There are others whose sacrifices are inspiring, to be sure. As we teach about them, however, we need to be careful not to center their voices and experiences or present them as more common figures than they were. Part of what makes it so incredible when people with dominant identities take risks for justice is that *so few do*. Learning about how to be in solidarity and leverage whatever privilege we have for justice *in ways both big and small* is a crucial element of anti-oppressive teaching, but these examples of solidarity should not take the place of lifting up the stories, voices, and perspectives of those most directly impacted by oppression.

Speaking of children, any opportunity to center youth activism in these stories is vital—both in historical and contemporary times. Children were *directly* involved in actions during the 1950s and 1960s fighting against racial segregation. The Birmingham Children's Crusade is a wonderful example, and Learning for Justice's *Mighty Times* film is a great resource (though, heads up, it contains the N-word so a conversation with children about that is crucial). Of course, highlighting local examples from students' neighborhoods or regions is especially good for helping them to see themselves in these histories. More recently, there are incredible youth leaders in struggles like the March for Our Lives fighting for gun control, as Dreamers protesting deportations of undocumented young people, and as water protectors fighting for sovereignty and sustainability at Standing Rock. In fact, educators must connect *current* struggles for justice to these historical movements so students can better understand what is happening in their communities right now. This is the "long Civil Rights struggle" (Hall, 2005) that so many social studies resources ignore to their detriment.

## Takeaways for the Problematics of Heroification: Diversification, Humanization, and Mobilization

It is easy to find examples of how the "Founding Fathers," suffragists, and Civil Rights Movement leaders are typically taught as heroified figures—extraordinary people beyond reproach who we should credit for social change. While there is value in highlighting the lives of individuals to help students better understand their communities and learn how to build a better world, we want to avoid the pitfall of heroification by which leaders' lives are oversimplified, their admirable qualities overemphasized, and their flaws and foibles erased. We also want to reconsider who gets identified as a hero in the first place by broadening the scope of whose leadership has made a difference. We must be sure to contextualize any figure we introduce to children within broader, multigenerational movements and organizations that made their accomplishments possible in the first place—as well as the broader, multigenerational movements and organizations that tried to stop them. See Table B.8 *Heroification Lesson/Unit Reflection Worksheet* in the appendix to apply these ideas.

Remember, *diversification, humanization,* and *mobilization* are not just about knocking white men off pedestals and replacing them with new canonized figures—though a more diverse cast of characters is certainly welcome. *The opposite of heroification is not demonization.* We can still appreciate and recognize the contributions of people without glorifying or sanctifying them. In fact, the *best* way to honor the lives of notable figures is to learn from their mistakes as much as we learn from their achievements, to humanize them and to honor the grassroots mobilization that made their achievements possible. It's also the best way to help youth recognize themselves as agents of change, able to build a better world.

## Putting These Ideas Into Practice

### Journey Box

Try creating a journey box that features counter narratives of social movements or influential organizations and figures, past or present. Initially developed by professors Linda Labbo and Sherry Field (1999) and modified by professor Cinthia Salinas and colleagues (Salinas, Blevins, & Sullivan, 2012; Salinas, Fránquiz, & Rodríguez, 2016) to emphasize counter narratives often omitted in textbooks, this collection of artifacts, photographs, and other primary sources uses "document-based questions" (DBQs) to draw students' attention to important details in each primary source. As students move through each primary source and respond to the DBQs, they are taken on a journey through the person's life, place, or historical event. Journey boxes can be physical or virtual, and can be designed around a compelling or a supporting question. These can also be designed as "breakout boxes" with students using information they learn to solve puzzles that unlock the next clue.

## Biography Audit

Conduct an audit of the biographies in your classroom or school's media center, either on your own or (even better!) with your students like elementary teacher Jess Lifshitz does (@Jess5th on Twitter). Is a diverse range of people included in your collection, or are dominant voices most prominent? Are the figures heroified, or are their lives presented in a way that honors their complexity? For the weaknesses that exist in your library, search out better biographies and request additions to your school library using the children's literature lists recommended on our website.

## Namesake Investigations

Is your school or a local site named after a historically significant figure? Do some digging to find out more about this person's life in all its complexity. Design an activity with students that avoids the pitfalls of heroification so they can deliberate about whether honoring them in this way is a good idea. This can easily be extended to a critique of local statues and monuments.

# 6

# Dramatization and Gamification: Immigration, "Westward Expansion," and Slavery

W e understand and appreciate educators' desire to make social studies instructional time "fun." We *want* students to look forward to social studies and be fully engaged in their lessons; we *love* these disciplines and want kids to love them, too. However, reenactments, simulations, and role plays focused on content that has anything to do with violence or trauma are *not fun*. They are explicitly harmful and even oppressive. Heads up: This chapter describes trauma related to genocide and racism. For some readers, the classroom examples of curricular violence may trigger memories of their own experiences as students or might hit close to home for other reasons.

### TYPES OF DRAMATIZATION AND GAMIFICATION
*Reenactments* are activities that ask students to act out an event as it actually happened. *Simulations* are activities that create the conditions to mimic an historical event or social phenomenon during which students make their own choices and experience the consequences through sustained teacher-mediated tasks (Wright-Maley, 2015). *Role-plays* are versions of reenactments or simulations during which students take on specific characters devised by themselves or the educators. Any of these

approaches can be face-to-face activities or virtual and can also be made into games ("gamified") by having students compete or earn some kind of credit toward a quantifiable goal.

To be clear, dramatization and gamification are powerful instructional approaches that can be incredibly meaningful and effective. But (and this is a *big* but), they also have the potential to do great harm if applied without a transformational, anti-oppressive social studies lens. They're like plants that can be lethal if eaten, but also serve as essential ingredients in lifesaving medicines when applied carefully and thoughtfully. You just have to know what you're doing.

Take, for instance, parent Karen Park Koenig's (2009) concerns after hearing about a Civil War reenactment in the local school district. Educators separated children into "Union" and "Confederate" sides and assigned them roles to play during a battle with uniforms and replica guns to play-fight. Children then pretended to be injured or die. After learning more about the activity, Koenig asked the principal why they were teaching war like this, and if teachers helped students process the mock battle and death. Ultimately, she wanted to know what the "pedagogical priorities" were—what did teachers want students to learn about war during this activity, why, and what were they *actually* learning? The principal assured her that the pedagogical goal was not "war is fun," despite that being the overwhelming response from students, but couldn't articulate what the goal *was*. In fact, the principal told Koenig, "I don't think we've ever talked about [the goal]" (para. 3). It should go without saying, if you don't have a clear pedagogical purpose for a lesson that dramatizes or gamifies content that is any way connected to trauma or violence, *then you are not ready to teach it.*

This chapter is a bit different than the others in Part 2 because, unlike normalization, idealization, and heroification, dramatization and gamification aren't *inherently* problematic. But they're consistently used in ways that can confuse kids and reinforce dominant narratives, trivialize trauma, or even retraumatize students with marginalized identities. We focus on three of the most common (though not the only) topics that educators use these tools to teach: immigration, American "Westward Expansion," and slavery. While each of these topics are taught in a range of problematic ways, we identify the pitfalls when educators try to dramatize or gamify them without an anti-oppressive lens. We also share creative solutions for using these tools more responsibly by suggesting ways teachers can *clarify* counter narratives, *honor* experiences rather than trivializing them, and *transform* rather than traumatize students. Lastly, we offer general advice for the responsible use of dramatization and gamification when applied to other content areas.

## Immigration

A dramatization activity that Noreen's daughter recently participated in, and many of our methods students fondly recall, is the Ellis Island Immigration Station. Whether conducted as a role-play or reenactment, students participate in a mock arrival to Ellis Island as fictional composite characters or historical figures. When Katy worked with fifth and sixth graders, this was a much anticipated activity. After reading books and examining primary sources about European immigration to Ellis Island, Katy and her colleagues posed as immigration agents who reenacted bureaucratic, harsh treatment to illustrate the various regulations preventing entry (literacy tests, trachoma exams) and the changing of names to sound "more English." Students seemed to enjoy the play acting, and no one ever questioned whether what we were doing was problematic in any way. In fact, it was a point of pride for the teaching team. Needless to say, it is not a point of pride now.

### Common Pitfalls

Despite educators' and students' delight, Ellis Island reenactments or role-plays can easily result in confusion for children. First, if the units are done without significant depth or the dramatization is done quickly, the lack of context and time compression can mislead students into thinking the act of immigration was relatively simple and quick— or even fun. The kind of play acting educators often encourage undermines the very serious reasons why many people were, and still are, compelled to leave their homes. For some, it could be for a new start or to appease a sense of adventure, but for many (including those who came through Ellis Island) it was about fleeing war, strife, and/or abject poverty. Immigrants may have felt fear or anxiety about starting life in an unknown country, especially if that meant learning a new language or seeing few, if any, familiar faces upon arrival.

Second, by focusing on Ellis Island, students only learn about immigration during a particular historical moment and from a very narrow region of the world. The Ellis Island Immigration Station operated from 1892 to 1924 and the millions of immigrants who passed through it were overwhelmingly from Europe. While this is an important story to teach students in order to understand a part of their communities or even some of their families, focusing *exclusively* on Ellis Island reinforces dominant narratives. When and how did people from other continents arrive in the United States? Why did they come? What challenges did they face? How are their experiences similar or different to those immigrants who passed through Ellis Island—and what accounts for those differences? How do all of these questions apply to immigration today? Unfortunately, elementary educators often begin and end immigration units with Ellis Island, leaving those questions unaddressed and the current demographics of the United States unexplained.

Third, educators rarely attend to the distinctions between the immigration laws in place during Ellis Island's operation and the immigration laws that exist today. Again, this can confuse students when they hear stories in the news or from adults in their lives about contemporary immigration—whether their own family is directly impacted by policies or voices a strong political stance. This fails to recognize the relatively recent idea of (un)documented immigration. Historian Mae Ngai (2006) notes that there was no such thing as "illegal immigration" in the early 19th and 20th centuries. Just 1% of the immigrants who landed at Ellis Island were barred from entry, primarily for health reasons. And if you hear students using the term *illegal immigrant*, correct them. As journalist Jose Antonio Vargas (2018), who is himself undocumented, reminds us, no human being is illegal.

After World War I, the United States imposed numerical limits on immigration for the first time. Congress allotted the smallest immigration quotas to eastern and southern Europeans, excluded Asians entirely, created the border patrol, and eliminated statutes of limitations on deportations (Ngai, 2006). The government *deliberately* deployed these actions to prevent the immigration of individuals from countries and continents deemed undesirable. These ideas continue in the 21st century with former President Trump's Executive Order 13769 (the so-called Muslim Ban) and other instances of hostility toward refugees from Syria and countries in Central America.

Sadly, U.S. immigration policy has long been built on legal definitions of whiteness based on bigoted views of which "races" were capable of assimilating into "American" culture and which were not (Ngai, 2004). Thus, the role-plays and reenactments that youth participate in bear almost no resemblance to the contemporary immigration experience—nor the historical immigration realities of people who came to the United States through a variety of ports of entry such as the large number of 19th-century immigrants who evaded inspection by crossing the U.S.–Canadian border, Operation Pedro Pan that secretly airlifted children from Cuba in the early 1960s, or the Tai Dam refugee resettlement program in Iowa in the 1970s. Neither do they reflect European immigration accurately—consider, for example, how the United States turned away Jewish asylum seekers during World War II.

### Creative Solutions

If a role-play or reenactment of Ellis Island is conducted, it must be richly contextualized and complemented by learning about other entry points and eras. Noreen (Rodríguez, 2015) taught third and fourth graders about Angel Island, a West Coast immigration station that processed immigrants from Central and South America, Asia, Russia, and Australia from 1907 to 1940 (Lee & Yung, 2010). Angel Island was established primarily to enforce the Chinese Exclusion Act of 1882, the first and only immigration law to exclude immigrants based on nationality. Given that immigrants were stripped naked for invasive and humiliating group exams and racially segregated for extended periods of time (like Kong Din Quong, who was detained for 756 days) it should be obvious that we do *not* recommend a role-play or reenactment for teaching this history.

Instead, Noreen screened short video tours of Ellis and Angel Islands for students to compare and contrast immigrant experiences, asking them to consider why the medical exams were conducted so differently and how that might make immigrants feel. Then they examined historical photographs and poems that detainees carved into the dormitory walls. Students drew from this historical evidence to write poems from the perspective of immigrants. These students were deeply engaged and doing rigorous work in a form of dramatization, but the focus was not on fun and students did not act in ways that denigrated or mocked the immigrant experience. Rather, they took this work quite seriously, learning a complex, nuanced history of immigration that deepened their understanding of ethnoracial injustice in the world (Rodríguez, 2015).

We caution educators to be especially careful with this topic. It is possible that students in your class have family members who are struggling with current immigration policies, whether they are seeking to become citizens, are separated from loved ones, or living under the threat of deportation. Some students (and their families) may not be willing to share their experiences as these stories can be haunting and traumatic. We also want to caution teachers against using language like "we are all immigrants" that collapses the diverse experiences of arrival (refugees, enslaved people, documented and undocumented immigrants) while simultaneously ignoring the presence of Indigenous Peoples since time immemorial. Anti-oppressive educators must be sensitive to these varied circumstances and consider them carefully when creating a caring space for students to ask questions and reflect on their own experiences.

## Westward Expansion

Another frequently taught topic in elementary schools is American "Westward Expansion." Remember why we put "Founding Fathers" in quotes? Same song, different verse. This time, think about how "westward" *and* "expansion" center settler perspectives—it's only "westward" if you're starting the story in the east; and it's only "expansion" for the group that was expanding while ignoring or trivializing Native Peoples' experiences. Elementary lessons typically focus on the experiences of non-Native settlers moving westward across the mainland United States in the 19th century instead of, say, a frank look at the centuries-long (and ongoing) settlement and displacement of Native Peoples and Nations. If and when Native Peoples are present in the dominant narrative, it's often only in relation to non-Natives or as victims who have since vanished. Think Manifest Destiny, Lewis and Clark, and, yes, the infamous Oregon Trail. For many readers, these two words transport them to their youth playing *Oregon Trail* on a computer. Since then, the role-play video game has seen multiple reissues with an intensely nostalgic fan base. Are we going to ruin this game for you? Yes, yes we are. This example of problematic gamification highlights the ways educators can trivialize traumatic events and reinforce deeply problematic dominant narratives.

Before we jump into the gamification of this historical event, we want to address the erasure of Native Peoples that typically occurs in units on "Westward Expansion" (and frankly, in almost all social studies teaching). This history may elicit painful emotions for students and educators alike. Teacher educator Leilani Sabzalian recognizes that it doesn't feel good to know about forced removal, dispossession through treaties, or illegal squatting coupled with settlers taking retroactive action to try to legalize their own presence—especially given that Native Nations have "inherent sovereignty that predate the United States" (Turtle Island Social Studies Collective, 2020, para. 39). However, Sabzalian implores, "[Knowing this history] makes us responsible for this legacy. It makes us responsible for redressing this violence. It makes us responsible for even considering repatriation" (para. 40). Furthermore, she considers youth to be the best positioned in our society to take on these responsibilities, as "they're not so deeply rooted in the system that we have inherited. They can think outside of it, and we should listen" (para. 82). Learning from, with, and about Native Nations and People through all of the social studies disciplines is crucial and can help foster feelings of obligation and interconnection.

**Common Pitfalls**

Invented by a student teacher and his roommates, *The Oregon Trail* game has sold over 65 million copies worldwide. Educators like Bill Bigelow (1997) have long taken the game to task for its reinforcement of white supremacist, settler colonial dominant narratives. First, the game presumes the protagonist to be white and male. While newer versions of the game include some Black characters, these portrayals erase the legalized and institutionalized oppression faced by Black people at the time, including exclusionary laws preventing Black settlement of Oregon. In addition, the game teaches "Westward Expansion" without ever engaging with the devastation of settler colonialism or offering much information about the Native Peoples on whose land the settlers were trespassing. According to children's literature professor Katharine Slater (2017), the game "perpetuates a racist narrative that privileges the ethos of white settlement through its refusal to engage directly with the geno- cidal consequences of westward expansion" (p. 381). Trivializing such a generationally traumatic era is actually itself an act of the settler colo- nial project. We'll just be as explicit as possible here: *Do not make genocide a game.*

Beyond *The Oregon Trail*, we should note that "Westward Expansion" is often dramatized in other problematic ways, for example when asking students to imagine settler perspectives as they write letters encouraging others to immigrate to the Great Plains, or to invent "Indian" names, build teepees, or wear construction paper headbands with zero respect or consideration of accuracy for Native traditions or the diversity of Native Peoples and Nations. All of this is bad. See educators Alison Schmitke, Leilani Sabzalian, and Jeff Edmundson's (2020) book *Teaching Critically About Lewis and Clark: Challenging Dominant Narratives in K–12 Curriculum* for a thorough and thoughtful critique of teaching about mid-19th century settlement, and Debbie Reese and Jean Mendoza's blog, *American Indians in Children's Literature* (www.americanindiansinchildrensliterature.blogspot.com) for suggestions to teach Native histories and Peoples with accuracy and authenticity.

## Creative Solutions

When we teach anything about settlement, we must consider how the phrasing of "westward expansion" makes invisible who was already in "the West" and how they responded to those who invaded. Katy asks the future teachers she works with, "How *should* educators refer to this era, and what does this mean for their curriculum?" With deeper background knowledge, all sorts of other names emerge, like "encounter" and "displacement and resistance." Instead of having students play games like *The Oregon Trail*, she partnered with Leah Slick-Driscoll (Meskwaki/Winnebago), a social studies teacher at the nearby Meskwaki Settlement School. In a simulation Slick-Driscoll designed and facilitates, students imagine that an alien invasion of the Midwest has begun. It is reminiscent of the Storyline or StoryPath techniques that involve educators (and sometimes students) constructing a setting and characters; as teachers present them with "incidents," students make decisions that change the course of the story. Given that she wants them to learn actual histories rather than general social phenomena, every part of Slick-Driscoll's story and every decision point she gives students is analogous to real events and dilemmas that have faced Native Peoples.

At the beginning, students receive slips of paper and record the names of loved ones, their favorite traditions or hobbies, and their favorite possessions. They also draw pictures of a special place in their community. As the simulation unfolds, Slick-Driscoll acts as a newscaster updating students on the aliens' actions. Students grapple with difficult decisions and face the consequences—like losing a loved one, never being able to do their hobby again, or destroying their special place. At one point, the aliens demand that the class remove themselves to a small territory or face war. Most students decide to move on given the losses they have already incurred. Later, she announces that their territory has a mineral the aliens need to fuel their spaceships, so they will have to move again. This time, many more students opt to take up arms and resist—what more do they have to lose? Since most of our candidates do not have a robust understanding of Native histories, they are blown away when Slick-Driscoll walks through each step of the simulation in the debrief to reveal how every incident reflects real histories of removal. The students are often incredibly moved; it powerfully expands their historical empathy and enriches their counter narrative content knowledge. Again, we want to caution educators to be exceptionally careful here. This is a simulation Slick-Driscoll brilliantly designed and facilitates—as a non-Native person descended from the very settlers that these histories document, Katy does not want to facilitate an activity like this without Slick-Driscoll's collaboration and leadership.

In addition to highlighting Native Peoples' and Nations' perspectives through simulations like Slick-Driscoll's, students need a more accurate historical understanding to avoid confusion. This means going beyond the stories of British and American colonists. Education professor Corey Sell, teacher Jennie Schmaltz, and content specialist Stephanie Hartman (2018) designed an inquiry unit for Spanish/English bilingual third graders that started off with a dramatized scenario to anchor the unit: a fight in the school's lunchroom, recounted by different people to help students understand historical interpretation. Using maps and primary source sets, students learn about Hispanos (the first wave of settlers to Colorado from Spain and Mexico) and how the U.S. border crossed *them*, not the other way around. As a culminating activity, students conducted family histories and presented them at a Family Engagement Night. These activities led to rich experiential learning without relying on problematic dramatization or gamification.

An accurate account of settlement and resistance cannot focus solely on settlers' perspectives and adventures. An anti-oppressive teaching of settlement must include Native and other marginalized histories, and these histories of genocide and displacement should *not* be recreated through gamification. Simulations and scenarios, however, can offer analogs to drive home concepts through experiential learning. Ultimately, dramatization tools must resist the temptation to whitewash or sidestep harms that reinforce settler colonial logics.

## Slavery

The genocidal enslavement of Africans is deeply woven into the fabric of U.S. history. Understandably, many elementary educators struggle with introducing this sordid past even as they recognize they must. Some educators only teach about Africa, Africans, and diasporic Black peoples in relation to slavery. In addition, many avoid talking about the people who deliberately constructed an exploitative economic system through chattel slavery. Chattel slavery is distinct from indentured servitude and other types of enslavement in that it renders the enslaved not as a person but as property. This means the enslaved had no rights, could be sold and moved, and any children they had were also enslaved. Quick note: You may hear the term *forced migration* to describe slavery. It's wrong. At best, that's a problematic euphemism for kidnapping. Same for *plantation*—they were actually *slave labor camps*. And we purposefully use the noun *enslaved* instead of *slave* to remind readers that enslavement is not an inherent condition but a deliberate act of oppressive violence within a system of dehumanization (see Hylton, 2020; Landis, 2015).

While slavery is an incredibly important part of the Black experience for African Americans *and* their ancestors who remained in Africa (e.g., the construction of Blackness itself), it is not the *only* part and should not be students' first nor only exposure to Black history. Especially in the elementary grades, it is important to share diverse stories of ancient and contemporary Africa *and* give plenty of examples of Black joy. And by Black joy, we do not mean the gross mischaracterization of the "happy slave," but the many incredible manifestations of creativity, resilience, and community that have nothing to do with the white gaze (Johnson, 2015).

In this section, we review how some teachers misguidedly attempt to gamify and dramatize the kidnapping and abuse of enslaved Africans in the classroom (Mitchell Patterson, 2019), from laying tightly packed on the floor with taped wrists to simulating a slave ship to picking cotton or pretending to be members of the Ku Klux Klan (Anderson, 2018; Jones, 2020). The company behind *The Oregon Trail* even created a short-lived slavery game called *Freedom!* but pulled it after a year due to significant pushback (Whitaker, 2020). As protesting parent Paulette Davis succinctly put it, "Slavery was not a game in our history" (West, 1993).

These are clear examples of what scholars Zeus Leonardo and

Ronald K. Porter (2010) call *educative-psychic violence*, the negative impact educators have on youth when they minimize or ignore racism by making European cultural values and practices the norm, representing BIPOC people as a monolithic group of subordinated victims of oppression who all think and act the same way, relegating BIPOC histories to certain eras and simplified figures, and telling stories that hide or explain away the individual and structural acts that oppress BIPOC communities. Scholars LaGarrett King and Ashley Woodson describe the superficial and reductive ways many youth learn about slavery as a "type of psychological violence . . . that keeps students of all racial and ethnic backgrounds from developing a full sense of their racial, historical, and political identities" (L. J. King & Woodson, 2017, p. 3). Professor Stephanie Jones (2020) has begun mapping examples of racial traumas in schools like those described above, including instances of curricular violence. Her *Mapping Racial Trauma* database online (www.facebook.com/mappingracialtrauma) is a heartbreaking read and lays bare the terrible harm that can happen through elementary social studies—especially when it comes to the teaching of African enslavement in the United States.

If you know of anything like this happening in a school near you, put this book down and immediately contact the educators and administrators to demand they stop. It is violence against children, plain and simple. Enough.

### Common Pitfalls

There are so, so many pitfalls here, but we want to focus on those that clearly threaten to retraumatize students. First, although some educators may think their dramatization of experiences related to slavery (the transatlantic Middle Passage, auctions, escape, etc.) is somehow anti-oppressive by foregrounding the trauma inflicted on Black people, these approaches can actually reinforce white supremacy and anti-Blackness. Lessons like these are designed through and for a white gaze for the purposes of teaching white students empathy, often at the expense of retraumatizing BIPOC youth, or to give white students grounds to disassociate themselves from this painful history.

Scholar Sadhana Bery (2014) gives a powerful example of this through the case of white educators at a predominantly white, private elementary school creating a student play about slavery. Bery recounts a meeting called by Black parents when they found out what was happening. At the meeting, the Head of School explained that some students, all white, had expressed a desire to experience what it was like to have been enslaved. Unsurprisingly, Black parents wanted to know why white students wanting to pretend to be enslaved was a sound pedagogical purpose, and why they had not been consulted given that "their children, the 'descendants' of the enslaved represented in the play, would be impacted in ways that white teachers could not know or fully understand" (p. 339). The Head defended the play by stressing that students got to choose between being enslaved or an owner. Unsurprisingly, all of the white students chose to play the roles of slaves or Harriet Tubman; none of them wanted to play anyone "responsible for the slave trade and the institutionalization of slavery" (Bery, 2014, p. 340). As a result, the white educators had to persuade the BIPOC students to play those roles. No. And then another no. Just *no*.

---

### WHAT WOULD YOU DO?

A white colleague is proud of her slavery unit that includes reenactments of the Middle Passage, escaping enslavement on the Underground Railroad, and a Civil War battle. She is convinced that the best way to teach students these histories is to have them "experience what it felt like." These activities have been positively covered by the local media and are considered by many families to be a rite of passage when their kids reach that grade. This teacher has even won an award from a local social studies organization for her "engaging methods." Given your identity and teaching context, what are your concerns and how do you voice them? What steps can you take to revise the curriculum?

---

Another pitfall is that reenactments, role-plays, simulations, and games focused on the horrors of slavery often frame Black people as objects of harm and helpless victims with no agency. In their review of K–12 textbooks focused on Black history, scholars LaGarrett King and Crystal Simmons (2018) found that texts often framed Black people as compliant victims or depicted oppression as if it was justified, suggesting that "Blacks did not exert agency unless it was through White philanthropy; if agency is explored, what is highlighted tends to align with acceptable Eurocentric standards" (p. 109). In addition, they identify how dominant narratives of slavery tend to paint Black people as a monolithic group with the same opinions and experiences, often avoiding any mention of sexism or other forms of oppression reproduced within Black communities. According to King and Simmons (2018), this *"Black history-as-oppression* paradigm" (p. 101) is inaccurate and can have negative psychological effects—especially on Black students.

Finally, in addition to the trauma that may occur when Black or Brown students are asked to reenact slavery (either as the enslaved or enslaver), watching their peers' interactions can produce another layer of harm. It is not unusual for children to get silly and laugh during dramatizations, but in the context of slavery, giggles make light of this painful history (Dack, van Hover, & Hicks, 2016). Imagine how a Black student might feel observing white peers laughing during a slavery simulation. To be clear, we're not pointing the finger at white children—these kinds of activities are set up for them to rely on broad stereotypes, and it is unlikely they have a sophisticated enough sense of their own racial identity to refuse to participate. We do, however, hold the educators responsible for putting all students in this impossible and inappropriate situation. We have to do better.

### Creative Solutions

It is possible to develop content knowledge and historical empathy without traumatizing students as they learn about slavery. Educator Adam Sanchez's (2019) lesson asks students to create a collective poem after taking on roles through a mixer activity to learn about enslaved peoples' various resistance strategies (work stoppages, armed revolt, running away, maintaining families, etc.). Role-plays can also be responsibly applied to current questions about how to reckon with the history of slavery, like designing a reparations bill (Wolfe-Rocca, 2020) or simulating a city council meeting to determine how to commemorate slavery-related history in the community.

> ### TEACHING THE HISTORY OF SLAVERY RESPONSIBLY
>
> Teaching about slavery responsibly is difficult, but there are wonderful digital resources to support teachers who are committed to this work. The New York Times' phenomenal The 1619 Project, conceived of by Nikole Hannah-Jones, includes curricular resources for teachers (www.pulitzercenter.org/lesson-plan-grouping/1619-project-curriculum). Learning for Justice's Teaching Hard History: American Slavery for K–5 (www.learningforjustice.org/frameworks/teaching-hard-history/american-slavery) has many helpful resources for responsible teaching of these histories including a podcast (learningforjustice.org/podcasts/teaching-hard-history). The Smithsonian National Museum of African American History and Culture's Talking About Race web portal (www.nmaahc.si.edu/learn/talking-about-race) as a wealth of information; the "Historical Foundations of Race" section has a collection of resources that trace the history of race and its role in the institution of slavery in the United States. And the Library of Congress' Voices Remembering Slavery: Freed People Tell Their Stories (www.loc.gov/collections/voices-remembering-slavery) houses invaluable recordings of interviews with formerly enslaved people. One special note with regards to teaching about slavery responsibly: For many white teachers in particular, it's tempting to teach about abolition or the Underground Railroad as a way to highlight "good" white people. Keep in mind that very few white people supported abolition, that lots of white abolitionists were also deeply racist (see Reynolds & Kendi, 2020), and that most Black people liberated themselves without help from white people.

Field trips are another experiential option. While many historical sites focused on slavery have exhibits and costumed employees who replicate dominant narratives that trivialize and reproduce trauma, some do *not* and have helpful anti-oppressive resources for educators. For example, the Whitney Plantation outside of New Orleans is the only plantation in Louisiana dedicated to the perspectives of enslaved people, the Middle Passage Ceremonies and Port Markers Project commemorates ancestors' arrival along the East and Gulf Coast, and the Legacy Museum in Montgomery, Alabama, features rare first-person accounts of the domestic slave trade. No matter where you live, there are local connections to be made to the history of slavery. Stops on the Underground Railroad extended throughout the Midwest and Northeast, for example, and many Confederate monuments have been erected across the United States years after the Civil War (see Wickenkamp, 2020). These experiential learning opportunities can complicate dominant narratives around slavery, center acts of resistance, illustrate the interstate web of enslaved labor, and reckon with the ongoing white supremacy that survived abolition.

One last time, we want to caution educators to be *extremely* careful here. Teaching the history of slavery is fraught enough—if your classroom community is not healthy, if your background knowledge is not strong, or if you do not have enough time for debriefing, then *most definitely* you should not apply dramatization or gamification tools. But don't let your fear of messing up dissuade you from attending to the topic in other responsible ways; remember, becoming an anti-oppressive educator is a *process*. Do your best to learn all you can, then seek out feedback from trusted critical friends, colleagues, and families to help you avoid the problems and pitfalls we outline here.

## General Advice for Dramatization and Gamification

As we illustrated with the examples of immigration, settlement, and slavery, dramatization and gamification can be taught in deeply problematic ways. Some of these pitfalls include confusing students by not explicitly linking their experiences to the learning objectives, reinforcing dominant narratives by decentering or erasing marginalized perspectives, trivializing trauma by prioritizing an activity's entertainment value over education, and retraumatizing youth by assigning problematic roles or tasks. However, if educators are intentional about using these experiences to clarify counter narratives, to honor experiences rather than trivialize them, and to create experiences that transform rather than traumatize students, they hold tremendous instructional potential.

Fifth-grade teachers Gabby Arca and Nina Sethi (Arca & Sethi, 2021) note that dramatization and gamification can help students make an emotional connection to the material through their engagement, including "negative" emotions like discomfort, anger, guilt, shame, or frustration that may be productive in activating students' empathy. This is especially profound with students who hold dominant identities in relation to the content being learned. Dramatization and gamification can also help make complex topics more accessible to young learners— especially highly abstract issues regarding structural oppression. Drawing from the pitfalls we've described and Arca and Sethi's (Arca & Sethi, 2021) advice, we highlight below several caveats for educators to consider when implementing simulations, role plays, and reenactments to keep from doing more harm than good. Remember, dramatization and gamification can be powerful teaching tools *if planned and executed as responsibly as possible.* If you don't feel ready to use them, that's

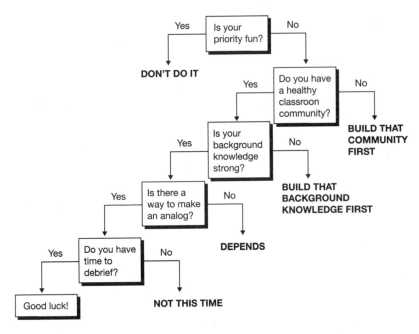

Gamification and Dramatization Flow Chart (CREATED BY KATY SWALWELL AND ALEX RODRÍGUEZ)

okay! There are other activities that can meaningfully engage students. If you want to try, however, consider the following advice as you plan using the flowchart below.

## Do Not Prioritize Fun

As you work your way through the flowchart, make sure your answers to the questions of what you want to teach and what you want students to learn are crystal clear—and, of course, are related to the anti-oppressive framework that centers and highlights counter (rather than dominant) narratives. If your priority is for students to have fun but the content has *anything* to do with violence or trauma (war, genocide, etc.), then *do not* use dramatization or gamification tools. If your priority is for students to develop deeper content knowledge, empathy, problem-solving skills, and so forth, then there *may* be a way to apply these tools effectively with regards to content related to violence or trauma—but, even then, it can be very tricky to do it well.

## Build Community

The success of dramatization or gamification is directly connected to the health of the classroom community. A strong sense of care and concern for each other and a belief that their teacher respects and loves them are nonnegotiables in an anti-oppressive classroom. In addition, students need vocabulary for and to practice explicitly talking about their emotions and oppression. If not, dramatization and gamification can exacerbate tensions and amplify any toxicity that exists within the group. If you have not yet built that kind of foundation among or relationship with your students, *do not use these instructional tools.* Instead, start building that community! And start laying the academic and emotional groundwork for them!

## Know Your Stuff

In order to actually help students accomplish your learning objectives, you must know your content backwards and forwards when creating an appropriately dramatized or gamified activity. Knowing the exact facts and figures or principles you want to highlight will help you develop meaningful and respectful analogs that keep kids from becoming confused, missing the point, or focusing on fun. Having deep content knowledge also prepares you to facilitate unscripted and unexpected directions that an activity may take based upon students' decisions and actions. This spontaneity and engagement is what helps make dramatization or gamification work, but it depends on the teacher being prepared to offer support and mediation to direct students to a deeper understanding of the content (Wright-Maley, 2015).

### Appropriately Adjust Verisimilitude

Responsible dramatization can have a degree of verisimilitude (i.e., direct connections to real events or phenomena). It is less risky in terms of retraumatizing students or reinforcing the dominant narrative, however, if presented as *analogs* to real events or phenomena that help break down something abstract or complex in a way that young children can understand. Analog activities can allow for a much stronger "aha moment" because they allow students to lose themselves in the experience, intentionally disconnecting from any preconceived notions, and ultimately helping them better understand the information you want to explicitly teach them in the debrief.

Additionally, educators should be careful with verisimilitude by *never* assigning individual students roles based on their actual identities. This can reinforce stereotypes and misconceptions and ultimately distract from the main purpose of simulations (Wright-Maley, 2015). Also remember that assigning roles to students with nondominant identities in traumatic scenarios has the potential to *re*traumatize them—like the Black students whose teacher assigned them to act as enslaved people while the white students in class pretended to buy their classmates at auction (Lockhart, 2019). *Do not do this.* If and when students start acting out in ways that reflect oppressive ways of being in the world, then it's time to set aside whatever the original learning goals were to address that with the class. Establishing ground rules ahead of time and identifying a way for students to stop the simulation, role-play, or reenactment if things start going awry can also help with this. We want to stress how our "good intentions" can in no way *ever* be an excuse for curricular violence. As Jones (2020) reminds us, "Intentionality is not a prerequisite for harmful teaching" (para. 7).

## Connect the Dots

Successful dramatization or gamification depends not just on what happens during the activity but on how teachers structure what comes before and after. It is crucial to frame what is about to happen with students beforehand and then provide ample time to debrief afterward—both to process emotions and restore a sense of community as students come back to the "real world," but also to make explicit what the content and skill takeaways are. It is especially important to identify and correct any misconceptions students may hold as a result of their participation in the activity. Even if it seems obvious to us as adults, students are not always quick to figure out the parallels between their experience and the content they are learning. Relatedly, it is important for educators to emphasize that any insight students gain through a dramatized or gamified activity is *not the same* as actually experiencing whatever event or phenomenon is the focus. See Table B.9 *Dramatization/Gamification Lesson/Unit Reflection Worksheet* in the appendix to apply these ideas.

## Putting These Ideas Into Practice

### Critical Analysis

Use the flowchart from this chapter to analyze how well examples of dramatization and gamification in the news hold up to our advice. These can be historical or contemporary activities, and may end up being good or bad examples. To illustrate, you could review recent examples on Stephanie Jones's *Mapping Racial Trauma* website or watch the documentary *A Class Divided* (Peters, 1985) about third-grade teacher Jane Elliott's famous simulation of racial discrimination with a class of white students after the assassination of Martin Luther King, Jr. How does your chosen simulation meet our criteria for anti-oppressive dramatization? How does it fall short? What would need to be in place for responsibly replicating this activity today?

### Try Something New

Review parts of your curriculum that need refreshing to see if responsible, anti-oppressive dramatization or gamification could improve it. This could be for activities that emphasize history, like the ones mentioned in this chapter, or could foreground the other social studies disciplines. If you're looking for more examples, check out Treick O'Neill and Tim Swinehart's (2008) role-play for an Indigenous Climate Summit that could easily be adapted for elementary students (see Shafer, 2017), teacher Brian Bigioni's (@MrBigioni308) use of Bill Bigelow's (n.d.) chocolate chip cookie "mining" simulation of mountaintop removal, Katy's (Swalwell, 2015) mixer activity where students interview each other in character to learn about labor actions from the 17th to 21st century in the United States, or scholars Jenni Gallagher and Christina Tschida's (2020) examination of how economic simulations can reinforce or disrupt dominant narratives.

# Part III

# Planning and Sustaining Anti-Oppressive Social Studies

At this point of the book, we hope we've convinced you that elementary social studies offers an incredibly important, not to mention immensely enjoyable, way to build a world that is more just, equitable, and thoughtfully interconnected (Part I). Now that we've warned you against the problems and pitfalls that are so common in the curriculum (Part II), we can begin to explore the practical logistics of creating learning opportunities for students that help build that better world and how to sustain our efforts in the face of resistance. You can do this! We promise!

Chapter 7 begins by assuring readers that feeling some anxiety as you think about how to find time to prepare for and teach anti-oppressive social studies is to be expected. But don't let insecurity or uncertainty stop you from doing better, bit by bit. We break down the steps of creating stimulating and accessible inquiries for students, advise how to best address state standards, and warn against the superficial and even oppressive online resources often found on Pinterest and Teachers Pay Teachers. We dive into tips for incorporating children's literature, like being sure to center #OwnVoices authors and illustrators. Lastly, we share ideas for leveraging the unique assets of your school and local community.

In Chapter 8, we acknowledge that many state legislatures

and district-level decisions can make this work challenging—if not dangerous. We stress the importance of having a radical imagination that helps us remember things have not always been this way and can always be better. We encourage everyone to embrace our professional expertise as educators, and to connect with others who are similarly committed—holding us accountable and backing us up as needed. We also share insights into how to engage with families, colleagues, students, and administrators in ways that foster trust and deep connection. This includes providing clear communication and transparency about our pedagogical decision-making, making room for everyone's growth and questions, having the humility that comes with genuine critical self-reflection, and appreciating critique from people pushing *for* rather than *against* anti-oppressive education.

Last, but not least, is our epilogue—a quick read that shares our final thoughts and ends with a rallying cry we hope lifts your spirits as much as it does for us. Don't miss it!

# 7

# Building Better Curriculum

W e understand how difficult it can be for educators to find the time to create and enact anti-oppressive social studies curriculum. It can be exhausting to continuously develop deep content knowledge, to design thoughtful activities, and implement what you plan. But don't put the book down! There are relatively easy ways to address these time crunches, we promise.

With regard to building content knowledge, we have to give ourselves some grace. The way to learn more (and *unlearn* so much) is to simply get started *somewhere* and recognize that there will always be more to learn. Doing a little bit all of the time builds huge results over the course of months or years. Listen to a podcast while you're doing the dishes or as you commute. Add an anti-oppressive social scientist or classroom teacher to your Twitter feed. There are so many great resources out there that are not dry and dusty academic tomes. We've done our best to only recommend sources that are super engaging and accessible *and* laser-focused on rich counter narratives in Appendix A ("Recommended Resources: The Tip of the Iceberg") and on www.ssfabw.com. Just start somewhere, and then don't stop!

As for the time it takes to plan . . . as former classroom teachers who are known to be fairly uptight perfectionists, we get how real this constraint can be. We want to stress that sometimes staying up until the wee hours tweaking a unit plan results in the most marginal of differences for the students. Instead, apply that economic thinking and prioritize what changes or new creations would be most impactful, get them in good working shape, and then just try them out. Things rarely go as planned anyway, so staying flexible leaves room for you to adapt based on students' questions and needs. Many educators spend hours decorating a bulletin board or creating "cute" props for a short activity. If there is time for that, then there is time to plan anti-oppressive social studies. Prioritize!

Lastly, we know that many administrators have relegated explicit time for social studies to the back burner or thrown it out the window entirely, in large part due to testing that prioritizes math and literacy (Fitchett, Heafner, & Lambert, 2014). However, students are *constantly* learning social studies regardless of whether we are deliberately teaching it to them. While it may be obvious that students learn from what we knowingly teach (the "explicit" curriculum), they also learn from what we choose to exclude or avoid (the "null" curriculum), and the "implicit" curriculum of interactions, physical spaces, and expectations (Eisner, 1985; Flinders, Noddings, & Thornton, 1986). Education professor Jennifer Hauver (2017) refers to this as the "in-between" and gives many examples of this: youth playing at recess, the posters hanging on walls, grouping and tracking, how teachers talk to students. All of these teach children "powerful lessons about being in community with others" (p. 376) and deserve our attention. Even if we don't have a ton of time for or control over explicit social studies, we can still apply an anti-oppressive framework to improve the null and implicit curriculum.

---

**USING OUR PROFESSIONAL VOICES**

Don't forget, we have the power to influence how much time districts allot to social studies time in elementary schools. Check out organizations that are working to push your local school board, state legislature, and/or state department of education to prioritize social studies. And if there isn't an organization yet, gather your fellow social studies lovers together and start one (Heafner et al., 2007)!

In addition to the implicit lessons "in-between" and the null curriculum, there are *so many* teachable social studies moments that unexpectedly occur through students' comments and questions. Try to take advantage of these as much as possible. Liz Kleinrock (2019) addresses this in her TED talk, "How to Teach Kids to Talk About Taboo Topics," as she describes her response to a white student's disturbing comment about race. In another example, methods instructor Amy Allen (2019) was teaching a math lesson on money in a second- and third-grade classroom when a student asked why there were no women on the money they were examining. This launched a meaningful inquiry with her students into the marginalization of female historical figures. We love it!

We also love the strategy of infusing social studies into protected curricular areas like language arts. For integration to be meaningful, however, it must be designed around the "interrelatedness of the subjects to each other and to the world outside the classroom" (Hinde, 2015, p. 23). Education professor Elizabeth Hinde (2005) views integration as one way to revive elementary social studies, but cautions against thin and weak versions of integration that waste time or perpetuate misconceptions through activities that relay inaccurate information, confuse students, or create busy work with no educational value (word searches, crafts). Healthy integration of social studies involves disciplinary thinking that clearly connects to students' lives *and* to other content areas.

Of course, don't forget to make sure integration is anti-oppressive. Scholars LaGarrett King and Ashley Woodson (2017) found appalling examples of third-grade math word problems like, "If Frederick [Douglass] got two beatings per day, how many beatings did he get in one week?" (p. 6). This question ticks all of the educative-psychic violence boxes: It obscures the people who perpetuated white supremacy through the use of passive voice, it presents Douglass as a victim without agency, and it reduces an important and complex figure to his enslavement. In other words, it is most definitely not anti-oppressive.

Regardless of whether your administration supports ample time for explicit social studies instruction or whether you have to strategically navigate the "in-between" time, there is *always* a way. And the more confidence and content knowledge you develop, the better you will be able to make meaningful connections and argue for more dedicated time.

## Planning Inquiry

A great curricular approach for engaging students in anti-oppressive learning is *inquiry*. If inquiry is new to you, most of the building blocks will not be—it's just a matter of repurposing the strategies you may already use, so you'll likely not be starting from scratch. So, what exactly do we mean by inquiry, and how do we plan for it to unfold in a meaningful, integrative, challenging, active, and value-based way?

> ### POWERFUL AND PURPOSEFUL PEDAGOGY
> In 2017, the National Council of Social Studies (NCSS) issued a statement for guiding "powerful and purposeful" elementary social studies. This includes pedagogy that is *meaningful* (relevant to the lives and questions of students), *integrative* (cross-disciplinary within the social studies as well as other subject areas), *challenging* (encouraging of critical and creative thinking), *active* (student-centered, engaging, and multimodal), and *value-based* (developing the skills and commitments necessary for a healthy, diverse democracy). Because it is issued from NCSS, a long-standing national nonpartisan professional organization, this statement can be very useful in garnering support for anti-oppressive teaching.

### What Is Inquiry?

The National Council of Social Studies and its partner organizations created the Civic, College, and Career Readiness (C3) Framework to provide a model for developing standards and curriculum rooted in inquiry. This framework identifies four steps to inquiry: (1) Develop questions that students will try to answer by the end of the unit; (2) Apply disciplinary concepts and tools to help students answer their questions (such as thinking about a problem from the perspective of a historian, geographer, economist, and political scientist); (3) Help students gather and evaluate sources to give them information to help them answer the questions; and (4) Support students in making evidence-based claims and taking some kind of informed action. The C3 Framework's "Inquiry Design Model" template, though not perfectly aligned with what we describe here, can be helpful when starting to plan inquiries (http://www.c3teachers.org/inquiry-design-model/). Whenever planning, we make sure to use a backwards design approach (McTighe & Thomas, 2003) that identifies objectives of the unit and determines what evidence will indicate students have met those goals before designing any instructional activities.

While we appreciate the C3 resources, we should note that there is nothing in the framework requiring an anti-oppressive framework that specifically addresses the long-standing issues of exclusion, erasure, and errors in the elementary social studies curriculum (Au, 2013), especially when it comes to Indigenous Peoples and histories (Sabzalian, 2019; Turtle Island Social Studies Collective, 2019), Black and Brown people (see Salinas, Rodríguez, & Lewis, 2015; Rodríguez, 2018a; Watson, Hagopian, & Au, 2018; Zapata et al., 2019), LGBTQ+ communities (e.g., Cruz & Bailey, 2017; Ryan, Patraw, & Bednar, 2013; Van Horn & Hawkman, 2018), women (see Brugar, Halvorsen, & Hernandez, 2014; Hubbard, Moore, & Christensen, 2020), and other marginalized groups. As a result, you may find that pre-built inquiries from your district or online educational platforms appear well-constructed, but actually reinforce dominant narratives in problematic ways. Don't use those. Instead, explicitly ground inquiry in an anti-oppressive framework. Our "critical inquiry" model merges the C3 Framework with scholar activist Bree Picower's (2012) social justice elementary curriculum design principles to make sure we are rooted in anti-oppressive teaching.

### SIX ELEMENTS OF SOCIAL JUSTICE CURRICULUM DESIGN

The six elements of social justice curriculum design include opportunities for all students to learn about self-love and self-knowledge, to gain respect for others, to learn about social movements and social change, to understand issues of social injustice, to develop skills to help raise others' awareness about what they have learned, and to take social action (Picower, 2012). See *Using Their Words* (www.usingtheirwords.org) for more resources, including sample units designed with these principles in mind.

## Step 1: Posing Questions

**Compelling Questions:** *What sets inquiry apart from other approaches to curriculum design is that it revolves around compelling questions.* Rooted in genuine curiosity, compelling questions can either be open-ended with multiple possible good answers or closed (yes/no) with legitimate claims to be made for either position. Compelling questions may be designed ahead of time by a teacher, but could also come from students. Scholar and educator Anna Falkner advises us to listen carefully to children's phrasing of questions to learn what would be compelling *to them*. She gives the example of a kindergartner asking, "What if polices do something bad?" (Falkner, 2020, p. 228). This can easily lead to the quandary of what *should* happen, and would lead students down a fascinating path of logistical and ethical supporting questions that genuinely interest them.

Ideally, an inquiry unit has only one compelling question to keep it simple and focused. Compelling questions should genuinely matter to students; they should fuel their drive to use disciplinary content and skills to figure something out. Often, educators new to planning inquiry come up with compelling questions that aren't actually compelling. "Why do people have jobs?" is one we've seen. Most students already know the most basic answer: "To make money." Inquiry over. Make sure that students either cannot already answer the compelling question or need the unit to help them develop more complex, sophisticated answers. Otherwise, what's the point? On the other end of the spectrum, compelling questions can be overly wordy and too complex for kids. Every student should know what the compelling question is and understand what it's asking. If *you* can't even remember what the compelling question is, that's not good.

Be careful: You want to make sure you do not pose any questions with possible answers you would find abhorrent. For example, don't create a unit that asks students to make an evidence-based claim for the question "Is slavery bad?" Their answer should be unequivocally *yes*. Instead, consider posing questions that give youth opportunities to grapple with controversial issues like *"What is the legacy of slavery?"* or *"Should there be reparations for slavery?"* or *"Did slavery end, or evolve?"* (See Chapter 2 for more about teaching "controversies").

> **WHAT WOULD YOU DO?**
> You have to teach a unit about regions of the United States. What are good possible compelling questions that would spark students' curiosity, draw their attention to counter stories, not shy away from controversy, and be worded in a kid-friendly way? *Hint*: You may want to revisit the section on geographic thinking in Chapter 1.

**Supporting Questions:** *After clarifying a compelling question, each inquiry unit needs supporting questions that provide the direction for each lesson, prompting students to find out information or develop skills that they can apply toward their pursuit of the compelling question.* Unlike compelling questions, supporting questions have clear answers and should be laid out in as logical a manner as possible. For instance, the best supporting questions to begin a unit are often definitional and help students understand terms found in the compelling question. Other good supporting questions are easily generated by applying different disciplinary lenses. Let's say your unit poses the compelling question, *"What is the legacy of slavery?"* Your supporting questions might include, *"What is slavery?" "When did slavery begin?" "Who was enslaved, and who enslaved them?"* and *"What was slavery like for enslaved people?"* Just like with compelling questions, supporting questions may be ones that students themselves generate—in fact, creating space for students to articulate their curiosity about a topic helps them connect to the material and hone their question-posing skills. It can also serve as a great way to start the unit or even as a form of pre-assessment. Just remember that they are questions with definitive answers that provide rich content for students.

## Step 2: Designing Assessments and Evaluations

**Pre-Assessment:** *Checking in with students to gauge what they already know (or think they know) about the relevant concepts and skills of a unit is essential.* It ought to be short and sweet: a quick conversation with students, a KWL chart, a mind map, or even drawing in response to a prompt. Not only is this a great chance to ask students what they want to know about a topic, but pre-assessment should inform how the rest of the unit takes shape.

Case in point: One of Katy's methods students, a white woman from Wisconsin whose family had immigrated from Europe in the 19th century, began to plan a unit about immigration focused on Ellis Island. Before she finalized anything, she interviewed students in her placement class to find out what they knew about "immigration." To her astonishment, the students (primarily children whose families recently immigrated from Central and South America) said things like: "Immigration? It's the people who come take your parents away," "I'm scared of Immigration," and "Immigration doesn't want us here." Instead of thinking of immigration as a process, her students equated the term with the federal agency Immigration and Customs Enforcement (ICE) tasked with enforcing immigration policy (Swalwell, 2015, p. 151). Needless to say, the teacher candidate dramatically shifted her plan to address her students' fears and incorporate their funds of knowledge. She still taught some content about Ellis Island, but within a totally different framing and context. Finding out what students know or wonder (or even worry) about is important to ensure you're planning something that is not too complex or too simple and is sensitive to their experiences, identities, and questions.

**Summative Assessment:** *Once a pre-assessment has shaped the direction of the unit, the next step is to figure out how students will answer the compelling question.* This is the summative assessment, and it should provide an opportunity for students to demonstrate what they've learned throughout the unit, communicate their claims (their responses to the compelling question), and take some kind of informed action. *Please* do not make this a test or some boring exercise with no authentic connection to anything. And do not ask them to do something that you aren't prepared to endure yourself. Do we want to watch every third grader present a PowerPoint slideshow answering the same question in the same way? No, we do not. That would be boring and a waste of precious classroom time. Instead, consider a range of authentic individual and group assessment tools that are differentiated and fit within the unit (writing a letter to the editor, creating a book to read to younger students, giving a speech, building a website to share what they learned, writing a reflection after presenting information to a public audience, making a zine, creating posters to hang in the hallway, etc.).

**Formative Assessments:** *Each supporting question should be linked to formative assessments.* These are opportunities for educators to check for understanding—to make sure your students are on the right track and to determine when you need to individually differentiate further or reteach something for the whole class. No doubt you have plenty of formative assessment ideas in your tool kit (thumbs up/down, short quiz, journal entries). Because each supporting question has definitive answers, students should be able to answer them correctly if they're understanding what you've been teaching. These should be low stakes, and can easily do double duty as instructional activities. For example, we often use graphic organizers to track a discussion, take notes during a short video, or analyze a primary source—all of that can provide evidence to a teacher of how well students are "getting it." Formative assessments can also help students practice making different claims for the compelling question. And don't forget: formative assessments are about content *and* skills. Whatever skills are needed to successfully complete the summative assessment should be practiced throughout the unit.

**Evaluation:** *Whenever we assess students, we must have a way to evaluate their work.* For tests and quizzes, this means assigning numerical value to questions with a cut score to determine baseline competence. For activities and projects, a rubric that educators and/

or students create and apply can be useful. Maybe it's as simple as verbal feedback. Whatever you choose, make sure you make your expectations and processes clear to students *before* they complete an assessment—especially if it's high stakes—and apply them in thoughtful, equitable ways.

**Standards:** *Some states or schools require teachers to address very specific content while others have more vague skill-based standards.* Regardless, we strongly recommend not letting the standards *wholly* dictate the curriculum—especially if you are in a position to create your own units. Instead, connect your inquiries to current events and/or children's lives, then find ways to organically weave in the standards so that you can assess them. While it is possible to start with the standards, be mindful about building meaningful inquiries around them rather than defaulting to direct instruction that could be mistaken for preparation for trivia night. Ideally, the standards are not an end in and of themselves, but rather a means for students to grapple with compelling questions.

As you consider which standards make sense for a unit, do not forget to integrate disciplinary standards beyond the social studies. In fact, this can be a way to fit more anti-oppressive social studies into the school day. Educators often feel most comfortable linking language arts standards to social studies, but consider the possibilities for linking to math and science standards as well. Of course, while it may be possible to connect all sorts of standards to a unit, keep in mind that officially connecting them means you're responsible for collecting evidence of student learning. As such, you may only want to address a handful of standards in any one unit to ensure that you are adequately assessing each one.

### LEARNING STANDARDS

We appreciate well-crafted standards that offer a thoughtful scope and sequence for elementary social studies and provide educators direction in what to teach. No one wants students to learn about ancient Rome three years in a row or get caught in their teacher's obsession about the

*Titanic* for nine weeks. However, standards vary state by state and some are less than ideal. With regards to the Texas state standards, former NCSS president and teacher Sue Blanchette (2010) remembers being "stunned and appalled at some of the changes being made to the standards, changes not based in scholarship but in partisan politics and religious fervor" (p. 199). While educators are required to address standards, they ought not revere or rely solely on them—remember, standards are documents humans create, so there is nothing sacred or neutral about them. While they may offer little guidance, vague standards can actually provide opportunities to insert anti-oppressive social studies and create space for topics that are otherwise not included in the curriculum. And check out Learning for Justice's Social Justice Standards (www.learningforjustice.org/frameworks/social-justice-standards) for examples of standards that are unapologetically supportive of anti-oppressive education.

## Step 3: Planning Instructional Resources and Activities

After clarifying the compelling and supporting questions and identifying what the different assessments and evaluation tools will be, it's time to figure out what resources and activities will help students answer questions in thoughtful, sophisticated ways. Remember, there is no such thing as a "great resource"—something is only "great" relative to its use. We have some terribly problematic children's books in our collections that we would never use as standalone read-alouds, but they work well in a critical media literacy unit to detect bias. This is where your treasure chest of resources becomes a pantry filled with ingredients to prepare wildly different meals. The clearer you are about the supporting question and a lesson's objective, the better you can choose which instructional approaches (guest speaker, read-aloud, mind map, debate, discussion, deliberation, role play, simulation) and which resources (primary sources, picture book, map, graph, video clip) make the most sense to help students learn content or develop a skill.

One more time for the people in the back: Selecting resources and planning instruction represents the *last* stage of planning. Often, our methods students will ask us if an activity is good, but without knowing the larger goals of the unit (the compelling question, summative assessment, standards), it's impossible to say. With backwards design, knowing where you're going is the only way to determine if your route makes any sense. Even if you do not know exactly how an inquiry unit will unfold, you can still plan ahead. For instance, maybe you want students to learn more about a controversial current event and then take some kind of action relevant to that issue. In any given year, there is no way to predict what the event will be or which kinds of actions students will decide to take. But it *is* possible to plan checkpoints along the way, to create a rubric for a summative assessment, to prepare activities to spark their event selection, and equip them with generally applicable skills.

## The Role of Children's Literature

We know that full-blown inquiry units like we described above may be a stretch for some readers. Maybe your district has a predetermined curriculum that you simply cannot modify, your grade-level team constrains your autonomy, or you're just not ready to plan an entire unit quite yet. Children's literature provides an easy way to incorporate anti-oppressive social studies into your teaching that can be part of any inquiry unit or stand on its own. With young children, this may involve reading aloud picture books to build community and practice literacy skills. With older students, this can take the form of reading aloud nonfiction passages or having students participate in historical fiction book clubs or reading groups. No matter where you teach, there is always protected time to read a book. The books we choose and the supplemental activities we do with students as we read them are powerful opportunities for anti-oppressive social studies to flourish. And because so many elementary social studies textbooks are boring, inaccurate, and biased, children's literature is an *invaluable* resource for anti-oppressive social studies.

While online bookstores and book lists offer educators unprecedented access to anti-oppressive books, the selections found in classrooms and school libraries remain focused on (surprise!) dominant identities and narratives. This is a long-standing problem and has been the subject of scholarly and practitioner critique for over a century

(Dahlen, 2020). In 1965, literacy educator Nancy Larrick published an article entitled, "The All-White World of Children's Literature," which began with the words of a five-year-old Black girl who asked, "Why are they always *White* children?" Larrick's (1965/1992) study revealed that only 6.7% of books published between 1962 and 1964 included one or more African Americans. Of course, this figure only relates to *inclusion*, not the substance or quality of the representation.

But that was a long time ago, right? Surely things must be better. Oh, how we wish this were true. This is why we need to build a better world! In the 1980s, the Cooperative Children's Book Center at the University of Wisconsin–Madison began to track statistics about children's literature, particularly around the race and ethnicity of authors as well as of main characters. In recent years, these statistics have gained mainstream attention thanks to infographics created by library and information science professor Sarah Park Dahlen and

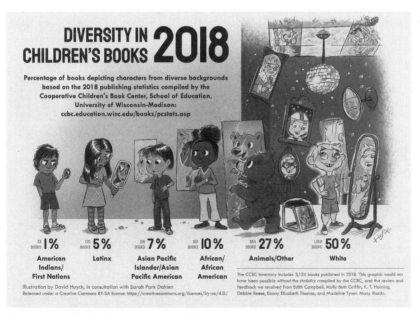

Diversity in Children's Literature 2018 (CREATED BY SARAH PARK DAHLEN AND DAVID HUYCK)

illustrator David Huyck (see figure below), which make clear that racial disparities in children's literature remain over 50 years after Larrick's article was published. As a reminder, the sheer presence of BIPOC in a book does not ensure that the character is represented accurately or in ways that are not stereotypical—particularly when the authors and illustrators are "cultural outsiders" (Rodríguez & Kim, 2018), which unsurprisingly also remains the norm.

While it is easy to blame the publishing industry for these shameful statistics related to ethnoracial and other forms of misrepresentation, educators play an essential role in deciding which books they feature with their students. Literacy scholar Rudine Sims Bishop (1990) used the metaphor of books as windows, mirrors, and sliding glass doors to describe the ways that readers engage with texts. Windows are those books that allow readers to view real or imagined worlds, both familiar and strange, while sliding glass doors allow readers to walk into such worlds. Mirrors, in contrast, provide readers with a reflection of themselves; these reflections are especially important for marginalized youth to see themselves reflected in the larger human experience (Bishop, 1990). Teachers must work to ensure that *all* students in their care have access to literature that serves as windows, sliding glass doors, *and* mirrors.

**FUN-HOUSE MIRRORS, BLIND SPOTS, AND CURTAINS**
Literacy scholars Mehmet Gultekin, Laura May, and Debbie Reese have added new metaphors to Bishop's taxonomy. Gultekin and May (2018) describe "fun-house mirrors" as books that distort reality and may be inaccurate (this notion is depicted in the figure), while "blind spots" occur when books only focus on a certain subset of a group, thereby omitting from view other experiences and perspectives. Reese's (2018) notion of "curtains" captures the information that a community may want to keep known just to its members; like curtains on a window, they prevent outside consumption of sacred beliefs.

Curating a diverse children's literature collection can be difficult given the limited number of picture books that feature marginalized characters; whiteness, in addition to other forms of dominance like classism, ableism, gender stereotyping, and an underrepresentation of female characters, continues to be normalized (Jones, 2008; Koss, 2015). Dominant group members benefit *tremendously* from books that offer them windows into the experiences of others, particularly given our multicultural and ethnoracially diverse society and world. If children of a dominant group (wealthy, white, cisgender, etc.) only see reflections of themselves in the books they read, "they will grow up with an exaggerated sense of their own importance and value in the world—a dangerous ethnocentrism" (Bishop, 1990, p. x).

So how can educators diversify their book selections to offer children a broader array of representations? It takes work and requires more than just a quick internet search. Vetting books through experts on children's literature, particularly experts of *diverse* children's literature, is essential to ensure cultural authenticity and accuracy—you don't want to present a book to a child in hopes that it will serve as a mirror, only to discover that it's actually perpetuating stereotypes and ultimately causes harm. The Children's Literature Assembly's Position Statement (2019) "On the Importance of Critical Selection and Teaching of Diverse Children's Literature" is a detailed guide that summarizes the ideas shared above (www.childrensliteratureassembly.org). We have also compiled a number of recommended websites, blogs, and book lists to support you on our website.

### #OWNVOICES

The #OwnVoices movement (Duyvis, 2015) emerged in response to misrepresentations in books authored by people who were outsiders of the communities described. Educators should be intentional about seeking out #OwnVoices books written and illustrated by members of the communities that are represented in texts, especially when they describe marginalized experiences. #OwnVoices books have become increasingly popular and accessible, and by continuing to demand quality texts that reflect accurate and authentic representations, we can all play an important role in pushing the publishing industry to do better.

The work is not over once you've found a great book. Children's literature expert Laura Jimenez reminds us that, "just having (diverse books) on the shelf does not . . . do that teaching or unlearning of the stereotypes that we are barraged with all the time" (Schwartz, 2019). Educators must engage students in meaningful conversations about texts, particularly those that feature identities, experiences, and histories that may be unfamiliar to students. Literacy scholar Angie Zapata (2020) leaves us with an important question to consider: "What conditions for young children might we nurture so that this new literature landscape fulfills its promise as a transformative space, a space where deficit assumptions of marginalized communities are challenged, and new mindsets emerge?" (para. 2).

One of these conditions is providing opportunities for students to go beyond the text to tell more complete narratives. For instance, children's literature has long been critiqued for an insistence on happy endings and whitewashing racial narratives. Two ways to counter this is to begin with the author's note or any available timelines, and to contextualize any histories students should understand prior to reading (Kellogg, 2019; Rodríguez & Kim, 2018). Primary sources are *excellent* extensions, and may even contradict the text and illustrations found in picture books, helping students develop more complex content knowledge and critical media literacy skills (Rodríguez & Vickery, 2020). Reading children's literature through strategic pairing or grouping (such as around a common historical event or theme) can ignite students' attention to comparisons and contrasts as they think across texts. For example, kindergarten teacher Meredith Labadie and education scholars Kathryn Pole and Rebecca Rogers (2013) created a text set focused on social class that helped young students identify and challenge economic inequality.

One final cautionary note: Beloved books that win awards or show up on recommended book lists can *fiercely* uphold dominant narratives. Historical fiction books are especially prone to whitewashing the past and promoting American exceptionalism. If you are new to this work, proceed carefully when someone tells you that they have a book that is "perfect" for teaching any social studies topic; it probably isn't. But that doesn't mean that those books should gather dust or go into the trash can. Even the best of books are enhanced with the supplements we've described here, and you can always read *against* problematic texts to practice those all-important critical media literacy skills.

## Celebrate the Unique Assets of Your Classroom and Community

Regardless of which instructional strategies you employ, your social studies units should take advantage of and lift up what makes you, your students, and your community unique. Even when you find well-researched, anti-oppressive curriculum (including thoughtful lessons from organizations we recommend), you will inevitably need to tailor it to your context. This requires you to know your context very well, including its counter histories, its demographics related to various forms of diversity, and organizations fighting for justice and equity.

For example, our shared curriculum for the social studies methods course we taught deliberately included counter stories relevant to our local area. Though Iowa is a state populated primarily by white, Christian settlers, it is much more diverse and complicated than what that description implies. It is the ancestral lands of many Native Peoples including the Báxoje and Očhéthi Šakówiŋ and surrounds the Meskwaki Settlement; has the oldest mosque in the United States; is home to refugee populations from across the world; has deep connections to labor, disability, and women's rights history; was one of the first states to legalize same-sex marriage; is at the heart of contentious debates around agricultural technologies, land rights, and animal rights; is a destination for families pushed out of their homes by gentrification in nearby cities like Chicago; was the site of the largest ICE raids in history; and is home to diverse Black and Brown communities whose members have made powerful contributions to the state.

We've built a network of community members who generously share their expertise as guest speakers, a list of field-trip sites, and connections with local organizations and museums to serve as resources for inquiries we plan. While we get how strapped educators' budgets are, we cannot stress enough the importance of expressing gratitude and trying to find some way to compensate people for their time—especially those from marginalized communities who too often face exploitation or co-opting of their labor and ideas. In addition, we pay attention to local news and connect our curriculum to local current events—especially controversial ones (Swalwell & Schweber, 2016). And while we worked from the same basic curriculum we codesigned, the shape our units took varied from semester to semester and between our courses, given our different identities, expertise, and interests as well as our students' questions and curiosities. As much as you can, find ways to honor that in your own classroom even if your curricular autonomy is restricted.

## Word of Warning

By advocating for an inquiry-based approach to social studies, we're trying to avoid the disjointed, random, vacuous crap (yep, that's the official term) that pervades so much social studies instruction and is overflowing on sites like Pinterest and Teachers Pay Teachers. While we certainly do not want educators to reinvent the wheel by designing their own curriculum from scratch, and we *have* found useful resources in our own searches, so much of what goes viral or is available online is problematic. Katy uses the metaphor of safe sex with her methods students. Because she knows it's futile to argue for abstinence—teachers are going to look for ideas online—she prefers to teach them how to do it safely. In an article with her colleagues Jenni Gallagher and Elizabeth Almond Bellows (J. L. Gallagher, Swalwell, & Bellows, 2019), Katy lays out a checklist to apply when considering whether to use or modify something found online. With her colleagues Michael Brown and Amanda Vickery, Noreen built on this work to encourage an explicitly anti-racist lens in this process—especially for those new to or unfamiliar with teaching (Rodríguez, Brown, & Vickery, 2020).

Table B.10 *Anti-Oppressive Filter for Online Resources* in Appendix B draws from these projects to offer readers an analytical tool for online resources.

Whether online or in your colleague's classroom, it's not hard to find elementary social studies that we wish we could send into a bottomless pit. We are especially frustrated with the elementary obsession with "cuteness." Social studies education professor Michelle Bauml notes that the "hands-on or playful" features of many elementary lessons often come at the "expense of striving for relevance, meaning, or substance" (2016, p. 56). She encourages her preservice teachers to ask themselves, "Is it cute, or does it count?" (2016, p. 58) as a reminder to make their curriculum "powerful and purposeful." While we agree with this sentiment, we want to caution against thinking of curriculum as "cute." A problematic craft like a construction paper feather headdress may look "cute" to a non-Native teacher, for example, but is *deeply* offensive and triggers harmful stereotypes. Regardless of whatever we call it, we want to—we *must*—do better. Whether we start small with a new read-aloud book or go big by tossing out our curriculum and planning something new, *you can do this.*

## Putting These Ideas Into Practice

### Sample Unit

If you're a preservice teacher, finish planning the unit about regions in the United States you started when you generated a compelling question earlier in the chapter. If you are an in-service teacher, revamp or create a new unit using the model we detail here. Challenge yourself to see if you can meaningfully link to other disciplines not commonly integrated with social studies like math, science, or physical education.

### State Standards

Investigate the history of standards in your state. What spaces do they offer for anti-oppressive social studies? Who wrote them? How have they changed over time? When are they scheduled for a rewrite, and what will that process be? How can the public offer input? How can you get involved?

### Children's Literature Review

As you begin to look for children's literature to teach social studies or to add to an inquiry unit, do so with a critical eye—even with (or, perhaps *especially* with) books that are promoted as "multicultural." Read the *Booktoss* blog post "Blackall's Bland as Blah" by literacy scholar Laura Jimenez (2020) as a model for how to do this. Another helpful resource to determine the anti-oppressive nature of the books you encounter are guiding questions like those in Table B.11 *Guiding Questions for a Critical Analysis of Children's Literature* in Appendix B. Keep in mind this kind of critical eye is not just for picture books—these questions can easily be applied to textbooks, popular media, news stories, and other resources for children. Katy has used a similar approach with children's atlases to identify bias against the Global South.

# 8

# How to Teach Anti-Oppressive Social Studies and Not Get Fired

We hope we've made our case for why anti-oppressive elementary social studies is both desirable *and* possible. Now, it's time to address the elephant in the room. We are well aware that there is no guarantee a school or district will support anti-oppressive elementary social studies. In fact, some of your colleagues or school leaders or community members will see it as a dangerous threat to their authority or the status quo and will pull out all the stops to undermine it. We don't want to sugarcoat it: This is hard work, even under the best of circumstances.

This situation is unlikely to get better anytime soon. The United States is increasingly polarized with extremists on the rise. More and more people consume news through siloed feeds, including sources with little to no commitment to objectivity or truth that instead unabashedly forward an ideological, partisan agenda (Long, Eveland, & Slater, 2019). Fueled by prominent politicians and media figures, "fake news" (Lazer et al., 2018) and conspiracy theories spread like wildfire on social media platforms.

While it may feel especially frustrating right now, social studies has *always* been hotly contested (Evans, 2004; Halvorsen, 2013), with a tug-of-war between camps advocating for an anti-oppressive framework like ours and others preaching the need for "cultural literacy" rooted in white, European, and Christian traditions (Buras, 2010) or a celebration of American exceptionalism that denounces questioning of the status quo as unpatriotic (Apple, 2006). Complicating matters lately is federal educational policy that incentivizes schools to prioritize literacy and math over other subject areas like social studies through high-stakes testing. All of this is amidst huge cuts to public education that have dramatically reshaped teachers' work so that they have less time and autonomy to plan *and* less pay—the perfect storm to encourage the uncritical consumption of whatever resources are easiest to implement and monetize their work on sites like Teachers Pay Teachers (J. L. Gallagher, Swalwell, & Bellows, 2019; Rodríguez, Brown, & Vickery, 2020; Schroeder, Curcio, & Lundgren, 2019).

No part of the current political situation outlined above is permanent—for better or worse. The only thing constant is change, right? Humans built these systems and invented these practices—we can create something different together, and we will. One way to look at that is not to get too comfortable thinking that any support or victories for anti-oppressive education are here to stay. People with a different normative vision of what constitutes a better world will always be advancing their vision, just like we will always be advancing ours. Laws, standards, or expectations can always be changed—*if* people strategically organize and push hard enough for long enough.

We say all of this not to depress you, but because we want to be frank about the challenges ahead and offer advice for the potential roadblocks. Anti-oppressive elementary social studies may not be easy, but it *is* absolutely worth it. This chapter lays out our suggestions for how to anticipate and respond to criticism from both within and outside classrooms and how to build a strong foundation for your practice.

## Nurture A Radical Imagination

Our first piece of advice is to nurture a radical imagination. Don't stop believing that a better world is possible, and don't stop imagining how our circumstances, our policies, and our practices can improve. If you find yourself saying, "Well, that's just how it is," tap into your inner toddler and ask, "But why?" Let's not take anything for granted or simply resign ourselves to social studies that is minimal, superficial, or oppressive. While we certainly can't fight every battle every time, neither can we forget the fact that things have *not* always been this way and they can be different. Better.

What makes this radical imagination easier is that there are many real-world examples of educators, children, and families engaging in anti-oppressive education. Communities who have long fought against oppression have used formal and informal schooling, and social studies curriculum specifically, to build a better world. This includes efforts to center Indigenous Knowledges in elementary schools and tribally controlled schools; a range of freedom schools and ethnic studies programs; Afrocentric schools; escuelitas in Chiapas, Mexico, run by an organization of grassroots activists in support of the Indigenous Zapatista communities; teacher pipelines for minoritized students and educators; and antibias bilingual elementary schools. There are several publications that help keep us abreast of the latest innovations—you can find our favorites on our website (www.ssfabw.com). Subscribing to these (most are free!) is a good way to ensure a steady diet of information to feed your radical imagination.

## Recognize Your Professional Obligation

In addition to keeping up to date on the latest innovations in anti-oppressive educational practices, we also need to be aware of the current challenges and harms kids face. It is our obligation to know what these are so that we can avoid and/or address them. Teachers know they are mandatory reporters of child abuse, but they're not necessarily empowered to report and stop the educative-psychic curricular violence we talked about earlier. We see it as our professional duty to make sure we are not doing harm to children through how and what we teach. Anything less is educational malpractice.

Thus, we must constantly sharpen our critical consciousness to be aware of problematic practices and build our tool kit to disrupt them. In addition to everything laid out in this book about curriculum and instruction, we must understand the bureaucracy and hierarchy of our states and districts so we can know where best to direct our change-making energies, buffer our credibility with ongoing meaningful professional development, and assess our own safety (mental, emotional, physical, financial) so we know exactly how far we are willing to go. Of course, there will be different stakes for different people based on their identities and contexts. And when we are in positions to risk more with fewer or less-intense consequences, we must be willing to do so as a way to be in solidarity with our colleagues who cannot.

---

### WHAT WOULD YOU DO?

You teach a unit asking, "How should we protect waterways?" In it, they learn about the Dakota Access Pipeline and protests against it at Standing Rock; the Flint Water Crisis; droughts due to overuse, and other examples of water rights, pollution, and protection efforts around the world. As a culminating activity, they test water from the school's sinks and a nearby stream and communicate their report to City Council. The students love it, and many families express excitement. A group of parents, however, is furious with your "propaganda" and expresses their rage through social media that goes viral, drawing the attention of conservative media and the local news. Your principal asks you to issue a formal apology and make changes to the unit that "presents both sides." How would you respond to the principal, to the small group of disgruntled parents, and to the students and families who have been deeply engaged and inspired by this unit?

---

We encourage readers to see enacting and standing up for anti-oppressive education as *fundamental* to what it means to be a "good" teacher of the highest professional standards. This is a fairly radical statement in some contexts, as many administrators increasingly define professionalism as compliance with mandates—no matter how awful they are for students. In their overview of elementary teachers' activism in Albuquerque, New Mexico, classroom teachers and teacher educators Katherine Crawford-Garrett, Michelle Perez, Rebecca M. Sánchez, Amanda Short, and Kersti Tyson (2015) offer a definition of professionalism *as activism:*

*Professionalism as activism recognizes that we enter our role as teachers in a democratic society with a set of commitments and responsibilities to advocate for children and for ourselves as educators. That means we must speak against policies and leadership decisions that undermine our work and devalue our expertise about children and learning. . . . Professionalism as activism, then, is characterized by action to defend and promote meaningful instruction and collaboration among teachers, action to inform families about current reform initiatives and their rights, and action as protesters against unsound policies that compromise the integrity of teaching and learning in our public schools. (para. 8)*

We want to be clear that educators should not consider themselves saviors, swooping in on behalf of people who did not ask us for help or who do not trust us to do right by them. There is a long history of this happening in ways that have caused tremendous harm, including attempted erasure of languages, cultures, and traditions. Professionalism as activism should be in *deep* solidarity with colleagues, families, and community organizations who are most directly impacted by oppressive education.

Of course, you may have colleagues who are openly hostile to this idea of professionalism. They may adamantly cling to antiquated, harmful curriculum and refuse any of the new ideas you're bringing to the table. "We've always done it this way!" or "You have an agenda!" We've heard it all. We've seen the eye rolls and felt the cold shoulders. While there's nothing quite as awesome as colleagues who are close collaborators, there's nothing quite as frustrating as colleagues who are not. If this is the case, we recommend that you prioritize when to push and when to compromise, and do as much as you can in ways that are healthy for you and your students.

Remember our emphasis on community? Build relationships and figure out your "in." Some colleagues might be more willing to tackle an existing unit related to the environment, while others might be compelled to shift their practices based on local events or politics. *Be strategic!* Sometimes, the best strategy is to let your work speak for itself. We've known teachers whose skeptical or dismissive colleagues have warmed up considerably after noticing students voluntarily extending their learning through deep discussion at recess, sophisticated and animated conversations heard through the classroom wall, and increased scholastic achievement. They're curious: What made that happen? And once they see how much more meaningful and rewarding this way of teaching is, they won't want to go back to the content or activities they relied on before. Not only is anti-oppressive social studies more engaging and relevant to youth, it makes the act of teaching so much richer and fulfilling for us as educators.

## Find Your People

It is much, much easier to muster the courage to fulfill our ethical professional obligations if we know there are others at our side. We first want to encourage readers to think of students' families as "their people." When our methods students express concern about families with regards to enacting anti-oppressive education, they often mean those who will complain or resist in some way—what they call "pushback." We urge readers to first and foremost consider the families who "push *for*" anti-oppressive education, those who have long been demanding something better for their children and who will go to bat for you if and when it comes under attack. These voices have long been crying out for a better world, and they are more than ready to have teachers be part of building it rather than staying on the sidelines or getting in the way.

Of course, we hope you have many colleagues excited to do this work. Though we have yet to meet someone who has *no* local ally or co-conspirator, we know from personal experience how hard it can be when you find yourself shouting into the wind during meetings with colleagues, administrators, or school board members who are determined to maintain the oppressive status quo. It's exhausting, to say the least. There are wonderful professional networks to support anti-oppressive elementary educators that are especially helpful if you find yourself alone in this approach within your building or district. See our website for our recommendations.

## Communicate and Be Transparent

While it is essential to have people in your corner who can share resources, troubleshoot, and have your back when the going gets rough, not everyone is going to understand or support anti-oppressive education. We recommend being clear and transparent about your vision for social studies, and regularly communicate with colleagues, families, and administrators about what you and your students are up to, and why. This means consistent and accessible email updates or newsletters, inviting people into the classroom, and providing an open door to discuss families' concerns or questions. While those conversations can be tough, they present opportunities to build relationships with families, to listen deeply to their hopes and dreams for their children, to genuinely reflect on whether your critics have a point, and to clarify any confusion or misunderstandings. Having a crystal clear, well-sourced philosophy of teaching for those conversations is critical. Knowing the school's mission and state standards backward and forward helps you connect them to anti-oppressive education. Even then, a caregiver may still leave angry or still accuse you of indoctrination. Hopefully, you've been keeping your administrators in the loop so they will have your back.

Elementary teachers Gabby Arca and Nina Sethi (Arca & Sethi, 2021) advise educators facing skeptical or resistant caregivers to "make it about the kids" by highlighting how they created curriculum in response to children's wonderful questions and curiosities. This is especially useful when defending against the argument that something is not "age appropriate"—if a kid asks about something, it's likely time to help them understand it. It doesn't mean we dive into graphic detail, but we can ask students about what they want to know to gauge what they're hoping to learn. No matter what your context, you must get to know your community to determine what framing will help families find reasons to support anti-oppressive social studies.

For the record, while we encourage teachers to engage in frequent, regular communication about what is happening in the classroom and why, we do *not* recommend sending letters home to alert parents to a topic you may think is especially sensitive. Not only does this have the potential to alienate families and students whose lives are reflected in that content, but we guarantee that you'll never be able to accurately predict what someone will find objectionable. Case in point: As Noreen's fifth graders began to learn how to multiply two-digit numbers, she encouraged them to use colored markers to track place values. One morning, a student submitted their math work with a long, angry parent note scrawled on the back. The parent was livid that Noreen would suggest that anything other than pencil might be appropriate for solving math problems. You may inevitably deal with similar baseless confrontations that are more about someone taking their anger out on you than anything you have done wrong. We caution educators from worrying too much about offending peers and parents who are in positions of advantage—you should genuinely listen to their concerns, but take them with a grain of salt.

That being said, some topics will be predictably controversial depending on where you are. For example, teaching about debates over fracking may be a nonissue in many places. In states like Texas, Oklahoma, or Pennsylvania, however, it may be deeply controversial as some students may have family members working in the oil or natural gas industry or who support fracking as they would profit from its economic contributions to the state, whereas others may suffer from devastating health problems as a result of fracking and oppose it. This doesn't mean we don't address these issues with our students (in fact, it is a reason to *highlight* them in our teaching). Rather, we want to be intentional about linking everything to the standards and providing explicit professional justifications for all of our decisions.

## Create Space for Questions and Growth

It likely won't just be caregivers who push against anti-oppressive teaching. There may be students who say or do things that throw wrenches in your best-laid plans. Sometimes this is intentional, and it's important to make every effort to build a relationship with students to find out what their concerns are and address them. While they cannot do harm to others in the class—or to us—we want to make it clear that we care about them, want to know what's going on with them, and that we are committed to figuring out a constructive way forward. Often, young students are simply repeating ideas they've heard from adults in their lives. They love their families, and we want to respect how hard it can be to square what they learn at school with what they learn at home when those ideas are in conflict. Taking their ideas and questions seriously and trusting that their thinking will develop and evolve not only creates a genuinely supportive learning environment for students but can also help assuage caregivers' concerns of indoctrination. It also helps keep us in check to make sure we're *not* actually indoctrinating students!

When intentional or unintentional harm occurs in the classroom, restorative justice practices can be a powerful way to help heal the community (see Wheeler-Bell & Swalwell, 2021; Winn & Winn, 2021). To be effective, however, restorative justice work cannot be a one-off or occasional behavior management solution—it is an entire philosophy that is grounded in mutual accountability that must be embedded in the culture of the classroom or school. Like any innovative educational approach, restorative justice has been used in transformative ways that uplift and strengthen school communities; it has also been taken up in ways that utterly disregard notions of justice and restoring relationships through a focus on discipline and control. We urge interested readers to learn more about this philosophy and classroom implementation before trying it out (see Zehr, 2015).

We want to point out that some student pushback may urge us to be *more* anti-oppressive. We've both learned a great deal from students (and their families), and have been called out in various ways over the years. It can be awkward and even embarrassing, but we urge readers to consider those moments as gifts. The honesty and care behind such feedback must be valued more than our feelings of embarrassment or defensiveness at realizing we've misstepped or caused harm, intentionally or not. Adopting an anti-oppressive stance means we must be trusted to do *something* with the feedback we are offered. Listen, take a step back, reflect, apologize, discuss, and/or learn more. This doesn't mean we always agree with critiques, but we *do* take them seriously as teachable moments for ourselves.

Student critiques may be evidence of deep, critical knowledge and skill—and courage! It's important to provide space for students to pose questions and communicate with us directly about what they're learning, whether through morning meetings, anonymous comment/question boxes, or writing opportunities like journals. These are vital tools for ensuring the ongoing dialogue needed to build relationships founded on trust and respect. When families offer critiques, do what you can to keep families' concerns front and center, be specific about what you plan to do, and thank them for their feedback. Constructive feedback is meant to make you do better next time. The worst thing an educator can do is dismiss it—it shows a lack of regard for families sharing their concerns and a refusal to grow in one's understanding of others' perspectives. Again, *you may not agree,* but that is also *not* the point.

Here's an example of a teacher's response to a parent concern about an assignment that asked students to compare which group had it worse during the 19th century in the United States: Black people or Indigenous people. At this point in the book, we hope we don't need to break down why asking students to compare oppressions is so heinous. We share this, however, because the teacher's response was exemplary. To protect the anonymity of those involved with this exchange, we have paraphrased this email but have maintained the spirit of each line.

*Thank you so much for reaching out to me about this assignment. You are absolutely right that this question was poorly written and out of line for all the reasons you outline. I am sorry that it has taken me so long to respond—I wanted to hear from the curriculum coordinator before writing you back. She created our lessons that the district mandates, so I wanted to make sure this was on her radar as we need to change it and learn from it. I've specifically asked her to rewrite this question so that it instead asks students to consider the impact of colonization on these groups and what they think ought to be done to rectify the problems that the colonizers created. I am excited that this reframing will also expose students to what is happening today in connection to these histories. I'm grateful you brought this up so in the future we can learn from this mistake and make sure the same issue isn't anywhere else in the curriculum. Your email has helped me grow and I hope it will help improve learning for students across the district. Please don't hesitate to reach out if you have any other concerns—I am constantly looking for ways to be a better educator and appreciate your perspective.*

Notice that this teacher doesn't make excuses, defend their intentions, or point to other less problematic stuff they are doing. They recognized the problem the parent identified, responded to it in a thoughtful way with clear short- and long-term solutions, and cultivated a relationship with the parent to deepen their trust and respect (Gorski & Swalwell, 2015). Teachable moment, nailed.

## Engage in Critical Self Reflection

Last, but most certainly not least, making space for our own ongoing growth is essential. None of us knows everything, none of us has got it all figured out. Not only is the world too vast to achieve that, but it's ever-changing. During the past 20 years of our respective careers, language around gender (terminology for various identities, pronoun usage, etc.) has expanded and evolved dramatically. We are still learning and growing in this area and many others! We remind each other to watch out for ableist language, and are constantly forwarding books, tweets, and podcasts to one another to learn more about an issue or our community. This can all be overwhelming, but we find it exciting and part of why we so deeply love what we do. Not knowing everything is not a shortcoming—it's an inevitability and an eternal opportunity to grow; it's also a foundational part of what it means to be in beloved community. We have an obligation to keep learning how to be more loving, thoughtful, responsive members of the human family and to be more respectful and caring to living and nonliving things that surround us.

For preservice teachers and educators who are early in their careers, we urge you to jump in, even if you think you have so much to learn. You *do. We all do.* This work is a *process.* We can't anticipate what will happen in the world after these words are published, but we are certain that educators will continue to be fiercely committed to doing right by youth. Honoring and affirming who they are and supporting their learning in ways that are rigorous, engaging, and bring joy, while teaching them a fuller story of how things came to be as they are. Most importantly, we know that educators can and will do the work to help youth build a world better than the one we live in now.

We hope this book can offer some measure of guidance and will mark a few signposts on your journey. We have tried to put into words the things that have driven us over the course of our careers as PK–12 educators and now as teacher educators, but no text could ever encapsulate the hopes and dreams we have for the next generation. Those lie in the power of the people and in beloved community. We hope that you will join us in building this better world together!

## Putting These Ideas Into Practice

### Conversations with Caregivers

If you are a preservice teacher, interview a diverse array of caregivers about their hopes and fears for what social studies their children will encounter. If you are an inservice teacher, reach out to the families of your students through a questionnaire, phone call, or face-to-face meeting in a time and place convenient for the families to have this conversation. Then figure out concrete ways to reflect those conversations in your practice, and don't forget to thank them for their time and care.

### Meet With Administration

As a follow-up to the caregiver interviews, advocate for families' needs and wants relative to social studies education by taking a meeting with administrators. Beforehand, strategize about how best to ask what steps the school is or can commit to taking as a way to attend to these issues, and what specific ideas you have for what you plan to do in your classroom with clear justifications that garner their support. If you are a preservice teacher, write a proposal asking for more social studies time or resources like money for books or a field trip as a way to practice making a case for anti-oppressive social studies to administrators. If possible, share it with an administrator for feedback on how to craft the strongest argument possible.

**Revise Your Manifesto**

Revisit the manifesto you wrote as an extension activity for Chapter 2. Now that you've finished the book, what do you want to delete, modify, or add before you share it with administrators and families?

**Attend, Subscribe, and Follow**

Review the resources we've recommended in this chapter, throughout the book, and on our website. Consider which medium of professional learning is your favorite and/or is most feasible for you right now. Maybe it's following some of the people we've mentioned on social media, maybe it's attending a conference, maybe it's listening to podcasts or reading a new book or two. Start somewhere, and then see how far you can get through the list of resources we recommend. And don't hesitate to reach out to us with suggestions to include on our website!

# • Epilogue •

*When we do this work of organizing against racism, hetero-*
*patriarchy, capitalism—organizing to change the world—*
*there are no guarantees . . . our work will have an immediate*
*effect. But we have to do it as if it were possible.*

—ANGELA DAVIS (2020)

The vision for anti-oppressive social studies that we have laid out in this book takes vision, time, resources, and a commitment to "evoke collective freedom dreaming" (Love, 2019, p. 12). In his book *Freedom Dreams: The Black Radical Imagination*, Robin D. G. Kelley (2002) explains that "the map to a new world is in the imagination, in what we see in our third eyes rather than in the desolation that surrounds us" (pp. 2–3). Much of the damage in the world around us has been wrought by colonial and settler projects, ultimately based on a thirst for power and money. It's easy to become discouraged and hopeless in the midst of it all. We've been there, particularly as we wrote this book in the fall of 2020. But we try to maintain a sense of critical hope, grounded in a deep sense of responsibility: to our families, to each other, to the communities of which we are a part, and to those living and nonliving who surround us (Boler, 2004). This includes fighting for justice even when there is no assurance that it will be achieved, and seeing ourselves in relationship to others. It is not easy, but it is how we build a better world that values everyone. Every. One.

We are certain that in this book, we have made mistakes. Part of equity and justice work is recognizing that you will likely mess up when you venture into new ways of thinking and knowing, particularly when those new ways are in opposition to what you've always learned and done. Moreover, this work is ever-evolving as new information comes to light, more people are willing to speak their truth and share it with others, and the language and approaches we use necessarily shift and change. Our work is ongoing, and although we know a lot about some things, we certainly don't know it all, and we have a great deal to learn—especially about communities of which we are not a part. And as academic writers, we know that the best way to find your mistakes, misspellings, and omissions is to submit something for publication; once your words are indelibly on a page, your errors become glaring. If we have misstepped, please let us know, and we will commit to doing better.

We wanted to include so much more than what you have read. We hope to include what didn't fit in the book on our website and in our future talks, lectures, and classes; we hope you may find any missing pieces there. Incredibly, this book is our first time writing together, despite four years of teaching and professional development collaborations, countless outlandish ideas, countable great ideas, and literal dozens of breakout boxes. We love connecting with others who share our passion for elementary social studies, anti-oppressive education, local histories, children's literature, and escape rooms. If any part of this book speaks to you, we hope you are willing to reach out. If you engage in teaching that our readers can learn from, we are always happy to uplift your work online. The more ways we can share our dreams of anti-oppressive education, the better we all will be.

We end this book with a rallying cry for our readers. Decades ago, a Filipino anti–martial law activist tradition was adopted by the United Farm Workers in the form of the unity clap, a ritual that ended community gatherings. The ritual begins with all members of the group forming a circle, then slowly clapping or stomping in unison as the rhythm quickens and rises to a crescendo. Teacher activist scholar Artnelson Concordia added another component of togetherness to the unity clap: As the clapping accelerates, someone yells, "Isang bagsak!"

followed by a final, single group-clap or stomp. In Tagalog, isang bag-sak means *one down,* and this cry represents the collective achievement of a goal. This book is the culmination of our many years of teaching about and for elementary social studies, and thus, this epilogue is our "one down." *Isang bagsak!*

Concordia and fellow teacher activist scholar Allyson Tintiangco-Cubales (2005) added two more layers to this tradition through their work with Pin@y Educational Partnerships in what they call the Tat-long Bagsak ritual. After someone yells "Isang bagsak!" and the community responds with one clap or stomp in recognition of their past together, another person yells "Dalawang bagsak!" (*two down*) followed by two community-claps or stomps in recognition of their present work and ongoing commitment to each other. We are committed to this work, and committed to you. *Dalawang bagsak!*

Finally, someone yells "Tatlong bagsak!" (*three down*) followed by three community-claps or stomps to represent the journey that lies ahead, together. Thank you for joining us on this journey. We look forward to building a better world, together. *Tatlong bagsak!*

Noreen and Katy

# • References •

Adams, E. C. (2020a, October 11). The way I see it: The current state of elementary economics. *Erin on Econ.* https://erinonecon.net/2020/10/11/the-way-i-see-it-the-current-state-of-elementary-economics/

Adams, E. C., (2020b). Whose (economic) knowledge is it, anyway? *Critical Education, 11*(12). https://ices.library.ubc.ca/index.php/criticaled/article/view/186542

Adichie, C. N. (2009). *The danger of a single story* [Video]. TED Conferences. https://www.ted.com/talks/chimamanda_adichie_the_danger_of_a_single_story

Ahmed, S. K. (2019). *Being the change: Lessons and strategies to teach social comprehension.* Portsmouth, NH: Heinemann.

Allen, A. (2019). Where are the women? A continuing absence on US currency. *Social Studies and the Young Learner, 31*(3), 19–23.

Alridge, D. P. (2006). The limits of master narratives in history textbooks: An analysis of representations of Martin Luther King, Jr. *Teachers College Record, 108*(4), 662.

An, S. (2017). Teaching race through AsianCrit-informed counterstories of school segregation. *Social Studies Research and Practice, 12*(2), 210–231.

Anderson, M. (2018, February 1). What kids are really learning about slavery. *The Atlantic.* https://www.theatlantic.com/education/archive/2018/02/what-kids-are-really-learning-about-slavery/552098/

Andrews, A. (2014). *The kid who changed the world.* Nashville, TN: Tommy Nelson.

Annamma, S. A., & Winn, M. (2019). Transforming our mission: Animating teacher education through intersectional justice. *Theory Into Practice, 58*(4), 318–327.

Apple, M. W. (2006). *Educating the "right" way: Markets, standards, God, and inequality.* New York, NY: Taylor & Francis.

Arca, G., & Sethi, N. (2021). We're afraid they won't feel bad: Teaching for social justice at the elementary level. In K. Swalwell & D. Spikes (Eds.), Anti-oppressive education in 'elite' schools: Promising practices and cautionary tales from the field (pp. 201–211). New York, NY: Teachers College Press.

Au, W. (2009). Decolonizing the classroom. In W. Au (Ed.), *Rethinking multicultural education* (pp. 247–254). Milwaukee, WI: Rethinking Schools.

Au, W. (2013). Coring social studies within corporate education reform: The Common Core State Standards, social justice, and the politics of knowledge in US schools. *Critical Education, 4*(5), 1-15.

Austin, R. (2004). Kwanzaa and the commodification of Black culture. *Black Renaissance, 6*(1), 8–18.

Ayers, W. (2004). *Teaching the personal and the political: Essays on hope and justice.* New York, NY: Teachers College Press.

Bajaj, M., Ghaffar-Kucher, A., & Desai, K. (2016). Brown bodies and xenophobic bullying in US schools: Critical analysis and strategies for action. *Harvard Educational Review, 86*(4), 481–505.

Baldwin, J. (1985). *The price of the ticket: Collected nonfiction, 1948-1985.* Macmillan.

Banks, J. A. (1971). Teaching Black history with a focus on decision making. *Social Education, 35*(7), 740–745.

Bauml, M. (2016). Is it cute or does it count? Learning to teach for meaningful social studies in elementary grades. *The Journal of Social Studies Research, 40*(1), 55–69.

Bednarz, S. W., Acheson, G., & Bednarz, R. S. (2006). Maps and map learning in social studies. *Social Education, 70*(7), 398–432.

Bery, S. (2014). Multiculturalism, teaching slavery, and white supremacy. *Equity & Excellence in Education, 47*(3), 334–352.

Bigelow, B. (1997). On the road to cultural bias: A critique of The Oregon Trail CD-ROM. *Language Arts, 74*(2), 84-93.

Bigelow, B. (n.d.). *Coal, chocolate chip cookies, and mountaintop removal.* Zinn Education Project. https://www.zinnedproject.org/materials/coal -mountaintop-removal/

Bishop, R. S. (1990). Mirrors, windows, and sliding glass doors. *Perspectives, 6*(3), ix–xi.

Blanchette, S. (2010). Education or indoctrination? The development of social studies standards in Texas. *Social Education, 74*(4), 199–203.

Blue, L. E., O'Brien, M., & Makar, K. (2018). Exploring the classroom practices that may enable a compassionate approach to financial literacy education. *Mathematics Education Research Journal, 30*(2), 143–164.

Boehm, R. G., & Petersen, J. F. (1994). An elaboration of the fundamental themes in geography. *Social Education, 58,* 211–218.

Boler, M. (2004). Teaching for hope: The ethics of shattering world views. In D. P. Liston & J. W. Garrison (Eds.), *Teaching, learning, and loving: Reclaiming passion in educational practice* (pp. 114–129). New York. NY: Routledge Falmer.

Bradshaw, C. P., Koth, C. W., Bevans, K. B., Ialongo, N., & Leaf, P. J. (2008). The impact of school-wide positive behavioral interventions and supports (PBIS) on the organizational health of elementary schools. *School Psychology Quarterly, 23*(4), 462–473.

Brown, K. D., & Brown, A. L. (2011). Teaching K–8 students about race: African Americans, racism, and the struggle for social justice in the US. *Multicultural Education, 19*(1), 9–13.

Brugar, K., Halvorsen, A. L., & Hernandez, S. (2014). Where are the women? A classroom inquiry into social studies textbooks. *Social Studies and the Young Learner, 26*(3), 28–31.

Buchanan, L. B., Tschida, C., Bellows, E., & Shear, S. B. (2020). Positioning children's literature to confront the persistent avoidance of LGBTQ topics among elementary preservice teachers. *The Journal of Social Studies Research, 44*(1), 169–184.

Buras, K. L. (2010). *Rightist multiculturalism: Core lessons on neoconservative school reform.* New York, NY: Routledge.

Busey, C. L., & Walker, I. (2017). A dream and a bus: Black critical patriotism in elementary social studies standards. *Theory & Research in Social Education, 45*(4), 456–488.

Butler-Wall, A., Cosier, K., & Harper, R. L. (2016). *Rethinking sexism, gender, and sexuality.* Milwaukee, WI: Rethinking Schools.

Carber, F. (2020, August 20). More than half of California's incarcerated firefighters are under lockdown as coronavirus sweeps through state prisons, resulting in a shortage of crews in fire season. *MSN Insider.* https://www.msn.com/en-us/weather/topstories/more-than-half-of-california-s-incarcerated-firefighters-are-under-lockdown-as-coronavirus-sweeps-through-state-prisons-resulting-in-a-shortage-of-crews-in-fire-season/ar-BB18aUUq

Catt, C. (1888). *The American sovereign* (Lyceum Lecture) [Speech text]. Iowa State University Archives of Women's Political Communication. https://awpc.cattcenter.iastate.edu/2018/12/03/the-american-sovereign-lyceum-lecture-1888/

Catt, C. C. (1917). Objections to the federal amendment. In C.C. Catt (Ed.), *Woman suffrage by federal constitutional amendment.* New York, NY: National Woman Suffrage Publishing Company. https://lccn.loc.gov/17004988

Children's Literature Assembly. (2019). *On the importance of critical selection and teaching of diverse children's literature* [Position Statement]. https://www.childrensliteratureassembly.org/uploads/1/1/8/6/118631535/clapositionstatementontheimportanceofcriticalselectionandteachingofdiversechildrensliterature.pdf

Chin, M. J., Quinn, D. M., Dhaliwal, T. K., & Lovison, V. S. (2020). Bias in the air: A nationwide exploration of teachers' implicit racial attitudes, aggregate bias, and student outcomes. *Educational Researcher, 49*(8), 566–578.

Ching, S. H. (2005). Multicultural children's literature as an instrument of power. *Language Arts, 83*(2), 128–126.

Cobb, J. C. (2018, April 4). Even though he is revered today, MLK was widely disliked by the American public when he was killed. *Smithsonian Magazine.* https://www.smithsonianmag.com/history/why-martin-luther-king-had-75-percent-disapproval-rating-year-he-died-180968664/

Collaborative for Academic, Social, and Emotional Learning. (2020). *SEL: What are the core competence areas and where are they promoted?* https://casel.org/sel-framework/

Collins, C. (2019, January 25). Why "both sides" of a story aren't enough. *Learning for Justice.* https://www.learningforjustice.org/magazine/why-both-sides-of-a-story-arent-enough

Collins, P. H. (2002). *Black feminist thought: Knowledge, consciousness, and the politics of empowerment.* New York, NY: Routledge.

Colón, J. (1982). *A Puerto Rican in New York, and other sketches.* New York, NY: International Publishers.

Combahee River Collective. (1977). *The Combahee River Collective Statement.* http://circuitous.org/scraps/combahee.html

Communities for Just Schools Fund. (2020, May 7). When SEL is used as another form of policing. *Medium.* https://medium.com/@justschools/when-sel-is-used-as-another-form-of-policing-fa53cf85dce4

Connor, M. A. (2003). Can we field questions honestly, or does "age appropriateness" require soft-pedaling the awful truth of war? *Rethinking Schools.* https://rethinkingschools.org/articles/straight-talk-with-kids-about-war/

Cooperative Children's Book Center. (2020). *Annual statistics on multicultural literature in publishing.* University of Wisconsin–Madison. https://ccbc.education.wisc.edu/books/pcstats.asp

Crampton, J. (1994). Cartography's defining moment: The Peters projection controversy, 1974–1990. *Cartographica: The International Journal for Geographic Information and Geovisualization, 31*(4), 16–32.

Crawford-Garrett, K., Perez, M., Sánchez, R. M., Short, A., & Tyson, K. (2015). Activism is good teaching. *Rethinking Schools.* https://rethinkingschools.org/articles/activism-is-good-teaching/

Crenshaw, K. W. (1988). Race, reform, and retrenchment: Transformation and legitimation in antidiscrimination law. *Harvard Law Review,* 1331–1387.

Crenshaw, K. (1991). Mapping the margins: Intersectionality, identity politics, and violence against women of color. *Stanford Law Review, 43,* 1241–1299.

Cronin, M., & Adair, D. (2004). *The wearing of the green: A history of St. Patrick's Day.* New York, NY: Routledge.

Cruz, B. C., & Bailey, R. W. (2017). An LGBTQ+ inclusive social studies: Curricular and instructional considerations. *Social Education, 81*(5), 296–302.

Dack, H., van Hover, S., & Hicks, D. (2016). "Try not to giggle if you can help it": The implementation of experiential instructional techniques in social studies classrooms. *The Journal of Social Studies Research*, *40*(1), 39–52.

Dahlen, S. P. (2020). "We need diverse books": Diversity, activism, and children's literature. In *Literary cultures and twenty-first-century childhoods* (pp. 83–108). London: Palgrave Macmillan, Cham.

Darder, A. (2017). *Reinventing Paulo Freire: A pedagogy of love.* New York, NY: Taylor & Francis.

De La Paz, S., Morales, P., & Winston, P. M. (2007). Source interpretation: Teaching students with and without LD to read and write historically. *Journal of Learning Disabilities, 40*(2), 134–144.

De Liscia, V. (June 18, 2020). Historical painting is altered to show most Declaration of Independence signatories were enslavers. *Hyperallergic.* https://hyperallergic.com/572035/historical-painting-is-altered-to -show-most-declaration-of-independence-signatories-were-enslavers/

de los Ríos, C. V., & Molina, A. (2020). Literacies of refuge: "Pidiendo Posada" as ritual of justice. *Journal of Literacy Research, 52*(1), 32–54.

Dreier, P. (2013). Martin Luther King was a radical, not a saint. *Huffington Post.* https://www.commondreams.org/views/2013/01/21/martin -luther-king-was-radical-not-saint

Dow, J. (2006). Deconstructing myths of 'the first Thanksgiving.' *Oyate.* http://oyate.org/index.php/resources/43-resources/thanksgiving

Dubois, B. E. (2011). Young children as activists: Celebrating Black history month and Marian Wright Edelman's work. *Social Studies and the Young Learner, 24*(2), 18–22.

Duckworth, A. (2016). *Grit: The power of passion and perseverance.* New York, NY: Scribner.

Dumas, M. J. (2016). Against the dark: Antiblackness in education policy and discourse. *Theory Into Practice, 55*(1), 11–19.

Dunbar-Ortiz, R. (2014). *An Indigenous peoples' history of the United States* (Vol. 3). New York, NY: Beacon Press.

Duyvis, C. (2015). #OwnVoices. *Corinne Duyvis: Sci-Fi and fantasy in MG & YA.* www.corinneduyvis.net/ownvoices

Eisner, E. W. (1985). *The educational imagination: On the design and evaluation of school programs.* New York, NY: MacMillan.

Elmore, P. G., & Coleman, J. M. (2019). Middle school students' analysis of political memes to support critical media literacy. *Journal of Adolescent & Adult Literacy, 63*(1), 29–40.

Evans, R. W. (2004). *The social studies wars: What should we teach the children?* New York, NY: Teachers College Press.

Falkner, A. (2020). *"Ain't gonna let nobody turn me around:" Learning about race in the early grades.* [Unpublished doctoral dissertation]. University of Texas at Austin.

Falkner, A., & Clark, A. (2018). Following Dylan's lead: Student-led discussion of gender variance in the elementary classroom. In S. B. Shear, C. M. Tschida, E. Bellows, L. B. Buchanan, & E. E. Saylor (Eds.), *(Re)Imagining elementary social studies: A controversial issues reader* (pp. 295–306). Charlotte, NC: Information Age.

Finchum, M. (2006). "I" is for Indian? Dealing with stereotypes in the classroom. *Social Studies and the Young Learner, 18*(4), 4–6.

Finkelman, P. (2014). *Slavery and the founders: Race and liberty in the age of Jefferson.* New York, NY: Routledge.

Fitchett, P. G., Heafner, T. L., & Lambert, R. (2014). Assessment, autonomy, and elementary social studies time. *Teachers College Record, 116*(10), n10.

Flannery, M. E. (2017, July 10). Fear and longing: Life for students with undocumented parents. *NEA News.* https://www.nea.org/advocating-for-change/new-from-nea/fear-and-longing-life-students-undocumented-parents

Flinders, D. J., Noddings, N., & Thornton, S. J. (1986). The null curriculum: Its theoretical basis and practical implications. *Curriculum Inquiry, 16*(1), 33–42.

Forest, D. E. (2014). From rags to "rich as Rockefeller": Portrayals of class mobility in Newbery titles. *Curriculum Inquiry, 44*(5), 591–619.

Fram, M. S., Frongillo, E. A., Jones, S. J., Williams, R. C., Burke, M. P., DeLoach, K. P., & Blake, C. E. (2011). Children are aware of food insecurity and take responsibility for managing food resources. *The Journal of Nutrition, 141*(6), 1114–1119.

Freire, P. (1994). *Pedagogy of hope.* New York, NY: Continuum.

Gainer, J. S., Valdez-Gainer, N., & Kinard, T. (2009). The elementary bubble project: Exploring critical media literacy in a fourth-grade classroom. *The Reading Teacher, 62*(8), 674–683.

Gallagher, J. L., & Kelly, E. (2019). Economic thinking with Jon Klassen's Animal Hat books. *Social Studies and the Young Learner, 32*(2), 16–18.

Gallagher, J. L., Swalwell, K. M., & Bellows, M. E. (2019). "Pinning" with pause: Supporting teachers' critical consumption on sites of curriculum sharing. *Social Education, 83*(4), 217–224.

Gallagher, J. L., & Tschida, C. (2020). Exploring master and counter narratives of economics through simulations with elementary teacher candidates. *Social Studies Journal, 40*(2), 21–30.

Gallagher, S., & Hodges, S. (2010). Let's teach students to prioritize: Reconsidering "wants" and "needs." *Social Studies and the Young Learner, 22*(3), 14–16.

Gold, J. (2017, November 29). The danger of the story of "both sides." *Learning for Justice.* https://www.learningforjustice.org/magazine/the-danger-of-the-story-of-both-sides

González, N., & Moll, L. C. (2002). Cruzando el puente: Building bridges to funds of knowledge. *Educational Policy, 16*(4), 623–641.

Gorski, P., & Swalwell, K. (2015). Equity literacy for all. *Educational Leadership.* http://www.edchange.org/publications/Equity-Literacy-for-All.pdf

Gotanda, N. (1991). A Critique of "Our Constitution is Color-Blind." *Stanford Law Review*, 1–68.

Gregory, A., Skiba, R. J., & Mediratta, K. (2017). Eliminating disparities in school discipline: A framework for intervention. *Review of Research in Education, 41*(1), 253–278.

Gregory, A., Skiba, R. J., & Noguera, P. A. (2010). The achievement gap and the discipline gap: Two sides of the same coin? *Educational Researcher, 39*(1), 59–68.

Gruenewald, D. A. (2003). The best of both worlds: A critical pedagogy of place. *Educational Researcher, 32*(4), 3–12.

Gultekin, M., & May, L. (2020). Children's literature as fun-house mirrors, blind spots, and curtains. *The Reading Teacher, 73*(5), 627–635.

Hagopian, J., & Jones, D. (2020). *Black lives matter at school.* Chicago, IL: Haymarket Books.

Hale, C. (2019). *Todos iguales/All equal: Un corrido de Lemon Grove/A ballad of Lemon Grove.* New York, NY: Lee & Low.

Hall, J. D. (2005). The long civil rights movement and the political uses of the past. *The Journal of American History, 91*(4), 1233–1263.

Halvorsen, A. L. (2013). *A history of elementary social studies: Romance and reality.* New York, NY: Peter Lang.

Hanes, R. (2020). How one 2nd-grader's story inspired climate justice curriculum. *Rethinking Schools, 34*(2). https://rethinkingschools.org/articles/how-one-2nd-grader-s-story-inspired-climate-justice-curriculum/

Hartenstein, J. M. (1992). A Christmas issue: Christian holiday celebration in the public elementary schools is an establishment of religion. *California Law Review, 80,* 981–1026.

Hauver, J. (2017). Attending to children's civic learning . . . in the in-between. *Social Education, 81*(6), 376–379.

Heafner, T. L., O'Connor, K. A., Groce, E. C., Byrd, S., Good, A. J., Oldendorf, S., Passe, J., & Rock, T. (2007). Advocating for social studies: Becoming AGENTS for change. *Social Studies and the Young Learner, 20*(1), 26–29.

Hess, D. E. (2004). Controversies about controversial issues in democratic education. *PS: Political Science and Politics,* 257–261.

Hess, D. E., & McAvoy, P. (2014). *The political classroom: Evidence and ethics in democratic education.* New York, NY: Routledge.

Hinde, E. T. (2005). Revisiting curriculum integration: A fresh look at an old idea. *The Social Studies, 96*(3), 105–111.

Hinde, E. R. (2015). The theoretical foundations of curriculum integration and its application in social studies instruction. In L. Bennett & E. R. Hinde (Eds.), *Becoming integrated thinkers: Case studies in elementary social studies* (pp. 21–29). Silver Spring, MD: National Council of the Social Studies.

Hobbs, R. (2020). *Mind over media: Propaganda education for a digital age.* New York, NY: W. W. Norton & Company.

Hoganson, K. L. (2001). "As badly off as the Filipinos": US women's suffragists and the imperial issue at the turn of the twentieth century. *Journal of Women's History, 13*(2), 9–33.

Hogg, L., & Volman, M. (2020). A synthesis of funds of identity research: Purposes, tools, pedagogical approaches, and outcomes. *Review of Educational Research, 90*(6), 862–895.

Hubbard, J., Moore, M. F., & Christensen, L. M. (2020). "Women are as important as men": Third graders investigate diverse women in US History. *Social Studies and the Young Learner, 32*(4), 16–21.

Hylton, B. (June 12, 2020). Why we must stop referring to people as "slaves." *Human Parts.* https://humanparts.medium.com/why-we-must-immediately-cease-and-desist-referring-to-enslaved-people-as-slaves-85b0ddfc5f7b

Immerwahr, D. (2019). *How to hide an empire: A short history of the greater United States.* New York, NY: Random House.

James, J. H. (2015). *Religion in the classroom: Dilemmas for democratic education.* New York, NY: Routledge.

Jeffries, H. K. (Ed.). (2019). *Understanding and teaching the civil rights movement.* Madison, WI: University of Wisconsin Press.

Jeffries, H. (Host) (2019, October 25). Teaching slavery through children's literature (Part 1 with E. E. Thomas). In *Teaching Hard History: American Slavery* [Audio podcast]. https://www.tolerance.org/podcasts/teaching-hard-history/american-slavery/teaching-slavery-through-childrens-literature-part-1

Jimenez, L. (2020, September 13). Blackall's bland as blah. *Booktoss.* https://booktoss.org/2020/09/13/blackalls-bland-as-blah/

Johansen, B. E. (1990). Native American societies and the evolution of democracy in America, 1600-1800. *Ethnohistory, 37*(3), 279–290.

Johnson, J. (2015). Black joy in the time of Ferguson. *QED: A Journal in GLBTQ Worldmaking, 2*(2), 177–183.

Jones, S. (2008). Grass houses: Representations and reinventions of social class through children's literature. *Journal of Language and Literacy Education, 4*(2), 40–58.

Jones, S. (2020). Ending curricular violence. *Learning for Justice.* https://www.learningforjustice.org/magazine/spring-2020/ending-curriculum-violence

Jones, T. (2018, October 25). There's nothing virtuous about finding common ground. *Time Magazine.* https://time.com/5434381/tayari-jones-moral-middle-myth/

Jordan, J. (2002). *Some of us did not die: New and selected essays.* New York, NY: Basic Books.

Joseph, P. E. (2020). *The sword and the shield: The revolutionary lives of Malcolm X and Martin Luther King Jr.* London, UK: Hachette UK.

Journell, W. (Ed.). (2019). *Unpacking fake news: An educator's guide to navigating the media with students.* New York, NY: Teachers College Press.

Kaba, M. (2021). *We do this 'til we free us: Abolitionist organizing and transforming justice.* Chicago, IL: Haymarket.

Kaiser, W. L., & Wood, D. (2001). *Seeing through maps: The power of images to shape our world view.* Amherst, MA: ODT.

Kann, M. (1999). *The gendering of American politics: Founding mothers, founding fathers, and political patriarchy.* ABC-CLIO.

Kaomea, J. (2005). Indigenous studies in the elementary curriculum: A cautionary Hawaiian example. *Anthropology & Education Quarterly, 36*(1), 24–42.

Kaur, V. (2020). *See no stranger: A memoir and manifesto of revolutionary love.* London, UK: One World.

Kelley, R. D. (2002). *Freedom dreams: The Black radical imagination.* Boston, MA: Beacon Press.

Kellogg, M. (2019). *The struggle continues: How the endings of children's literature create false narratives of social movements.* Teaching for Change. https://socialjusticebooks.org/the-struggle-continues/

Kent, S. (1999). Saints or sinners? The case for an honest portrayal of historical figures. *Social Education, 63*(1), 8–12.

King, L. J. (2017). The status of Black history in US schools and society. *Social Education, 81*(1), 14–18.

King, L. J., & Simmons, C. (2018). Narratives of Black history in textbooks: Canada and the United States. In S. A. Metzger & L. M. Harris (Eds.), *The Wiley international handbook of history teaching and learning,* 93–116. New York, NY: Wiley.

King, L. J., & Womac, P. (2014). A Bundle of silences: Examining the racial representation of Black founding fathers of the United States through Glenn Beck's founders' Fridays. *Theory & Research in Social Education, 42*(1), 35–64.

King, L. J., & Woodson, A. N. (2017). Baskets of cotton and birthday cakes: Teaching slavery in social studies classrooms. *Social Studies Education Review, 6*(1), 1–18.

King, M. L. (1960). *Stride toward freedom: The Montgomery story.* New York, NY: Ballantine Books.

Kleinrock, E. (2018, September 27). How my third graders and I address consent. *Learning for Justice.* https://www.learningforjustice.org/magazine/how-my-thirdgraders-and-i-address-consent

Kleinrock, L. (2019, January). How to teach kids to talk about taboo topics. [Video] TED Conferences. https://www.ted.com/talks/liz_kleinrock_how_to_teach_kids_to_talk_about_taboo_topics/transcript?language=en#t-328670

Kleinrock. L. [@teachntransform]. (2020, December 2). *Educators, please remember that "de-centering Christmas" in the classroom doesn't mean "no celebrations." It means to dismantle the religious hierarchy with Christmas at the top- even if all of your students are Christian. Anti-BIAS work includes reflecting on your religious/spiritual beliefs and practices. For example, we often call December holidays, "THE holidays" even though the month does not hold major holidays for non-a Christian religions.* [Tweet]. Twitter/https://twitter.com/teachntransform/status/1334163706473828353

Koenig, K. P. (2009). 'It was so much fun! I died of massive blood loss!' The problem with Civil War reenactments for children. *Rethinking Schools, 23*(4). https://rethinkingschools.org/articles/it-was-so-much-fun-i-died-of-massive-blood-loss/

Kohl, H. R. (2005). *She would not be moved: How we tell the story of Rosa Parks and the Montgomery bus boycott.* New York, NY: The New Press.

Koss, M. D. (2015). Diversity in contemporary picturebooks: A content analysis. *Journal of Children's Literature, 41*(1), 32–42.

Kruse, K. M. (2015). *One nation under god: How corporate America invented Christian America.* New York, NY: Basic Books.

Krutka, D. G. (2017). " Remixing" current events: Navigating the transmedia terrain with fifth graders. *Social Studies and the Young Learner, 29*(4), 27–31.

Kushner, R. (2019, April 17). Is prison necessary? Ruth Wilson Gilmore might change your mind. *The New York Times.* https://www.nytimes.com/2019/04/17/magazine/prison-abolition-ruth-wilson-gilmore.html

Labadie, M., Pole, K., & Rogers, R. (2013). How kindergarten students connect and critically respond to themes of social class in children's literature. *Literacy Research and Instruction, 52*(4), 312–338.

Labbo, L. D., & Field, S. L. (1999). Journey boxes: Telling the story of place, time, and culture with photographs, literature, and artifacts. *The Social Studies, 90*(4), 177–182.

Ladson-Billings, G. (1995). Toward a theory of culturally relevant pedagogy. *American Educational Research Journal, 32*(3), 465–491.

Ladson-Billings, G. (2015). *American Educational Research Association social justice in education award lecture* [Video]. YouTube. https://www.youtube.com/watch?v=ofB_t1oTYhI

Lagerwerff, K. (2016, Spring). Prizes as curriculum: How my school gets students to "behave." *Rethinking Schools, 30*(3). https://rethinkingschools.org/articles/prizes-as-curriculum-how-my-school-gets-students-to-behave/

Landis, M. T. (2015, September 4). These are words scholars should no longer use to describe slavery or the Civil War. *History News Network.* https://historynewsnetwork.org/article/160266

Largey, M. (2016, March 11). *What's the story behind the 'Fair sailing tall boy' memorial?* ATXplained. KUT/Austin Public Radio. https://www.kut.org/austin/2016-03-11/whats-the-story-behind-the-fair-sailing-tall-boy-memorial

Larrick, N. (1965/1992). The all-white world of children's books. *Journal of African Children's and Youth Literature, 3*(5), 1–10.

Lazarus, E. (1883/1987). *An epistle to the Hebrews.* New York, NY: Jewish Historical Society of New York.

Lazer, D. M., Baum, M. A., Benkler, Y., Berinsky, A. J., Greenhill, K. M., Menczer, F., Metzger, M.J., Nyhan, B., Pennycook, G., Rothschild, D., Schudson, M., Sloman, S. A., Sunstein, C. R., Thorson, E. A., Watts, D. J., & Zittrain, J. L. (2018). The science of fake news. *Science, 359*(6380), 1094–1096.

Lee, E., & Yung, J. (2010). *Angel Island: Immigrant gateway to America.* New York, NY: Oxford.

Leonardo, Z. (2004). The color of supremacy: Beyond the discourse of 'white privilege'. *Educational Philosophy and Theory, 36*(2), 137–152.

Leonardo, Z., & Porter, R. K. (2010). Pedagogy of fear: Toward a Fanonian theory of "safety" in race dialogue. *Race Ethnicity and Education, 13*(2), 139–157.

Levin, S. (2019, June 21). Compton's cafeteria riot: A historic act of trans resistance, three years before Stonewall. *The Guardian.* https://www .theguardian.com/lifeandstyle/2019/jun/21/stonewall-san-francisco -riot-tenderloin-neighborhood-trans-women

Lewis, B. A. (1998). *The kid's guide to social action: How to solve the social problems you choose—and turn creative thinking into positive action.* Golden Valley, MN: Free Spirit Publishing.

Library of Congress. (n.d.). Tactics and techniques of the National Woman's Party suffrage campaign. *Women of protest: Photographs from the records of the National Woman's Party.* https://www.loc.gov/static/ collections/women-of-protest/images/tactics.pdf

Lockhart, P. R. (2019, May 30). American schools can't figure out how to teach kids about slavery. *Vox.* https://www.vox.com/ identities/2019/3/13/18262240/mock-slave-auction-new-york-school -teacher-investigation

Loewen, J. W. (2008). *Lies my teacher told me: Everything your American history textbook got wrong.* New York, NY: The New Press.

Loga, S. (2020, September 3). Does 'Midwest nice' breed racism? *Medium.* https://medium.com/an-injustice/does-midwest-nice-breed-racism -b9c54aaf6cbf

Long, J. A., Eveland Jr., W. P., & Slater, M. D. (2019). Partisan media selectivity and partisan identity threat: The role of social and geographic context. *Mass Communication and Society, 22*(2), 145–170.

Love, B. L. (2019). *We want to do more than survive: Abolitionist teaching and the pursuit of educational freedom.* Boston, MA: Beacon.

Love, B. L., & Bradley, R. N. (2015). Teaching Trayvon: Teaching about racism through public pedagogy, hip-hop, Black trauma, and social media. In J. L. Martin (Ed.), *Racial battle fatigue: Instances from the front line of social justice* (pp. 255–268). Santa Barbara, CA: ABC-CLIO.

Lovgren, S. (2010, May 6). Cinco de Mayo history: From bloodshed to beer fest. *National Geographic.* https://www.nationalgeographic.com/ news/2010/5/100505-cinco-de-mayo-history/

Lucey, T. (2018). A critically compassionate approach to financial literacy: A pursuit of moral spirit. *Education Sciences, 8*(4), 152.

Luft, S. (2016, December 16). Media literacy is critical. *Literacy Now.* https://www.literacyworldwide.org/blog/literacy-now/2016/12/16/media-literacy-is-critical

Lyiscott, J. (2019). *Black appetite. White food. Issues of race, voice, and justice within and beyond the classroom.* New York, NY: Routledge.

Malecki, C. K., Demaray, M. K., Smith, T. J., & Emmons, J. (2020). Disability, poverty, and other risk factors associated with involvement in bullying behaviors. *Journal of School Psychology, 78,* 115–132.

Marable, M. (2015). *How capitalism underdeveloped Black America: Problems in race, political economy, and society.* Chicago, IL: Haymarket Books.

Martino, W., & Cumming-Potvin, W. (2016). Teaching about sexual minorities and "princess boys": A queer and trans-infused approach to investigating LGBTQ-themed texts in the elementary school classroom. *Discourse: Studies in the Cultural Politics of Education, 37*(6), 807–827.

Mascareñaz, L. [@laurynmaria]. (2020, November 16). *The phrase "INVITE marginalized people to the table" assumes a white, dominant culture as the hosts of the table/conversation.* [Tweet]. Twitter. https://twitter.com/laurynmaria/status/1328442578107310083

McArthur, S. A. (2019). "It's like black and white!": Critical media literacy and social justice in the elementary classroom. *The International Journal of Critical Media Literacy, 1*(1), 118–127.

McCoy, M. L., Sabzalian, L., & Ender, T. (2021). Alternative strategies for family history projects: Rethinking practice in light of Indigenous perspectives. *The History Teacher, 54*(3), 473–508.

McDaneld, J. (2013). White suffragist dis/entitlement: The revolution and the rhetoric of racism. *Legacy: A Journal of American Women Writers, 30*(2), 243–264.

McTighe, J., & Thomas, R. S. (2003). Backward design for forward action. *Educational Leadership, 60*(5), 52–55.

Menkart, D., Murray, A. D., & View, J. L. (2004). *Putting the movement back into civil rights teaching.* Washington, DC: Teaching for Change.

Menon, S. J., & Saleh, M. (2018). Borders. In D. Krutka, A. M. Whitlock, & M. Helmsing (Eds.), *Keywords in the social studies* (pp. 53–64). New York, NY: Peter Lang.

Merryfield, M. (2012). Four strategies for teaching open-mindedness. *Social Studies and the Young Learner, 25*(2), 18–22.

Mitchell Patterson, T. (2019, February 1). 3 ways to improve slavery education in the US. *The Conversation.* https://theconversation.com/3 -ways-to-improve-education-about-slavery-in-the-us-110013

Mizielinska, A., & Mizielinski, D. (2013). *Maps.* New York, NY: Big Picture Press.

Moll, L. C., Amanti, C., Neff, D., & Gonzalez, N. (1992). Funds of knowledge for teaching: Using a qualitative approach to connect homes and classrooms. *Theory Into Practice, 31*(2), 132–141.

Morris, E. W. (2005). "Tuck in that shirt!" Race, class, gender, and discipline in an urban school. *Sociological Perspectives, 48*(1), 25–48.

Mulholland, L., & Fairwell, A. (2016). *She stood for freedom: The untold story of a civil rights hero, Joan Trumpauer Mulholland.* Salt Lake City, UT: Shadow Mountain Publishing.

Muller, M. (2018). Justice pedagogy: Grade 1–3 students challenge racist statues. *Social Studies and the Young Learner, 31*(2), 17–23.

National Council of Social Studies. (2017). Powerful, purposeful pedagogy in elementary social studies. https://www.socialstudies.org/ position-statements/powerful-purposeful-pedagogy-elementary -school-social-studies

Ngai, M. M. (2004). *Impossible subjects: Illegal aliens and the making of modern America.* Princeton, NJ: Princeton University Press.

Ngai, M. (2006, May 16). How grandma got legal. *Los Angeles Times.* https://www.latimes.com/archives/la-xpm-2006-may-16-oe-ngai16 -story.html

North, A. (2020, August 18). The 19th Amendment didn't give women the right to vote: It's language—and effects—were much narrower. *Vox.* https://www.vox.com/2020/8/18/21358913/19th-amendment -ratified-anniversary-women-suffrage-vote

Nxumalo, F. (2019). *Decolonizing place in early childhood education.* New York, NY: Routledge.

Nxumalo, F., & Villanueva, M. (2019). Decolonial water stories: Affective pedagogies with young children. *International Journal of Early Childhood Environmental Education, 7*(1), 40–56.

O'Neill, J. T., & Swinehart, T. (2010). " Don't take our voices away":

A role play on the Indigenous Peoples' Global Summit on Climate Change. *Rethinking Schools, 24*(3), 54–58. https://rethinkingschools .org/articles/don-t-take-our-voices-away-a-role-play-on-the-indigenous -peoples-global-summit-on-climate-change/

Okonofua, J. A., Walton, G. M., & Eberhardt, J. L. (2016). A vicious cycle: A social–psychological account of extreme racial disparities in school discipline. *Perspectives on Psychological Science, 11*(3), 381–398.

Paris, D. (2012). Culturally sustaining pedagogy: A needed change in stance, terminology, and practice. *Educational Researcher, 41*(3), 93–97.

Paris, R., DeVoe, E. R., Ross, A. M., & Acker, M. L. (2010). When a parent goes to war: Effects of parental deployment on very young children and implications for intervention. *American Journal of Orthopsychiatry, 80*(4), 610.

Payne, K. A. (2020). Starting with children's democratic imagination. A response to "That's my voice! Participation and citizenship in early childhood." *Democracy and Education, 28*(2), 1–6.

Pearcy, M. (2020). "The most insidious legacy": Teaching about redlining and the impact of racial residential segregation. *The Geography Teacher, 17*(2), 44–55.

Pelo, A., & Pelojoaquin, K. (2006). Why we banned legos: Exploring power, ownership, and equity in an early childhood classroom. *Rethinking Schools, 21*(2), 20–25.

Peters, W. (Director & Producer). (1985). A class divided. *Frontline,* episode 9. [Motion picture]. Boston, MA: Public Broadcasting System.

Picower, B. (2012). Using their words: Six elements of social justice curriculum design for the elementary classroom. *International Journal of Multicultural Education, 14*(1), 1–17.

Randolph, B., & DeMulder, E. (2008). I didn't know there were cities in Africa. *Teaching Tolerance, 34,* 36–43.

Reese, D. (2018). Critical Indigenous literacies: Selecting and using children's books about Indigenous Peoples. *Language Arts, 95*(6), 383–393.

Reynolds, J., & Kendi, I. X. (2020). *Stamped: Racism, antiracism, and you—A remix of the National Book Award-winning* Stamped from the beginning. New York, NY: Little, Brown Books for Young Readers.

Roberts, S. L., Strachan, S. L., & Block, M. K. (2019). "The room where it happens:" Using the "great/not so great" framework for evaluating the founders in lower elementary social studies. *Oregon Journal of the Social Studies*, 15.

Rodríguez, N. N. (2015). Teaching about Angel Island through historical empathy and poetry. *Social Studies and the Young Learner, 27*(3), 22–25.

Rodríguez, N. N. (2018a). From margins to center: Developing cultural citizenship education through the teaching of Asian American history. *Theory & Research in Social Education, 46*(4), 528–573.

Rodríguez, N. N. (2018b). Not all terrorists: A teacher educator's approach to teaching against Islamophobia and for religious toler- ance. In S. B. Shear, C. M. Tschida, E. Bellows, L. B. Buchanan, & E. E. Saylor (Eds.), *(Re)Imagining elementary social studies: A con- troversial issues reader* (pp. 129–152). Charlotte, NC: Information Age.

Rodríguez, N. N. (2020). Transformative justice in social studies. *Trans- formative justice in education working paper series*, 1–23. Davis, CA: Transformative Justice in Education Center.

Rodríguez, N., Brown, M., & Vickery, A. (2020). Pinning for profit? Examining elementary preservice teachers' critical analysis of online social studies resources about Black history. *Contemporary Issues in Technology and Teacher Education (CITE), 20*(3), n3.

Rodriguez, N. N., & Kim, E. J. (2018). In search of mirrors: An Asian critical race theory content analysis of Asian American picturebooks from 2007 to 2017. *Journal of Children's Literature, 44*(2), 17–30.

Rodriguez, N. N., & Salinas, C. S. (2019). "La lucha todavía no ha termi- nado"/The struggle has not yet ended: Teaching immigration through testimonio and difficult funds of knowledge. *Journal of Curriculum Theorizing, 34*(3), 136–149.

Rodríguez, N. N., & Vickery, A. (2020). Much bigger than a hamburger: Disrupting problematic picturebook depictions of the civil rights move- ment. *International Journal of Multicultural Education, 22*(2), 109–128.

Ryan, C. L., Patraw, J. M., & Bednar, M. (2013). Discussing princess boys and pregnant men: Teaching about gender diversity and transgender experiences within an elementary school curriculum. *Journal of LGBT Youth, 10*(1–2), 83–105.

Sabzalian, L. (2019). *Indigenous children's survivance in public schools*. New York, NY: Routledge.

Salinas, C., Blevins, B., & Sullivan, C. C. (2012). Critical historical thinking: When official narratives collide with other narratives. *Multicultural Perspectives, 14*(1), 18–27.

Salinas, C., Fránquiz, M. E., & Guberman, S. (2006). Introducing historical thinking to second language learners: Exploring what students know and what they want to know. *The Social Studies, 97*(5), 203–207.

Salinas, C., Fránquiz, M., & Rodríguez, N. N. (2016). Writing Latina/o historical narratives: Narratives at the intersection of critical historical inquiry and LatCrit. *The Urban Review, 48*(3), 419–439.

Salinas, C., Rodríguez, N. N., & Lewis, B. A. (2015). The Tejano history curriculum project: Creating a space for authoring Tejanas/os into the social studies curriculum. *Bilingual Research Journal, 38*(2), 172–189.

Sanchez, A. (2019). Poetry of defiance: How the enslaved resisted. In A. Sanchez (Ed.), *Teaching a people's history of abolition and the Civil War* (pp. 19–39). Milwaukee, WI: Rethinking Schools.

Sanchez, A., & Hagopian, J. (2016, October 19). What we don't learn about the Black Panther Party—but should. *Zinn Education Project.* https://www.zinnedproject.org/if-we-knew-our-history/black-panther -party-significance/

Sanders, S., & Young, K. (2020, July 28). A Black mother reflects on giving her sons 'The Talk' . . . again and again. *NPR Life Kit.* https:// www.npr.org/2020/06/28/882383372/a-black-mother-reflects-on -giving-her-3-sons-the-talk-again-and-again

Saunt, C. (2014). *West of the revolution: An uncommon history of 1776.* New York, NY: W. W. Norton & Company.

Savage, A., & Wesson, S. (2016). " What makes you think that?" Kindergarten students analyze primary sources from the Library of Congress. *Social Studies and the Young Learner, 29*(1), 24–26.

Sayers, J. F., & MacDonald, K. A. (2001). A strong and meaningful role for First Nations women in governance. *First Nations women, governance and the Indian Act: A collection of policy research reports, 11.*

Saylor, E. E., & Schmeichel, M. (2020). Breaking the "bronze ceiling": Investigating a monumental inequality. *Social Studies and the Young Learner, 32*(4), 22–26.

Schaeffer, K. (2020, October 5). *Key facts about women's suffrage around the world, a century after U.S. ratified 19th Amendment.* Pew Research Center. https://www.pewresearch.org/fact-tank/2020/10/05/key-facts-about-womens-suffrage-around-the-world-a-century-after-u-s-ratified-19th-amendment/

Scheibe, C., & Rogow, F. (2011). *The teacher's guide to media literacy: Critical thinking in a multimedia world.* Thousand Oaks, CA: Corwin.

Schmidt, S. (2020, August 9). Thousands of women fought against the right to vote. Their reasons still resonate today. *Washington Post.* https://www.washingtonpost.com/graphics/2020/local/history/anti-suffrage-women-vote-19-amendment/

Schmitke, A., Sabzalian, L., & Edmundson, J. (2020). *Teaching critically about Lewis and Clark: Challenging dominant narratives in K–12 curriculum.* New York, NY: Teachers College Press.

Schroeder, S., Curcio, R., & Lundgren, L. (2019). Expanding the learning network: How teachers use Pinterest. *Journal of Research on Technology in Education, 51*(2), 166–186.

Schultz, B. D. (2018). *Spectacular things happen along the way: Lessons from an urban classroom* (2nd ed.). New York, NY: Teachers College Press.

Schwartz, S. (2019, June 11). Teachers push for books with more diversity, fewer stereotypes. *Education Week.* https://www.edweek.org/ew/articles/2019/06/12/teachers-push-for-more-diverse-books-fewer.html

Seixas, P., & Peck, C. (2004). Teaching historical thinking. In A. Sears & I. Wright (Eds.), *Challenges and prospects for Canadian social studies* (pp. 109–117). Vancouver, CA: Pacific Educational Press.

Sell, C. R., Schmaltz, J., & Hartman, S. (2018). We came to Colorado: Third graders inquire into the past to honor their present. *Social Studies and the Young Learner, 30*(3), 26–31.

Sensoy, O., & DiAngelo, R. (2017). *Is everyone really equal? An introduction to key concepts in social justice education.* New York, NY: Teachers College Press.

Shafer, R. (2017). The (young) People's Climate Conference. *Rethinking Schools, 31*(4). https://rethinkingschools.org/articles/the-young-people-s-climate-conference/

Shalaby, C. (2017). *Troublemakers: Lessons in freedom from young children at school.* New York, NY: The New Press.

Simmons, D. (2019). Why we can't afford whitewashed social-emotional learning. *ASCD Education Update, 61*(4). http://www.ascd.org/publications/newsletters/education_update/apr19/vol61/num04/Why_We_Can't_Afford_Whitewashed_Social-Emotional_Learning.aspx

Simpson, L. B. (2017). *As we have always done: Indigenous freedom through radical resistance.* Minneapolis, MN: University of Minnesota Press.

Slater, K. (2017). Who gets to die of dysentery? Ideology, geography, and *The Oregon Trail*. *Children's Literature Association Quarterly, 42*(4), 374–395.

Sonu, D., & Marri, A. R. (2018). The hidden curriculum in financial literacy: Economics, standards, and the teaching of young children. In T.A. Lucey and K.S. Cooter's (Eds.), *Financial Literacy for Children and Youth (Second Edition)*, 7–26. New York, NY: Peter Lang.

Stewart, D-L. (2017, March 30). Language of appeasement. *Inside Higher Ed*. https://www.insidehighered.com/views/2017/03/30/colleges-need-language-shift-not-one-you-think-essay

Strachan, S. L., Block, M. K., & Roberts, S. L. (2016). Cardboard Airplanes: Authentic ways to foster curiosity about geography in early childhood. *Social Studies and the Young Learner, 29*(2), 17–20.

Swalwell, K. M. (2015). What are they thinking? Investigating student views to build a stronger curriculum. *Social Education, 79*(3), 151–154.

Swalwell, K. (2021). Noticing and questioning capitalism with elementary students. In T. A. Lucey (Ed.). Financialization, financial literacy, and social education (pp. 42–60). New York, NY: Routledge.

Swalwell, K., & Gallagher, J. (n.d.). The myth-busting history of Edna Griffin. *Civil Rights Teaching*. https://www.civilrightsteaching.org/edna-griffin

Swalwell, K., Lambert, M., & Oliva, J. (2018). Teaching wealthy children about economic inequality. In L. Willox & C. Brant (Eds.) *It's being done in social studies: Race, class, gender and sexuality in the pre/K-12 curriculum* (pp. 73–82). Charlotte, NC: Information Age.

Swalwell, K., & Pellegrino, A. M., & View, J. (2015). Teachers' curricular choices when teaching histories of oppressed people: Capturing the US civil rights movement. *The Journal of Social Studies Research, 39*(2), 79–94.

Swalwell, K., & Schweber, S. (2016). Teaching through turmoil: Social studies teachers and local controversial current events. *Theory & Research in Social Education, 44*(3), 283–315.

Sweeney, J. (1996/2018). *Me on the map*. New York, NY: Knopf Books for Young Readers.

Takaki, R. (2012). *A different mirror: A history of multicultural America*. Newport Beach, CA: Back Bay Books.

Taylor, A. (2015, August 17). This interactive map shows how 'wrong' other maps are. *The Washington Post*. https://www.washingtonpost .com/news/worldviews/wp/2015/08/18/this-interactive-map-shows -how-wrong-other-maps-are/

Templeton, T. N. (2020). Family photography. In D. T. Cook (Ed.), *SAGE Encyclopedia of Children and Childhood Studies* (Vol. 1, pp. 750–753). Thousand Oaks, CA: Sage.

Theoharis, J. (2018). *A more beautiful and terrible history: The uses and misuses of civil rights history*. Boston, MA: Beacon Press.

Thomson, S. L. (2017). Thomas Jefferson, slavery, and the language of the textbook: Addressing problematic representations of race and power. *Language Arts Journal of Michigan, 32*(2), 5.

Tintiangco-Cubales, A. G. (2005). Pinayism. In M. L. de Jesús (Ed.), *Pinay power: Theorizing the Filipina/American experience* (pp. 137-148). New York, NY: Routledge.

Trouillot, M. R. (1995). *Silencing the past: Power and the production of history*. Boston, MA: Beacon.

Tschida, C. M., & Buchanan, L. B. (2017). What makes a family? Sharing multiple perspectives through an inclusive text set. *Social Studies and the Young Learner, 30*(2), 3–7.

Tschida, C. M., Ryan, C. L., & Ticknor, A. S. (2014). Building on windows and mirrors: Encouraging the disruption of "single stories" through children's literature. *Journal of Children's Literature, 40*(1), 28–39.

Tudor, A., Tudor, K., & J. EagleSpeaker. (2018). *Young Water Protectors: A story about Standing Rock*. Scotts Valley, CA: CreateSpace.

Turtle Island Social Studies Collective. (2019). Beyond Pocahontas: Learning from Indigenous women changemakers. *Social Studies and the Young Learner, 31*(3), 7–13.

Turtle Island Social Studies Collective. (2020, February). Groundwork for teaching Indigenous enslavement—with the Turtle Island Social Studies Collective (Episode 10, Season 2). *Teaching Hard History: American Slavery* [Audio podcast]. https://www.learningforjustice.org/podcasts/teaching-hard-history/american-slavery/groundwork-for-teaching-indigenous-enslavement

Ulrich, L. T. (2007). How Betsy Ross became famous: Oral tradition, nationalism, and the invention of history. *Common Place*. http://commonplace.online/article/how-betsy-ross-became-famous/

U.S Government Accountability Office. (2018, March). *Discipline disparities for Black students, boys, and students with disabilities.* https://www.gao.gov/assets/700/690828.pdf

Van Horn, S. E., & Hawkman, A. M. (2018). First comes love, then comes marriage (equality): Welcoming diverse families in the elementary classroom. *Social Studies and the Young Learner, 31*(2), 24–32.

VanSledright, B. (2008). Narratives of nation-state, historical knowledge, and school history education. *Review of Research in Education, 32*(1), 109–146.

Vargas, J. A. (2018). *Dear America: Notes of an undocumented citizen.* New York, NY: HarperCollins.

Vasquez Heilig, J., Brown, K., & Brown, A. (2012). The illusion of inclusion: A critical race theory textual analysis of race and standards. *Harvard Educational Review, 82*(3), 403–424.

Vaught, C. (2017). Inclusivity is not a guessing game. *Rethinking Schools, 32*(2), 23–25.

Vazquez, T. (2019, September 12). Rethinking 'muffins with moms' and 'donuts with dads.' *Yes! Magazine*. https://www.yesmagazine.org/social-justice/2019/09/12/school-kids-family-inclusive/

Vickery, A. E. (2015). It was never meant for us: Towards a black feminist construct of citizenship in social studies. *The Journal of Social Studies Research, 39*(3), 163–172.

Vizenor, G. R. (1999). *Manifest manners: Narratives on postindian survivance.* Lincoln, NE: University of Nebraska Press.

Waters, M. W. (2020). *For beautiful Black boys who believe in a better world.* Louisville, KY: Flyaway Books.

Watson, D., Hagopian, J., & Au, W. (2018). *Teaching for Black lives.* Milwaukee, WI: Rethinking Schools.

Weatherford, C. B. (2016). *Voice of freedom: Fannie Lou Hamer.* Holland, OH: Dreamscape.

Weber, C. A., & Hagan, H. N. (2020). Is the "Right to clean water" fake news? An inquiry in media literacy and human rights. *Social Studies and the Young Learner, 33*(1), 3–9.

Weeks, L. (2015, October 22). American women who were anti-suffragettes. *NPR History Department.* https://www.npr.org/sections/npr-history-dept/2015/10/22/450221328/american-women-who-were-anti-suffragettes

West, P. (1993, March 24). Reaction to software on slavery raises issues surrounding new types of media. *EducationWeek.* https://www.edweek.org/ew/articles/1993/03/24/26soft.h12.html

Westheimer, J., & Kahne, J. (2004). Educating the" good" citizen: Political choices and pedagogical goals. *PS: Political Science and Politics, 37*(2), 241–247.

Wheeler-Bell, Q. (2014). Educating the spirit of activism: A "critical" civic education. *Educational Policy, 28*(3), 463–486.

Wheeler-Bell, Q. (2021). Combating the pathology of class privilege: A critical education for the elites. In K. Swalwell & D. Spikes (Eds.), Anti-oppressive education in 'elite' schools: Promising practices and cautionary tales from the field (pp. 15–26). New York, NY: Teachers College Press.

Wheeler-Bell, Q. & Swalwell, K. (2021). "How could we solve that problem?" Cultivating a healthy democracy through democratic classrooms. In R. Evans (Ed.). Handbook of teaching social issues (2nd ed., pp. 17–24).

Whitaker, R. (2020, November 3). The 'Oregon Trail' studio made a game about slaver. Then parents saw it. *Vice.* https://www.vice.com/en/article/3annjy/the-oregon-trail-studio-made-a-game-about-slavery-then-parents-saw-it

Whitlock, A. M. (2019). Elementary school entrepreneurs. *Interdisciplinary Journal of Problem-Based Learning, 13*(1). Retrieved at https://docs.lib.purdue.edu/cgi/viewcontent.cgi?article+1780&context=ijpbl

Wickenkamp, G. (2020, June 15). Confederate monuments in Iowa: Their monsters and the movements they require. *Iowa Informer.* http://iowainformer.com/politics/2020/06/confederate-monuments-iowa-bentonsport-bloomfield-john-brown/

Wilkins, R. (2002). *Jefferson's pillow: The founding fathers and the dilemma of Black patriotism.* Boston, MA: Beacon.

Wills, J. S. (2001). Missing in interaction: Diversity, narrative, and critical multicultural social studies. *Theory and Research in Social Education, 29*(1), 43–64.

Winkler, E. N. (2009). Children are not colorblind: How young children learn race. *PACE: Practical Approaches for Continuing Education, 3*(3), 1–8.

Winn, M. T. (2018). *Justice on both sides: Transforming education through restorative justice.* Cambridge, MA: Harvard Educational Press.

Winn, M. T., & Winn, L. T. (Eds.) (2021). *Restorative justice in education: Transforming teaching and learning through the disciplines.* Cambridge, MA: Harvard Educational Press.

Wolfe-Rocca, U. (2020). Repair: Students design a reparations bill. *Zinn Education Project.* https://www.zinnedproject.org/wp-content/uploads/2020/09/Repair_Students_Design_Reparations_Bill.pdf

Woodson, A. N. (2016). We're just ordinary people: Messianic master narratives and Black youths' civic agency. *Theory & Research in Social Education, 44*(2), 184–211.

Wright-Maley, C. (2015). Beyond the "Babel problem": Defining simulations for the social studies. *The Journal of Social Studies Research, 39*(2), 63–77.

Yosso, T. J. (2005). Whose culture has capital? A critical race theory discussion of community cultural wealth. *Race Ethnicity and Education, 8*(1), 69–91.

Young, I. M. (1990). *Justice and the politics of difference.* Princeton, NJ: Princeton University Press.

Zapata, A. (2020, November 4). Shifting the elementary classroom linguistic landscape through picturebooks. *National Council for Teachers of English Blog.* https://ncte.org/blog/2020/11/shifting-elementary-classroom-linguistic-landscape-picturebooks/?fbclid=IwAR1G6hlETAKgRJU_3BaD1cbLOgJtRZCWoeLt_WiuzBxFjHWmpQmLqfxBIi0

Zapata, A., King, C., King, L., & Kleekamp, M. (2019). Thinking with race-conscious perspectives: Critically selecting children's picture books depicting slavery. *Multicultural Perspectives, 21*(1), 25–32.

Zehr, H. (2015). *The little book of restorative justice.* Good Books.

Zembylas, M. (2017). Teacher resistance to engage with 'alternative' perspectives of difficult histories: The limits and prospects of affective disruption. *Discourse: Studies in the Cultural Politics of Education, 38*(5), 659–675.

Zinn, H. (1980/2013). *A people's history of the United States* (3rd ed.) New York, NY: Routledge.

Zipin, L. (2009). Dark funds of knowledge, deep funds of pedagogy: Exploring boundaries between lifeworlds and schools. *Discourse: Studies in the Cultural Politics of Education, 30*(3), 317–331.

# • Appendix A •

## Recommended Resources:
## The Tip of the Iceberg

This appendix includes the resources we've referenced in the book, but it's just the tip of the iceberg. For many more of our favorite resources (books, websites, podcasts, etc.) and sample units, visit www.ssfabw.com.

### Curricular Resources

*The 1619 Project* by *The New York Times*, https://www.nytimes.com/ interactive/2019/08/14/magazine/1619-america-slavery.html

Erin Adams's blog, erinonecon.net

Children's Literature Assembly, Position Statement on the Importance of Critical Selection and Teaching of Diverse Children's Literature, https://www.childrensliteratureassembly.org

Civic, College, and Career Readiness (C3) Framework, https://www .socialstudies.org/standards/c3

Cooperative Children's Book Center, https://ccbc.education.wisc.edu

Facing History and Ourselves, https://www.facinghistory.org

National Council of Social Studies, "Powerful and Purposeful Pedagogy in Elementary Social Studies," https://www.socialstudies.org/position -statements/powerful-purposeful-pedagogy-elementary-school-social -studies

*Native Land Teacher Guide*, https://native-land.ca/wp/wp-content/ uploads/2019/03/teacher_guide_2019_final.pdf

The News Literacy Project, www.thenewsliteracyproject.org

Debbie Reese and Jean Mendoza's blog, American Indians in Children's Literature, americanindiansinchildrensliterature.blogspot.com

Smithsonian National Museum of African American History and Culture's Talking About Race Web Portal, https://nmaahc.si.edu/learn/talking-about-race

Teaching Hard History: American Slavery for K–5 by Learning for Justice, https://www.learningforjustice.org/frameworks/teaching-hard-history/american-slavery/k-5-framework

Learning for Justice Digital Literacy Framework, www.learningforjustice.org/frameworks/digital-literacy

Learning for Justice Social Justice Standards, www.learningforjustice.org/frameworks/social-justice-standards

Using Their Words, www.usingtheirwords.org

Wisconsin Teachers of Local Culture, https://wtlc.csumc.wisc.edu

Zinn Education Project, www.zinnedproject.org

## Readings to Inspire Educators

Sara Ahmed, *Being the Change* (2019)

James Baldwin, "A Talk to Teachers" (1963)

Valarie Kaur, *See No Stranger*

Barbara A. Lewis, *The Kid's Guide to Social Action* (1998)

Bettina Love, *We Want to Do More Than Survive* (2019)

Noreen N. Rodríguez and Transformative Justice in Education Center, *Transformative Justice in Social Studies* [white paper], https://tje.ucdavis.edu/practitioner-residence-white-paper-series

Carla Shalaby, *Troublemakers* (2017)

## Media

Chimamanda Ngozi Adichie, "The Danger of a Single Story," TED Talk (2009)

Liz Kleinrock, "How to Teach Kids to Talk About Taboo Topics," TED Talk (2019)

*Mighty Times: The Children's March* film kit by Learning for Justice

## Build Your Content Knowledge

Jesse Hagopian, Wayne Au, and Dyan Watson (Editors), *Teaching for Black Lives* (2018)

Hasan Kwame Jeffries, *Understanding and Teaching the Civil Rights Movement* (2019)

Denisha Jones and Jesse Hagopian (Editors), *Black Lives Matter at Schools* (2020)

Stephanie Jones, *Mapping Racial Trauma in Schools,* https://www.facebook.com/mappingracialtrauma/

Deborah Menkart, Alana Murray, and Jenice View, *Putting the Movement Back Into Civil Rights Teaching* (2014)

Leilani Sabzalian, *Indigenous Children's Survivance in Public Schools* (2019)

Alison Schmitke, Leilani Sabzalian, and Jeff Edmundson, *Teaching Critically About Lewis and Clark: Challenging Dominant Narratives in K–12 Curriculum* (2020)

Özlem Sensoy and Robin DiAngelo, *Is Everyone Really Equal?* (2017)

Jeanne Theoharis, *A More Beautiful and Terrible History: The Uses and Misuses of Civil Rights History* (2018)

## Recommended Children's Literature

Andy Andrews, *The Kid Who Changed the World* (2014)

Christy Hale, *Todos Iguales/All Equal: Un Corrido de Lemon Grove/A Ballad of Lemon Grove* (2019)

Tom Jackson and Cristina Guitian, *Fake News* (2020)

Aslan Tudor, Kelly Tudor, and Jason EagleSpeaker, *Young Water Protectors: A Story About Standing Rock* (2018)

Michael W. Waters, *For Beautiful Black Boys Who Believe in a Better World* (2020)

Carol Boston Weatherford, *Voice of Freedom: Fannie Lou Hamer* (2016)

## Professional Networks

Abolitionist Teaching Network, www.abolitionistteachingnetwork.org/

Badass Teachers Association, www.badassteacher.org

Education for Liberation Network, https://www.edliberation.org

Institute for Teachers of Color Committed to Racial Justice, http://www
.instituteforteachersofcolor.org

National Association of Multicultural Educators, https://www.nameorg
.org

Morningside Center for Teaching Social Responsibility, https://www
.morningsidecenter.org

Rethinking Schools, http://www.rethinkingschools.org

Teaching for Change, http://www.teachingforchange.org

# Appendix B

## Educator Tools and Guides

Table B.1 Empirical and Normative Questions in the Disciplines

|  | Empirical Questions | Normative Questions |
|---|---|---|
| **Definition** | Can be answered with evidence | "Forever struggles" about priorities, values, and ethics |
| **History** | What happened in the past? Why? What stories do people tell about the past? Why? | Whose history matters? What stories should get told? |
| **Economics** | What is scarce, and why? How do people allocate scarce resources? What are the consequences of our decisions? | What should people want and need? What should we do when there isn't enough? What consequences are fair and just? |

## Table B.1 Empirical and Normative Questions in the Disciplines
### (continued)

| | | |
|---|---|---|
| **Behavioral Sciences** | What identities exist, and what diversity exists within those identities? How do people interact within and across groups, and why? Who has power and who doesn't, and why? What disparities exist, and why? How do advantages and disadvantages compound for people with intersecting dominant and marginalized identities? | What identities should be recognized? How should people interact? Who should have power? What should we do about inequities, especially those that exist across various intersections of identities? |
| **Civics** | Who is in our community? How do people govern themselves? What are a community's rules and consequences for breaking them? How does social change occur? What tools do people have to identify and solve a problem? | Who should be in our circle of care and concern? What does that mean for our obligations for how to treat others and expectations of how others will treat us? How should people govern and organize themselves? What are fair and just rules and consequences? What social change should occur? What is a problem in our community, and how should we solve it? |

| Geography | What places matter to people, and why? How do people represent places? What makes places similar and different? What connections do people and places have, and why? | Who should get to access or claim a place? How should people represent places? What makes a place good or bad? What are our obligations to particular places and the life that inhabits them, and why? |

**Table B.2 Disciplinary Concepts and Tools**

| Discipline | Major Concepts | Ways to Center Counter Narratives |
|---|---|---|
| History | – Chronology<br>– Cause and effect<br>– Change and continuity<br>– Turning points | – Explicitly include attention to the experiences and perspectives of marginalized communities.<br>– Apply historical thinking skills to primary sources and artifacts to consider bias.<br>– Analyze secondary sources for whose experiences and perspectives are missing.<br>– Inquire into how and why people constructed systems of oppression. |

**Table B.2 Disciplinary Concepts and Tools (*continued*)**

| Economics | – Scarcity<br>– Wants and needs<br>– Production, distribution, and consumption<br>– Opportunity costs<br>– Independence and interdependence | – Contextualize needs and wants.<br>– Notice and critique capitalism and the myth of meritocracy.<br>– Interrogate the consequences of resource distribution and consumption.<br>– Highlight examples of collectivity, mutual aid, and interdependence. |
|---|---|---|
| Behavioral Sciences | – Social identities<br>– Power and oppression<br>– Patterns of disparity<br>– Culture and cultural universals<br>– Intersectionality, stereotypes, and perspective-taking | – Explicitly acknowledge various forms of intersecting oppressions.<br>– Make space for students and families to share their own unique identities and traditions to the degree they're comfortable.<br>– Engage in critical content analysis and interviews.<br>– Identify and interrupt bias.<br>– Apply statistics to look for disparities.<br>– Avoid stereotyping and "single stories" of groups or communities.<br>– Make cross-cultural interactions ordinary for students.<br>– Value the knowledge of "ordinary" people.<br>– Seek out multiple perspectives. |

| | | |
|---|---|---|
| **Civics** | – Deliberation, discussion, and debate<br>– Changemaking strategies<br>– Surveys and observations<br>– Restorative justice<br>– Branches and functions of local, state, and federal government<br>– Rights and responsibilities of citizens | – Stress the need to consider the common good.<br>– Interrogate the status quo and the consequences of current events for various communities.<br>– Utilize critical media literacy skills.<br>– Make connections to social movements.<br>– Identify a range of community problems.<br>– Highlight various ways to take action to collectively solve problems. |
| **Geography** | – Cartography (globes, grids, graphs, maps)<br>– Physical and human characteristics of place<br>– Absolute and relative location<br>– Human–environment interaction<br>– Movement<br>– Regions<br>– Distribution<br>– Orientation<br>– Landforms and waterways<br>– Local and global<br>– Sustainability | – Expose different approaches for and consequence of spatially reasoning and representing places.<br>– Center power struggles related to place (e.g., land claims, naming, settlement, access, resource use, etc.).<br>– Include more-than-human life in considering who inhabits and matters in a place.<br>– Cultivate a love for and responsibility to specific places. |

**Table B.3 Identity and Power Chart**

| Identity | Definition/ Categories | Oppression | Who Is Advantaged? | Who Is Disadvantaged? | Your Own Identity |
|---|---|---|---|---|---|
| Ability | | | | | |
| Age | | | | | |
| Ethnicity | | | | | |
| Gender | | | | | |
| Language | | | | | |
| Race | | | | | |
| Religion | | | | | |
| Sexual Orientation | | | | | |
| Social class | | | | | |
| Other? | | | | | |

*Note:* See the figure in Chapter 1 (p. 15), and its corresponding explanation for help when using this chart.

**Table B.4 Connect Disciplinary Questions to Your Life**

| Discipline | Question | Your Response |
|---|---|---|
| History | What historical event or figure is important to your family and why? (e.g., "My family wouldn't be the same if ___ hadn't happened/lived.") | |
| Geography | Where is a place that you have felt like you belong(ed), and why? Where is a place that you *haven't* felt a sense of belonging, and why? | |
| Economics | What has been a pivotal choice in your life, and what shaped your decision? | |
| Behavioral Sciences | What social identity or combination of identities is most important in your life, and why? | |
| Civics | What community rules, levels of government, or social movements impact your life most? | |

**Table B.5 Connect Disciplinary Questions to Your Life—Noreen and Katy's Sample Responses**

| Disciplinary Questions | Noreen's Response | Katy's Response |
|---|---|---|
| What historical event or figure is important to your family and why? (In other words, "My family wouldn't be the same if ___ hadn't happened/lived.") | My family wouldn't be the same if the Immigration and Nationality Act of 1965 had not been passed. Both of my parents immigrated to the U.S. from Asia in the 1970s, and prior to this act, immigration from Asia, Africa, and Latinx America was heavily restricted. | My family wouldn't be the same if my dad had accepted a job in Moscow in the early 1980s. Because of the Cold War, my mom was scared to move, so we stayed in Iowa—a state whose history of settlement has also dramatically shaped my family as both sides took advantage of the displacement of Indigenous communities 4 generations ago. |
| Where is a place that you have felt like you belong(ed), and why? Where is a place that you *haven't* felt a sense of belonging, and why? | I felt like I truly belonged at the first elementary school where I taught. Although the city of Austin has long been majority-white, students at this school were almost entirely children of color and there were bilingual education classes at every grade level and many teachers of color. Students often asked if I was sisters with two other teachers, because we all had dark brown skin and black hair. I taught there for 5 years, and in that short time I taught many siblings and felt incredibly welcomed by their families. A place where I didn't feel like I belonged was the town of Ankeny, where I lived during my first year in Iowa. The town is the epitome of suburban white flight, and literally *no one* on the street where we rented a home spoke to us for the entire year that we lived there. | Because I am white and have always attended and taught at predominantly white institutions, I've felt like I've belonged in most places I've lived and worked. When in the racial or linguistic minority, I have enjoyed feeling "out of place"—though recognize how my dominant identities have shaped that enjoyment, and appreciate how people I've met have lovingly pushed me out of my comfort zone in ways that caused much-needed growth. One place where I felt like I didn't belong was the Catholic church I attended in grad school. The priest used each homily to share his misogynistic and homophobic opinions. Coupled with rules that Eucharist had to include gluten (I am gluten-intolerant), it was quite painful to realize that the church I had been born into was a place I regularly felt angry and excluded. |

| What has been a pivotal choice in your life, and what shaped your decision? | Choosing to take a faculty position in Iowa offered my family some unexpected benefits. While the salary I was offered was not particularly high, the cost of living in the state was significantly lower than what we were accustomed to in Austin, Texas. My husband works in tech, and we were surprised that he had many more opportunities available to him in Iowa than in Austin. Daycare and afterschool care fees were also significantly cheaper. | Choosing to start a family later in life has been the best and most impactful decision of my life. Where I grew up, most women my age were married years before I met my husband. I've had a mix of emotions about that over the years. All sorts of resources and advantages supported my decision to defer this stage—and helped me both pick and be a better partner. In particular, I couldn't have made this choice without family planning technologies like birth control and IVF. |
| --- | --- | --- |
| What social identity or combination of identities is most important in your life, and why? | I was raised Muslim. My father is Muslim and my mother is Catholic, so while I attended Arabic school on weekends, I also went to church from time to time. Although I was never particularly devout and have not practiced any religion for two decades, the prayers that I turn to in times of fear and sorrow are in Arabic and I now identify as a cultural Muslim. I have witnessed a great deal of anti-Muslim racism and Islamophobia although I have been personally subjected to very little of it. I don't think many of my colleagues know this about me, but it absolutely impacts the way I view the world and the importance of religious freedom and interfaith alliances. | When I've lived elsewhere, my identity as an Iowan has connected me with others from the Midwest and provided an outsider perspective to help undercut the regional elitism I've felt in bigger coastal cities. In those spaces, I've been extremely proud and defensive of my Midwestern identity. Once I moved back to Iowa, however, I dove into its history as a site of deep-seated racism and toxic passive aggression. When I'm "home," I feel much more frustrated with and conflicted about this part of my identity and find myself more often than not drawn to people who aren't from here—or who moved away and came back like I did. |

**Table B.5 Connect Disciplinary Questions to Your Life—Noreen and Katy's Sample Responses (*continued*)**

| What community rules, levels of government, or social movements impact your life most? | Since I am writing this during the COVID-19 pandemic, I've found that in the months we've been self-quarantining at home, honoring and relying upon our neighbors has never been so important to us. We recently got a puppy and several of our neighbors are dog owners who have been incredibly kind and supportive as we struggle with potty training and biting. They are the kind of people who drop off treats unexpectedly and will let us know if a package has been sitting on our porch for awhile. At a time when we feel very isolated, it's so nice to know that if there was an emergency, we could count on them to help and we would certainly do the same for them. | I am a political junkie and listen to at least five different politics podcasts regularly. As we just finished the 2020 presidential election, I am trying to take a break—I've been consumed with news about the federal government (scandals, protests, etc.) for the past 4 years and am exhausted trying to figure out the best way to engage . . . especially since I also had a new baby this past spring. In fact, while I was up during late night feeds, I connected with an online group of moms who are similarly politics-obsessed and trying to use their "mom" status as political leverage for justice-oriented social change. That has helped me channel my civic energy! |

## Table B.6 Normalization Lesson/Unit Reflection Worksheet

| Normalization | | |
|---|---|---|
| **Lesson/Unit Topic:** | | |
| **General Problems** | **General Pitfalls** | **General Solutions** |
| – Reinforces supremacy for some kids and deviance or inferiority for others | – Expansion of inclusion that is superficial or inaccurate<br><br>– Exoticization<br><br>– Tokenization | – Expansion that is deep and accurate<br><br>– Contextualization |
| **Reflections on Normalization in Current Lesson/Unit** | | |
| *Which of these problems exist in the existing lesson/unit?* | *What pitfalls have you witnessed or can you anticipate?* | *Have you seen any solutions in action? What can you do to make these changes and adjustments come to life?* |

**Table B.7 Idealization Lesson/Unit Reflection Worksheet**

| *Idealization* | | |
|---|---|---|
| **Lesson/Unit Topic:** | | |
| **General Problems** | **General Pitfalls** | **General Solutions** |
| – Ignores reality | – Compliance with authority<br>– Only focuses what exists<br>– Doesn't question the ideal put forth | – Realization<br>– Balance ideal with reality<br>– Reimagine the ideal<br>– Co-construction |
| **Reflections on Idealization in Current Lesson/Unit** | | |
| *Which of these problems exist in the existing lesson/unit?* | *What pitfalls have you witnessed or can you anticipate?* | *Have you seen any solutions in action? What can you do to make these changes and adjustments come to life?* |

### Table B.8 Heroification Lesson/Unit Reflection Worksheet

| Heroification | | |
|---|---|---|
| **Lesson/Unit Topic:** | | |
| **General Problems** | **General Pitfalls** | **General Solutions** |
| – Erases complexity of canonical figures<br>– Fails to acknowledge other important figures | – Makes canonical figures more complex, but doesn't acknowledge other historically significant figures or social movements/ everyday people<br>– Presents nondominant people as saints or whitewashes them | – Diversification<br>– Humanization: Examine the complicated lives of diverse individuals with historical significance<br>– Mobilization: Appreciate the role of social movements and everyday people in social change |
| **Reflections on Heroification in Current Lesson/Unit** | | |
| *Which of these problems exist in the existing lesson/unit?* | *What pitfalls have you witnessed or can you anticipate?* | *Have you seen any solutions in action? What can you do to make these changes and adjustments come to life?* |

### Table B.9 Dramatization and Gamification Lesson/Unit Reflection Worksheet

| Dramatization and Gamification | | |
|---|---|---|
| **Lesson/Unit Topic:** | | |
| **General Problems** | **General Pitfalls** | **General Solutions** |
| – Trivializes and traumatizes<br>– Prioritizes an activity's entertainment value over education<br>– Reinforces dominant narratives by decentering or erasing marginalized perspectives | – Confuses students by not explicitly linking their experiences to the learning objectives (which can reinforce dominant narratives)<br>– Trivializes trauma and/or retraumatizes kids by assigning problematic roles or tasks | – Honors marginalized perspectives<br>– Transforms dominant narratives |
| **Reflections on Dramatization and Gamification in Current Lesson/Unit** | | |
| *Which of these problems exist in the existing lesson/unit?* | *What pitfalls have you witnessed or can you anticipate?* | *Have you seen any solutions in action? What can you do to make these changes and adjustments come to life?* |

## Table B.10 Anti-Oppressive Filter for Online Resources

| Anti-Oppressive Components | Yes/No? | Ideas for Modification |
|---|---|---|
| Does this content reinforce oppressive norms, stereotypes, or trauma? | *If the answer is yes, don't use this resource!* | |
| Is the resource supportive of the predetermined inquiry, standard, or learning objective? | | |
| Is the resource clearly connected to one or more of the social studies disciplines? | | |
| Does the resource have any elements of normalization, idealization, heroification, and/or problematic dramatization and gamification? | | |
| Is the information included accurate and does it attend to issues of power and oppression honestly? | | |
| Is the resource created by someone with a deep knowledge of the community of focus? If not, is there an #OwnVoices resource that you can use instead or alongside the resource? | | |
| Does the resource engage students in critical thinking and questions that are relevant to them? | | |

**Table B.10 Anti-Oppressive Filter for Online Resources (*continued*)**

| | | |
|---|---|---|
| Do you have enough content knowledge to answer questions that might emerge and/or make connections for kids when using this resource? If not, what resources should you consult before teaching? | | |
| For which students might this resource serve as a window? For which students might this resource serve as a mirror? | | |
| Who might you need to talk with before teaching this resource to ensure that marginalized students don't feel tokenized or targeted by the topic? | | |
| What questions, connections, and confusions do you anticipate students having based on previous discussions and your knowledge of their interests and learning? | | |
| Which family and community members and local connections would make this resource more impactful? | | |

**Table B.11 Guiding Questions for a Critical Analysis of Children's Literature**

| Guiding Questions for Text Selection | Guiding Questions to Begin Engaging Students |
|---|---|
| From whose perspective is the story told? | How are you like _____ [character]? |
| Whose voices and experiences are present/absent from the text? | How are you not like _____ [character]? |
| What moral values and sociopolitical messages are dominant in the text? | How does this book make you feel? |
| How are cultural practices depicted? | [After selecting a particularly important spread in the book] If you could draw yourself anywhere in this picture, where would you be? What would you be doing? What would you be saying? How would you be feeling? |
| What is the overall tone of the illustrations? The written narrative? | Whose voices are present in this book? Whose aren't? |
| How are the lived experiences of historically minoritized populations represented in the text? | Whose experiences are represented? Whose aren't? |
| To what degree are complex social situations oversimplified in the text? | How are the issues in this book relevant to you today? To your community? To others? |
| How are complex relationships between characters represented in the text? | What does this book have to say about the world? |

# • Index •

# • About the Authors •

**Noreen Naseem Rodríguez** (she/her) is the daughter of Asian immigrants and was a bilingual elementary educator in Austin, Texas before becoming a teacher educator at the University of Texas at Austin and Iowa State University. She is currently an Assistant Professor of Teacher Learning, Research and Practice in the School of Education at the University of Colorado Boulder. Noreen engages in tsundoku—the art of collecting books but not reading them—and enjoys baking and cooking. **Katy Swalwell** (she/her) is the descendent of European settlers in Iowa and was a middle and high school social studies teacher before becoming a professor in elementary education programs at universities in the Midwest and Mid-Atlantic. She is currently Lead Equity Specialist for the Equity Literacy Institute and founder of Past Present Future Consulting & Media. She looks forward to road trips with her family, tries to garden, and co-hosts a podcast called "Our Dirty Laundry." Noreen and Katy bonded over their love of escape rooms, theme parties, breakout boxes, and dessert. When together, they are bound to burst into song and dance and gesticulate wildly.